Black Southerners in Confederate Armies

Copyright 2001. Southern Lion Books, Inc.

Library of Congress Cataloging-in-Publication Data

Black Southerners in Confederate Armies
Complied and edited by J. H. Segars and Charles Kelly Barrow

ISBN 0-966245-1-5

CIP 00-135048

Front Cover: Confederate veterans meet for a reunion barbeque at Florence, Alabama in August 1921; *Florence Times*, Sept. 2 edition 1921, page 5. (Courtesy of Darrell Glover.) The 3 black men are: Reuben Patterson (1843-1928) of the 5th Alabama Cavalry. Reuben was Company Bugler and Body Servant of Col. Josiah Patterson. George Washington Seawright (1848-1931) of Co. K, 7th Alabama Infantry & Co. F, 4th Alabama Cavalry Peter Stewart (1825-1925).

Back Cover: Reunion photograph of the Egbert Jones Camp, United Confederate Veterans, Huntsville, Alabama; *Confederate Veteran*, January, 1928 edition, page 97.

Black Southerners in Confederate Armies

Compiled & Edited
by
J. H. Segars and Charles Kelly Barrow

Southern Lion Books, Inc.
Post Office Box 347163
Atlanta, GA 30334

CONTENTS

Preface

PREFACE

Readers of military history continue to be captivated by one of the greatest of all epochs, the American Civil War, and publishers are attempting to meet the perpetual demand for new material. Unfortunately, many of the more recent studies remain focused on subjects that are well-worn and oft covered - the major battles, Eastern military campaigns, and the exploits of commanding generals. Some topics as "the Battle of Gettysburg" and "Sherman's March to the Sea" are revisited quite often. Nevertheless, there are other important subjects that need and deserve closer scrutiny and examination.

Eminent historians such as Bell I. Wiley and James I. Robertson, Jr. have provided detailed studies about ordinary men and women who were pulled into the vortex of our greatest national struggle. But since the late 1960s, few scholars have delved into the human aspects of the American Civil War. As a result, there is a shortage of notable books about common soldiers, women in the war, and ethnic minorities. Furthermore, if we take into consideration the hundreds of thousands of books published about this period, we continue to find that the story of *all* participants has yet to be fully told. For example, very little is written about the role of African Americans in military campaigns of the United States -- yet, men and women of color were involved in all national conflicts beginning with the Revolutionary War. Modern history texts do not always mention that large numbers of slaves chose to fight with their colonial masters instead of accepting British offers of freedom during the American Revolution. This leads to an interesting parallel: In the 1860s, could black Southerners have also supported the war efforts of their homeland -- the Confederacy?

While historians are willing to acknowledge that African Americans did serve in support of Confederate armies there continues to be debate over the count of how many men were involved and whether significant military contributions were made. On the surface the thought of black men and women serving the Confederacy seems beyond comprehension and reason, and is a vexation for many. Based on modern interpretations of history, persons of color who served within Confederate units (termed in today's vernacular as Black Confederates) are, indeed, a paradox and this phenomenon contradicts much of what we thought we knew about the Civil War . . . and the South.

Some scholars feel that Black Confederates were few in number so the subject is not worthy of serious study. Others strongly disagree. Nevethleless, extant source material provides information about slaves and freedmen who were Southern allies, and in some instances, who served as enlisted soldiers. The debate over this issue, like so many others relating to the Civil War, is not likely to be settled anytime soon. For many, the possibility-and the historical reality-of "Black Confederates" is not only intriguing but remains as one of the great ironies of American history.

How do we learn about Black Confederates? Considering the scarcity of official records and published unit histories, this is not an easy question to answer. One way is to view the surviving accounts, narratives, and writings of Civil War veterans and their family members. A number of notable books written between 1865 and 1925 contain important passages about blacks who worked in Confederate military units as cooks, teamsters, bodyguards, construction workers, porters, artillerists, sailors, and soldiers. Also, the archival records, recorded minutes, and group photographs of United Confederate Veterans camps provide documentation of the postwar presence of Black Confederates. (The *Confederate Veteran* magazine, the official organ of the UCV, is an invaluable source for learning about socio-military activities of veterans -- black and white.)

Surprisingly, Confederate pension records include the names of African Americans and the accompanying affidavits filed in support of these pension applications offer statements about the military service of applicants that can not be found anywhere else. Reliable information can also be gleaned from period newspapers, historical papers, and volumes of the *Official Records*. Genealogists and historical researchers have identified Black Confederates in their research and source material. County histories, family papers, and personal correspondence are also valuable sources. Newspaper articles and published obituaries tell readers about the military service of hometown heroes; and, recorded tributes to Black Confederates offer heartfelt sentiments and historical information that should not be ignored. Cemetery memorials, markers, and obelisks serve as tangible reminders of those who served their country.

In this volume an attempt has been made to present selections from a wide variety of reliable sources, and with a minimal amount of editorial opinion and analysis. Also, readers are encouraged to do additional research by viewing archival and library source material that can be found in their local areas. Regardless of the debate over this subject, or any other single issue of the Civil War, there seems to be at least one constant to which we can all agree: the historical impact of this great struggle is mind-boggling.

J. H. Segars

Acknowledgements

Since the 1995 publication of *Forgotten Confederates: An Anthology about Black Southerners,* Charles Kelly Barrow has continued to collect source material for this second volume. Subscribers of *Confederate Veteran* magazine responded to Barrow's classified ads and many of these selections are now included. We offer thanks to Greg White, Civil War author and historian, for his outstanding research and for the extraordinary "gems" he sent our way. Also, we appreciate the editorial contributions of Cyndy Coan, a Georgia educator and writer. And for production and technical assistance we are indebted to Brenda Brothers of Independent Typestyles of Christiana, Tennessee.

Special acknowledgement to Sheldon Vanauken and the editors of Southern Partisan Magazine for allowing us to reprint a wonderful article "Black Fighters for the South" from the 4th Quarter 1992 edition. We are indebted to Rebecca Maksel of *Smithsonian Magazine* for J.K. Obatala's classic, "The unlikely story of blacks who were loyal to Dixie" which appeared in the March 1979 edition. (Attempts were made by the staff of Smithsonian and Southern Lion Books to locate the author, Mr. Obatala, and we are still trying to contact him for an interview.)

Two exceptional selections, originally scheduled for inclusion in *Forgotten Confederates,* were saved for this volume. The first, "The Employment of Negroes as Soldiers in the Confederate Army" by Charles H. Wesley appeared as an article in the *Journal of Negro History,* Vol. IV, July, 1919: permission to reprint is granted by The Association for the Study of African-American Life and History, Inc. The second, "Understanding the Stillness," appeared on national wire services in 1994 and was reprinted in newspapers around the country. We are grateful to Bill Maxwell, an outstanding Florida journalist, for the contribution of his timeless essay.

We have included the words of a modern-day Black Confederate, the late Eddie Brown Page, who reminds us that the phenomenon of men of color supporting the South is not relegated to the forgotten ages but remains as real - and as misunderstood - today as in the past. We were privileged to hear Eddie speak on a favorite topic, "Black Confederates," and to hear his moving performances of "Dixie" which were always presented with passion and heartfelt emotion. We will continue to miss Eddie Page's long telephone conversations: his enthusiasm was infectious, his knowledge of the South remarkable, and his devotion and love for history (and fellow countrymen) was inspiring. Special thanks to Calvin Johnson, Eddie's good friend and compatriot, for keeping Page's memory and important work from slipping into the narrow corners of lost history.

Special thanks to the following contibutors.

CALIFORNIA
Dr. Lawrence Fletcher Talbott

DOMINION OF CANADA
Tom Brooks

FLORIDA
James F. Hull Camp #1347, SCV
Robert Mann
Hewitt J. Dupont

GEORGIA
Greg C. White
Andrew M. Thompson
John B. Carroll III
Calvin Johnson, Jr.

INDIANA
Dr. Duane W. H. Arnold

KANSAS
Jesse R. Estes

LOUISIANA
Keith Bernard

MICHIGAN
Stephen D. Lutz

NEW YORK
Khalid Hashim Bey

SOUTH CAROLINA
Charles Parks
The Confederate States of America-Historical Preservation Society
Isabel Vandervelde

Chapter I

Encountering Black Confederates in History

The feelings that existed between us can only be understood by Southern men; by a Northern man, never.

Capt. M.P. Usina,

A Confederate blockade runner, tells of the courage and fidelity of his slave, a skilled seaman, who refused freedom in order to stay in service aboard ship.

Savannah Morning News, February 18, 1899.

The Employment of Negroes As Soldiers In The Confederate Army
by Charles H. Wesley

The Journal of Negro History discusses the arming and service of Negroes in the Confederate army. Vol. IV, July, 1919 - No. 3

The problem of arming the slaves was of far greater concern to the South, than to the North. It was fraught with momentous consequences to both sections, but pregnant with an influence, subtle yet powerful, which would affect directly the ultimate future of the Confederate Government. The very existence of the Confederacy depended upon the ability of the South to control the slave population. At the outbreak of the Civil War great fear as to servile insurrection was aroused in the South and more restrictive measures were enacted.[1]

Most of the Negro population was living in the area under rebellion, and in many cases the slaves outnumbered the whites. To arm these slaves would mean the lighting of a torch which, in the burning, might spread a flame throughout the slave kingdom. If the Negro in the midst of the oppression had been in possession of the facts regarding the war, whether the slaves would have remained consciously faithful would have been a perplexing question.[2]

The South had been aware of its imminent danger and, with its traditional methods, strove to prevent the arming of the Negroes. With the memories of Negro insurrections ever fresh in the public mind, quite a change of front would be required to bring the South to view with favor such a radical measure.

The South, however, was not alone in its unwillingness to employ Negroes as soldiers. For the first two years of the war, the North, represented by President Lincoln and Congress, refused to consider the same proposal. In the face of stubborn opposition, loyal Negroes had been admitted into the Engineer and Quartermaster Departments of the Union armies, but their employment as soldiers under arms was discountenanced during the first years of the war.

In the North this discrimination caused much discontent among the Negroes, but those living in the states in rebellion did not understand the issues in the war and would not understand until the Union forces had invaded the hostile sections and spread the gradually developing point of view that the war was for exterminating the institution of slavery. During the opening days of the war, slaves captured by the Union forces were returned to their disloyal masters, an act that provides sufficient concrete evidence that slavery was not the avowed cause of the conflict.[3] If there was this uncertain notion of the cause of the war among northern sympathizers, how much more befogged must have been the minds of the southern slaves in the hands of men who imagined that they were fighting for the same principles involved in our earlier struggle with Great Britain! To the majority of the Negroes, as to all the South, the invading armies of the Union seemed to be ruthlessly attacking independent States, invading the beloved homeland and trampling upon all that these men held dear.[4]

The loyalty of the slave in guarding home and family during his master's absence has long been eloquently orated.[5] The Negroes' loyalty extended itself even to service in the Confederate army. Believing their land invaded by hostile foes, slaves eagerly offered themselves for service in actual warfare. In the early days of the war, Negroes who volunteered were received into the fighting forces by the rebelling States, especially during those years in which the North was academically debating the advisability of arming the Negro.[6]

In the first year of the war, large numbers were received into the service of the Confederate laboring units. In January, a dispatch from Mr. Riordan at Charleston to Hon. Percy Walker at Mobile stated that large numbers of Negroes from the plantations of Alabama were at work on the redoubts, which, when complete, were described as very substantially made, strengthened by sand-bags and sheet-iron.[7] Negroes were employed in the army throughout the South to build fortifications.[8] In 1862, the Florida Legislature conferred authority upon the Governor to impress slaves for military purposes—if authorized by the Confederate Government. The owners of the slaves were to be compensated for this labor and, in turn, were to furnish one good suit of clothes for each of the slaves impressed. The wages were not to exceed twenty-five dollars a month.[9] In February 1864 the Confederate Congress provided for the impressment of 20,000 slaves for menial service in the Confederate army.[10] President Davis was so satisfied with their labor that he suggested in his annual message in November 1864 that this number should be increased to 40,000,[11] with the promise that the slaves would be emancipated at the end of their service.

Before the outbreak of the war and the beginning of actual hostilities, the local authorities throughout the South had permitted the enrollment for military service of organizations formed of free Negroes although no action had been taken or suggested by the Confederate Government. Some of these troops are said to have remained in the service of the Confederacy during the period of the war, but not to have taken part in any important engagements. For example, the Adjutant-General's Office of the Louisiana Militia issued an order stating that "the Governor and the Commander-in-Chief relying implicitly upon the loyalty of the free colored population of the city and State, for the protection of their homes, their property and for southern rights, from the pollution of a ruthless invader, and believing that the military organization which existed prior to February 15, 1862, and elicited praise and respect for the patriotic motives which prompted it, should exist for and during the war, calls upon them to maintain their organization and hold themselves prepared for such orders as may be transmitted to them."[13]

These "Native Guards" joined the Confederate forces, but they did not leave the city with these troops who retreated before General Butler and the invading Union army. When General Butler learned of the bravery of this organization after his arrival in New Orleans, he sent for several of the most prominent colored men of the city and asked why they had accepted service "under the Confederate Government which was set up for the purpose of holding their brethren and kindred in eternal slavery." They replied that they dared not to refuse, that they had hoped by serving the Confederates to advance nearer to equality with the whites, and that they had longed to throw the weight of their class with the Union forces and with the cause in which their own dearest hopes were identified.[14]

At the outbreak of the war, an observer in Charleston noted the war-time preparations and called particular attention to "the thousand Negroes who, so far from inclining to insurrections, were grinning from ear to ear at the prospect of shooting the Yankees."[15] In the same city, one of the daily papers stated in early January, 150 free colored men had offered their services to hasten the work of throwing up redoubts along the coast.[16] At Nashville, Tennessee, in April 1861, a company of free Negroes offered their services to the Confederate Government, and at Memphis a recruiting office was opened.[17] In June 1861 the Legislature of Tennessee authorized Governor Harris to receive into the state military service all male persons of color between the ages of fifteen and fifty and to provide them with eight dollars a month, clothing, and rations. The sheriff of each county was required to report the names of these persons, and in case the number tendering their services was not sufficient to meet the needs of the county, the sheriff was empowered to impress as many as were needed.[18] In the same state, under the command of Confederate officers, marched a procession of several hundred colored men carrying shovels, axes, and blankets. The observer adds, "they were brimful of patriotism, shouting for Jeff Davis and singing war songs."[19] A paper in Lynchburg, Virginia, commenting on the enlistment of seventy free Negroes to fight for the defense of the State, concluded with "three cheers for the patriotic Negroes of Lynchburg."[20]

Two weeks after the firing on Fort Sumter, several companies of volunteers of color passed through Augusta, Georgia, on their way to Virginia to engage in actual war. Sixteen well-drilled companies of volunteers and one Negro company from Nashville composed this group.[21] In November of the same year, a military review was held in New Orleans, where twenty-eight thousand troops passed before Governor Moore, General Lowell, and General Ruggles. The line of march extended beyond seven miles and included one regiment comprised of 1,400 free colored men.[22] *The Baltimore Traveler* commented on arming Negroes at Richmond: "Contrabands who have recently come within the Federal lines at Williamsport, report that all the able-bodied men in that vicinity are being taken to Richmond, formed into regiments, and armed for the defense of that City."[23]

During February 1862 the Confederate Legislature of Virginia was considering a bill to enroll all free Negroes in the state for service with the Confederate forces[24] as did the legislatures of other states. Military and civil leaders and the Confederate Congress and its perplexed War Department debated among themselves the relative value of employing Negroes as soldiers. Slowly the ranks of those at home were made to grow thin by calls to the front. In April 1862 President Davis was authorized to call out and place in service all white men between the ages of eighteen and thirty-five; in September the ages were raised to include the years, of thirty-five and, forty-five; and finally in February 1864 all white males between the years of seventeen and fifty were made liable to military service. The Negroes were liable for impressment in the work of building fortifications, producing war materials, and the like.[25]

The demand became so urgent for men that quite a controversy arose over the advisability of employing the Negroes as soldiers. Some said that the Negro belonged to an inferior race and, therefore, could not be a good soldier, that the Negro could do menial work in the army, but that fighting was the white man's task. Those who supported the idea in its incipiency always urged the necessity of employing Negroes in the army. In a letter to the Secretary of War, a native Georgian supported the employment of these troops recommending after the war was over freedom to those who fought, compensation to the owners, and the continuation of the institution of slavery by retaining as slaves "boys and women, and exempted or detailed men." The statement concludes: "[O]ur country requires a quick and stringent remedy. Don't stop for reforms."[26]

In November 1864 in his message to the Confederate Congress, Jefferson Davis spoke of a possible time when slaves would be needed in the Confederate army: "The subject is to be viewed by us, therefore, solely in the light of policy and our social economy. When so regarded, I must dissent from those who advise a general levy and arming of slaves for the duty of soldiers. Until our white population shall prove insufficient for the armies we require and can afford to keep the field, to employ as a soldier the Negro, who has merely been trained to labor, and as a laborer under the white man, accustomed from his youth to the use of firearms, would scarcely be deemed wise or advantageous by any; and this is the question before us. But should the alternative ever be presented of subjugation or of the employment of the slave as a soldier, there seems no reason to doubt what should be our decision."[27] In the same month, J. A. Seddon, Secretary of War, refused permission to Major E. B. Briggs of Columbus, Georgia, to raise a regiment of Negro troops, noting the improbability that any such policy would be adopted by Congress.[28]

In response to an inquiry from Secretary of War Seddon as to the advisability of arming slaves, General Howell Cobb presented the point of view of one group of the Confederates when he opposed the measure to arm the Negroes: "I think that the proposition to make soldiers of our slaves is the most pernicious idea that has been suggested since the war began . . . you cannot make soldiers of slaves or slaves of soldiers. The moment you resort to Negro soldiers, your white soldiers will be lost to you, and one secret of the favor with which the proposition is received in portions of the army is the hope when Negroes go into the army, they [the whites] will be permitted to retire. It is simply a proposition to fight the balance of the war with Negro troops. You can't keep white and black troops together and you can't trust Negroes by themselves. . . . Use all the Negroes you can get for all purposes for which you need them but don't arm them. The day you make soldiers of them is the beginning of the end of the revolution. If slaves make good soldiers, our whole theory of slavery is wrong." General Beauregard, Commander of the Department of Georgia, South Carolina, and Florida, wrote to a friend in July 1863 that the arming of the slaves would lead to the atrocious consequences which have ever resulted from the employment of "a merciless servile race as soldiers."[30] General Patton Anderson declared that the idea of arming the slaves was a "monstrous proposition revolting to southern sentiment, southern pride and southern honor."[31]

The opposite point of view was expressed by the group of Southerners led by General Pat Cleburne who wrote in a petition presented to General Joseph E. Johnson by several Confederate Officers: "Will the Slaves fight?—the experience of this war has been so far, that half-trained Negroes have fought as bravely as many half-trained Yankees."[32] J. P. Benjamin, Secretary of State, urged that the slaves would be certainly made to fight against the Southerners if not armed for southern defense. He advocated also the emancipation of those who would fight—if they should fight for southern freedom. According to Benjamin, they were entitled to their own. In keeping with the necessity of increasing the army, the editor of a popular newspaper in Charleston, South Carolina, was besought to commence a discussion on this point in his paper so that "the people might learn the lesson which experience was sternly teaching."[33]

In a letter to President Davis, another correspondent argued that since the Negro had been used from the outset of the war to defend the South by raising provisions for the army, that the sword and musket be put in his hands, and added, "I would not make a soldier of the Negro if it could be helped, but we are reduced to this last resort."[34] Sam. Clayton of Georgia wrote: "The recruits should come from our Negroes, nowhere else. We should away with pride of opinion, away with false pride, and promptly take hold of all the means God has placed within our reach to help us through this struggle—a war for the right of self-government. Some people say that Negroes will not fight. I say they will fight. They fought at Ocean Pond (Olustee, Fla.), Honey Hill and other places. The enemy fights us with Negroes, and they will do very well to fight the Yankees."[35]

The pressure to fill the depleted ranks of the Confederate forces became greater as the war continued. Congress and the State legislatures had called into service all able-bodied whites between the ages of seventeen and fifty years; later the ages were extended both ways to sixteen and sixty years. Grant remarked that the Confederates had robbed "the cradle and the grave" in order to fill the armies.[36] Jefferson Davis began to see the futility of a hypothetical discussion as to the advisability or values in the use of Negroes as soldiers and in a letter to John Forsythe in February 1865 stated "that all arguments as to the positive advantage or disadvantage of employing them are beside the question, which is simply one of relative advantage between having their fighting element in our ranks or in those of the enemy."[31]

A strong recommendation for the use of Negroes as soldiers was sent to Senator Andrew Hunter at Richmond by General Robert E. Lee, in January, 1865. "I think, therefore," said he, "we must decide whether slavery shall be extinguished by our enemies and the slaves be used against us, or use them ourselves at the risk of the effects which may be produced upon our social institutions. My own opinion is that we should employ them without delay. I believe that with proper regulations they may be made efficient soldiers. They possess the physical quali- fications in a marked degree. Long habits of obedience and subordination coupled with the moral influence which in our country the white man possesses over the black furnish an excellent foundation for that discipline which is the best guaranty of military efficiency. Our chief aim should be to secure their fidelity. There have been formidable armies composed of men having no interest in the cause for which they fought beyond their pay or the hope of plunder. But it is certain that the surest foundation upon which the fidelity of an army can rest, especially in a service which imposes hardships and privations, is the personal interest of the soldier in the issue of the contest. Such an interest we can give our Negroes by giving immediate freedom to all who enlist and freedom at the end of the war to the families of those who discharge their duties faithfully (whether they survive or not), together with the privilege of residing in the South. To this might be added a bounty for faithful service."[38] This word was influential, coming as it did from the Commander-in-Chief of the Confederate forces. Even if the Confederate Congress had immediately moved upon this suggestion, the measure would have been en- acted too late to be of any avail.[39]

On February 7, 1865, the Confederate Senate refused to pass a resolution calling on the committee on military affairs to report a bill to enroll Negro soldiers. Later in the same month the Senate indefinitely postponed the measure.[40] As the House and Senate met in secret session, much of the debate cannot be found. General Lee wrote to Representative Barksdale of Mississippi that the employment of Negro soldiers was declared not only expedient but necessary and reiterated his opinion that they would make good soldiers as had been shown in their employment in the Union armies.[41] With recommendations from General Lee and Governor Smith of Virginia and, with the approval of President Davis, an act was passed by the Congress, March 13, 1865, enrolling slaves in the Confederate army.[42] Each state was to furnish a quota of the total 300,000.[43] The Preamble of the act reads as follows: "An Act to increase the Military Force of the Confederate States: The Congress of the Confederate States of America so enact, that, in order to provide additional forces, to repel invasion, maintain the rightful possession of the Con- federate States, secure their independence and preserve their institution, the Presi- dent be, and he is hereby authorized to ask for and accept from the owners of slaves, the services of such number of able-bodied Negro men as he may deem expedient, for and during the war, to perform military service in whatever capacity he may direct. . . ."

The language used in other sections of the act seems to imply that volunteering also made one a freedman.[44]

After the passage of the measure by the Confederate Congress, General Lee cooperated in every way with the War Department in facilitating the recruiting of

Negro troops.[45] Recruiting officers were appointed in each state. Lieutenant John L. Cowardin, Adjutant, 19th Batallion, Virginia Artillery was ordered on April 1, 1865, to proceed recruiting Negro troops according to the act. On March 30, 1865, Captain Edward Bostick was ordered to raise four companies in South Carolina, others in Alabama, Florida, and Virginia.[41] Lee and Johnson, however, surrendered before this plan could be carried out. If the Confederate Congress could have accepted the recommendation in the fall of 1864, the war might have been prolonged at least a few months by the use of the Negro troops. President Davis's opinion on learning of the passage of the act was that less was accomplished than would have been if the act had been passed sufficiently early to drill and make ready the slaves for the spring campaign of 1865.

Under the guidance of the local authorities came the enlistment of thousands of Negroes in the State Militias and in the Confederate Army who served with satisfaction; however there is no evidence that they took part in any important battles. Initally, the Confederate Government could not bring itself to acknowledge the right or the ability of the slave to serve with the white man as a soldier, but necessity forced the acceptance of the Negro as a soldier. In spite of the long years of controversy with its arguments of racial inferiority,[47] out of the muddle of fact and fancy came the deliberate decision to employ Negro troops. This act, in itself, as a historical fact, refuted the former theories of southern statesmen. That the Negro was a factor in both the Union and Confederate armies in the War of the Rebellion leads to the conclusion that the he is an American not only because he lives in America, but because his life is closely connected with every important movement in American history.

ENDNOTES

[1] Davis, *The Civil War and Reconstruction in Florida*, p. 220.

[2] For summary of such legislation to prevent this, see J.C. Hurd, *The Law of Freedom and Bondage in the United States*, Vol. II. In Florida, 1827, a law was enacted to prevent trading with Negroes. In 1828, death was declared the penalty for inciting insurrection among the slaves and in 1840 there was passed an act prohibiting the use of firearms by Negroes. In Virginia as early as 1748 there was enacted a measure declaring that even the free Negroes and Indians enlisted in the militia should appear without arms; but in 1806 the law was modified to provide that free Negroes should not carry arms without first obtaining a license from the county or corporation court. One who was caught with firearms in spite of this act was to forfeit the weapon to the informer and receive thirty-nine lashes at the whipping-post. *Hening, Statutes-at-Large*, Vol. V, p. 17; Vol. XVI, p. 274.

[3] General W. S. Harney, commanding in Missouri, responded to the claims of slaveholders for the return of runaway slaves with the works: "Already, since the commencement of these unhappy disturbances, slaves have escaped from their owners and have sought refuge in the camps of the United States troops from the Northern States, and commanded by a Northern general. They were carefully sent back to their owners." General D.C. Buell, commanding in Tennessee, in reply to the same demands states: "Several applications have been made to me by persons whose servants have been found in our camps; and in every instance that I know of the master has removed his servant and taken him away." William Wells Brown, *The Negro in the Rebellion*, pp. 57-58

[4] Secretary Seddon, War Department, wrote: "They [the Negroes] have, besides, the homes they value, the families they love, and the masters they respect and depend on to defend and protect against the savagery and devastation of the enemy." - *Official Rebellion Records,* Series IV, Vol. III, pp. 761-762.

[5] Governor Walker of Florida, himself a former slaveholder, said before the State legislature in 1865 that "the world had never seen such a body of slaves, for not only in peace but in war they had been faithful to us. During much of the time of the late unhappy difficulties, Florida had a greater number of men in her army than constituted her entire voting population. This of course, stripped many districts of their arms-bearing inhabitants and left our females and infant children almost exclusively to the protection of our slaves. They proved true to their trust. Not one instance of insult, outrage, or indignity has ever come to my knowledge. They remained at home and made provisions for the army." John Wallace, *Carpet-Bag Rule in Florida*, p. 23.

[6] For more than two years, Negroes had been extensively employed in belligerent operations by the Confederacy. They had been embodied and drilled as rebel soldiers and had paraded with white troops at a time when this would not have been tolerated in the armies of the Union." - Greely, *The American Conflict,* Vol. II, p. 524.

[7] Ibid., Vol. II, p. 521.

[8] Jones, *A Rebel War Clerk's Diary*, Vol. I, p. 237; Schwab, *The Confederate States of America*, p. 194.

[9] *Laws of Florida, 12th Session,* 1862, Chap. 1878.

[10] *Confederate War Department, Bureau of Conscription*, Circular No. 36, December 12, 1864. *Off. Red. Reb.*, Series IV, Vol. III, p. 933.

[11] *Off. Red. Reb.*, Series IV, Vol. III, p. 780. Journals of Congress, IV, 260.

[12] Washington, *The Story of the Negro,* Vol. II, p. 321.

[13] *Order No. 426. Adjutant-General's Office, Headquarters Louisiana Militia, March 24, 1862.* Cf. Brown, *The Negro in the Rebellion*, pp. 84-85.

[14] Parton, *History of the Administration of the Gulf,* 1862-1864; General Butler in New Orleans, p. 517.

[15] Greely, *The American Conflict*, p. 521.

[16] The *Charleston* Mercury, January 3, 18861;

[17] The announcement of the recruiting read: "Attention, volunteers: Resolved by the Committee of Safety that C. Deloach, D.R. Cook and William B. Greenlaw be authorized to organize a volunteer company composed of our patriotic free men of color, of the city of Memphis, for the service of our common defense. All who have not enrolled their names will call at the office of W. B. Greenlaw & Co. "

F. W. Forsythe, Secretary.   F. Titus, President.

Williams, *History of the Negro*, Vol. II, p. 277.

[18] Greely, *The American Conflict*, Vol. II, p. 521.

[19] *Memphis Avalanche*, September 3, 1861.

[20] Greely, *The American Conflict*, Vol. II, p. 522.

[21] *Ibid.*, p. 277.

[22] Ibid., Vol. II, p. 522

[23] The *Baltimore Traveler*, February 4, 1862

[24] Greely, *The American Conflict,* Vol. II, p. 522.

[25] Schwab, *The Confederate States of America*, p. 193. Moore, Rebellion Records, Vol. VII, p. 210. Jones, Diary, Vol. I, p. 381.

[26] An indorsement from the Secretary of war reads: "If all white men capable of bearing arms are put in the field, it would be as large a draft as a community could continuously sustain, and whites are better soldiers than Negroes. For war, when existence is staked, the best material should be used." - *Off. Reds. Rebell.*, Series IV, Vol. III, pp. 693-694

[27] *Off. Reds. Rebell*, Series IV, Vol. III, p. 799.

[28] *Ibid*, Series IV, Vol. III, p. 846. J.A. Seddon to Maj. E. B. Briggs, Nov. 24, 1864.

[29] *Ibid*, Series IV, Vol. III, p. 1009.

[30] *Off. Reds. Rebell*, Series I, Vol. XXVIII, Pt. 2, p. 13.

[31] *Ibid.*, Series I, Vol. LII, Pt. 2, p. 598.

[32] Davis, *Civil War and Reconstruction in Florida*, p. 226.

[33] *Off. Reds. Rebell.*, Series IV, Vol. III, pp. 959-960

[34] *Ibid.*, p. 227

[35] *Off. Reds. Rebell.*, Series IV, Vol. III, pp. 1010-1011

[36] Rhodes, *History of the United states since the Compromise of 1850*, Vol. IV, p. 525.

[37] *Off. Reds. Rebell.*, Series IV, Vol. VIII, p. 1110

[38] *Off. Reds. Rebell.*, Series IV, Vol. VIII, p. 1013.

[39] Williams, *Negro Troops in the War of the Rebellion,* Journals of Congress, Vol. IV, pp. 572-573.

In the *American Historical Review,* January, 1913, N.W. Stephenson has an article upon "The Question of Arming the Slaves." The article is concerned particularly with the debate in the Confederate Congress upon this perplexing question and with the psychology of the statements made by President Davis, Secretary Benjamin, General Lee and by various Congressmen. The author has searched the Journals of the confederate Congress, newspaper files and personal recollections and gives conclusions which show that "the subject was discussed during the last winter of the Confederate regime," and by inference the dissertation shows that the fear of the consequences of arming the slaves was alike in the minds of all southern people. The treatise is a study in historical psychology; and, as in similar works by men of the type of the author, the point of view of the South and of the Confederacy is presented and the Negro and his actual employment as a soldier is neglected. The author contends that a few southern leaders attempted to force the arming of the blacks upon an unwilling southern public. He neglects the evidence contained in the action of local authorities in arming the Negroes who were free and their attitude concerning those who were slaves. He neglects also the sentiment of southern leaders who favored the measure. The Journals of the Confederate Congress, therefore, will be more valuable to those desiring information concerning the debates on this questions.

[40] *Journal of Congress of Confederate States,* Vol. IV, p. 528 and Vol. VII, p. 595; Jones, *Diary*, Vol. II, p. 431.

[41] *Richmond Dispatch,* February 24, 1865; Jones *Diary*, vol. II, p. 432.

[42] *Journal of Congress of Confederate States,* Vol. VII, p. 748.

[43] *Richmond Examiner*, December 9, 1864 - Gov. Smith's Message. Jones, *Diary*, Vol. II, p. 43; pp. 432-433. Schwab, *The Confederate States of America,* p. 194.

44 Off. Reds. Rebell., Series IV, Vol III, p. 1161.

Ibid., Series III, Vol. V, pp. 711-712; Davis, Confederate Government, Vol. II, p. 660.

[45] Rhodes, *History of U.S.*, Vol. V, 1864-1865, p. 81.

[46] *Off. Reds. Rebell.*, Series IV, Vol. III, pp. 1193-1194 and Appendix.

[47] *Cf. Southern Correspondence throughout the Rebellion Records.*

NEGROES IN OUR ARMY.

The following article, taken from Southern Historical Society Papers, Vol. XXXI, relates the thoughts and efforts of General Pat Cleburne on the issue of Negroes in the Confederate Army:

GENERAL PAT CLEBURNE THE FIRST TO ADVOCATE THEIR USE. HIS PLAN WAS TURNED DOWN.

But a similar one was afterwards adopted—some interesting reminiscences on the subject, which show the circumstances prompting the suggestion.

In the spring of 1879 I had a letter from the War Department at Washington, asking me to authenticate a document in the files of the Confederate Record Office. Considering that paper of the first interest and value, I send, herewith, a copy, and will give your readers the circumstances surrounding it, viz: After the disgraceful defeat of the Confederate army, at Missionary Ridge, in front of Chattanooga, on the 25th of November, 1863, the bulk of it retreated to Dalton, Ga. Cleburne's Division, which was the rear guard, on the 27th made a stand a Ringgold Gap, and without assistance, and single handed, checked and defeated the attempt of the pursuing army under General Hooker to capture the wagon, artillery, and ordnance train of Bragg's army. Holding the position until the safety of these were assured, the division retired, under orders to Tunnel Hill, some ten miles north of Dalton, where it remained on outpost.

CLEBURNE ABSORBED.

In December following, I noticed that General Cleburne was for several days deeply preoccupied and engaged in writing. Finally he handed me his MS., which upon reading, I found to be an advocacy of freeing the negroes and their enlistment in our military service. In reply to his question as to what I thought of it, I said while I fully concurred in his opinion as to the absolute necessity of some such step to recruit the army, and recognized the force of his arguments, still I doubted the expediency, at that time, of his formulating these views. First, because the slave holders were very sensitive as to such property, and were totally unprepared to consider such a radical measure, and many, not being in our service, could not properly appreciate that it had become a matter of self-preservation that our ranks should be filled to meet, in some degree, the numerical superiority of the enemy— consequently, it would raise a storm of indignation against him. And next that one of the corps of our army was without a lieutenant-general, that he, General Cleburne, had already achieved, unaided, a signal success at Ringgold, for which he had received the thanks of Congress, and stood in reputation first among the major-generals, and might justly expect to be advanced to this vacancy, and I felt assured the publicity of this paper would be used detrimentally to him, and his chances of promotion destroyed.

To that he answered that a crisis was upon the South, the danger of which he was convinced could most quickly be averted in the way outlined, and feeling it to be his duty to bring this before the authorities, he would try to do so, irrespective of any personal result. To my question as to whether or not the negroes would make efficient soldiers, he said that with reasonable and careful drilling, he had no doubt they would, and as deep as was his attachment to his present command he would cheerfully undertake that of a negro division in this emergency.

COPIES OF THE PLAN.

Under his instructions I made, from his notes, a plain copy of the document, which was read to, and free criticisms invited from members of his staff, one of whom, Major Calhoun Benham, strongly dissented, and asked for a copy with the purpose of writing a reply in opposition.

The division brigadiers were then called together, and my recollection is, that their endorsement was unanimous—namely: Polk, Lowery, Govan, and Granberry. Later, a meeting of the general officers of the army, including its commander, General Joseph E. Johnston, was held at General Hardee's headquarters, and the paper submitted. It was received with disapproval by several, and before this assemblage Major Benham read his letter of protest. Not having been present, I am unable to state the individual sentiment of the higher officers, but my impression is, that Generals Hardee and Johnston were favorably disposed, though the latter declined to forward it to the War Department, on the ground that it was more political than military in tenor.

That was a sore disappointment to Cleburne, who supposed his opportunity of bringing the matter before the President was lost, as he was too good a soldier and strict a disciplinarian to think of sending it over the head of his superior.

The day following, Major-General W. H. T. Walker addressed him a note, stating that this paper was of such a dangerous (I think he said incendiary) character, that he felt it his duty to report it to the President, and asking if General Cleburne would furnish him a copy and avow himself its author.

Both requests were promptly complied with, Cleburne remarking that General Walker had done him an unintentional service, in accomplishing his desire, that this matter be brought to the attention of the Confederate authorities. Communication with Richmond was then very slow and uncertain. General Cleburne, naturally, felt somewhat anxious as to the outcome of the affair, though manifesting no regrets, and in discussing the matter and possibilities, said the worst that could happen to him would be court-martial and cashiering, if which occurred, he would immediately enlist in his old regiment, the 15th Arkansas, then in his division; that if not permitted to command, he could at least do his duty in the ranks.

After the lapse of some weeks the paper was returned endorsed by President Davis, substantially, if not verbatim, as follows:

"While recognizing the patriotic motives of its distinguished author, I deem it inexpedient, at this time, to give publicity to this paper, and request that it be suppressed. J. D."

Upon receipt of this, General Cleburne directed me to destroy all copies, except the one returned from Richmond. This was filed in my office desk, which was subsequently captured and burned with its contents by the Federal cavalry during the Atlanta campaign.

COMES TO LIGHT.

After the war, I was several times solicited, from both Confederate and Federal sources, to furnish copies, which was impossible, as I felt sure the only one retained had been destroyed, as above stated, and that no other existed. A few years ago Major Benham died in California, and to my extreme surprise and delight, a copy—the one supplied him at Tunnel Hill—was found among his papers. This was forwarded to Lieutenant L. H. Mangum, Cleburne's former law partner and afterwards aide-de-camp, who sent it to me to identify, which I readily did. Mangum afterwards placed it in the hands of General Marcus J. Wright, agent of the War Department, for collection of Confederate records, and it was this paper I was called upon to authenticate, the reason for which being that as it is a copy and not an original, some such official certification was desirable.

HIS POLICY ADOPTED.

A short while before his death, on the fatal field of Franklin, Cleburne had the gratification of knowing that a bill, embodying exactly his proposition, was advocated upon the floor of the Confederate Congress. This was subsequently passed and became a law, by executive approval.

It is scarcely a matter of speculation to tell what the result of this measure would have been, had it gone promptly into effect early in the spring of 1864. General Hood, whose opinion is entitled to weight, probably states it correctly in his book, *Advance and Retreat* (page 296), when referring to Cleburne, says:

He was a man of equally quick perception and strong character, and was, especially in one respect, in advance of many of our people. He possessed the boldness and wisdom to earnestly advocate at an early period of the war the freedom of the negro and enrollment of the young and able-bodied men of that race. This stroke of policy and additional source of strength to our armies would, in my opinion, have given us our independence.

> **IRVING A. BUCK,** Former Assistant Adjutant-General
> Cleburne's Division, Hardee's Corps, Army of Tennessee.

THE PAPER IN QUESTION.

Here is the document referred to:

To the Commanding General, the Corps, Division, Brigade, and Regimental Commanders of the Army of Tennessee:

GENERAL, - Moved by the exigency in which our country is now placed, we take the liberty of laying before you, unofficially, our views on the present state of affairs. The subject is so grave and our views so new, we feel it a duty both to you and the cause that before going further we should submit them for your judgment, and receive your suggestions in regard to them. We, therefore, respectfully ask you to give us an expression of your views in the premises. We have now been fighting for nearly three years, have spilled much of our best blood, and lost, consumed, or thrown to the flames an amount of property equal in value to the specie currency of the world.

LONG LISTS OF DEAD AND MANGLED.

Through some lack in our system, the fruits of our struggle and sacrifices have invariably slipped away from us and left us nothing but long lists of dead and mangled. Instead of standing defiantly on the borders of our territory, of harassing those of the enemy, we are hemmed in today into less than two-thirds of it, and still the enemy menacingly confronts us at every point with superior forces. Our soldiers can see no end to this state of affairs except in our own exhaustion hence, instead of rising to the occasion, they are sinking into a fatal apathy, growing weary of hardships and slaughters, which promise no results.

In this state of things it is easy to understand why there is a growing belief that some black catastrophe is not far ahead of us, and that unless some extraordinary change is soon made in our condition we must overtake it. The consequences of this condition are showing themselves more plainly every day—restlessness of morals spreading everywhere, manifesting itself in the army in a growing disregard for private rights; desertion spreading to a class of soldiers it never dared to tamper with before; military commissions sinking in the estimation of the soldier; our supplies failing, our finances in ruins. If this state continues much longer we must be subjugated. Every man should endeavor to understand the meaning of subjugation before it is too late. We can give but a faint idea when we say it means the loss of all we now hold most sacred—slaves and all other personal property, lands, homesteads, liberty, justice, safety, pride, manhood. It means that the history of this heroic struggle will be written by the enemy; that our youth will be trained by Northern school teachers; will learn from Northern school-books their version of the war; will be impressed by all the influences of history and education to regard our gallant dead as traitors, our maimed veterans as fit objects for derision. It means the crushing of Southern manhood, the hatred of our former slaves, who will, on a spy system, be our secret police. The conqueror's policy is to divide the conquered into factions and stir up animosity among them, and in training an army of negroes the North, no doubt, holds this thought in perspective.

THE THREE GREAT CAUSES.

We can see three great causes operating to destroy us:

1. The inferiority of our armies to those of the enemy in point of numbers.
2. The poverty of our single source of supply, in comparison with his several sources.
3. The fact that slavery, from being one of the chief sources of strength at the commencement of the war, has now become, in a military point of view, one of our chief sources of weakness.

The enemy already opposes us at every point with superior numbers, and it is endeavoring to make the preponderance irresistible.

President Davis, in his recent message, says the enemy "has recently ordered a large conscription and made a subsequent call for volunteers, to be followed, if ineffectual, by a still further draft." In addition, the President of the United States announces that "he has already in training an army of 100,000 negroes as good as any troops," and that every fresh raid he makes and new slice of territory he wrests from us will add to this force. Every soldier in our army already knows and feels our numerical inferiority to the enemy. Want of men in the field has prevented him from reaping the fruits of his victories, and has prevented him from having the furlough he expected after the last reorganization, and when he turns from the wasting armies in the field to look at the source of supply, he finds nothing in the prospect to encourage him.

Our single source of supply is that portion of our white men fit for duty and not now in the ranks. The enemy has three sources of supply; first, his own motley population; secondly, our slaves; and, thirdly, Europeans, whose hearts are fired into a crusade against us by fictitious pictures of the atrocities of slavery, and who meet no hindrance from their governments in such enterprise, because these governments are equally antagonistic to the institution.

In touching the third cause, the fact that slavery has become a military weakness, we may rouse prejudice and passion, but the time has come when it would be madness not to look at our danger from every point of view and to probe it to the bottom.

A SOURCE OF STRENGTH.

Apart from the assistance that home and foreign prejudice against slavery has given to the North, slavery is a source of great strength to the enemy in a purely military point of view by supplying him with an army from our granaries; but it is our most vulnerable point, a continual embarrassment, and in some respects an insidious weakness. Wherever slavery is once seriously disturbed, whether by the actual presence or the approach of the enemy, or even by a cavalry raid, the whites can no longer with safety to their property openly sympathize with our cause. The fear of their slaves is continually haunting them, and from silence and apprehension many of these soon learn to wish the war stopped on any terms. The next stage is to take the oath to save property, and they become dead to us, if not open enemies. To prevent raids we are forced to scatter our forces, and are not free to move and strike like the enemy. His vulnerable points are carefully selected and fortified depots; ours are found in every point where there is a slave to set free. All along the lines slavery is comparatively valueless to us for labor, but of great and increasing worth to the enemy for information. It is an omnipresent spy system, pointing out our valuable men to the enemy, revealing our positions, purposes, and resources, and yet acting so safely and secretly that there is no means to guard against it. Even in the heart of our country, where our hold upon this secret espionage is firmest, it waits but the opening fire of the enemy's battle-line to wake it, like a torpid serpent, into venomous activity.

In view of the state of affairs, what does our country propose to do? In the words of President Davis:

"No effort must be spared to all largely to our effective force as promptly as possible. The sources of supply are to be found in restoring to the army all who are improperly absent, putting an end to substitution, modifying the exemption law, restricting details, and placing in the ranks such of the able-bodied men now employed as wagoners, nurses, cooks, and other employees as are doing service for which the negroes may be found competent."

MEN IMPROPERLY ABSENT.

Most of the men improperly absent, together with many of the exempts and men having substitutes, are now without the Confederate lines and cannot be calculated on. If all the exempts capable of bearing arms were enrolled, it will give us the boys below 18, the men above 45, and those persons who are left at home to meet the wants of the country and the army; but this modification of the exemption law will remove from the fields and manufactories most of the skill that directed agri-cultural and mechanical labor, and, as stated by the President, "details will have to be made to meet the wants of the country," thus sending many of the men to be derived for this source back to their homes again. Independently of this, experi-ence proves that striplings and men above conscript age break down and swell the sick lists more than they do the ranks. The portion now in our lines of the class who have substitutes is not, on the whole, a hopeful element, for the motives that created it must have been stronger than patriotism, and these motives, added to what many of them will call breach of faith, will cause some to be not forthcoming and others to be unwilling and discontented soldiers.

The remaining sources mentioned by the President have been so closely pruned in the Army of Tennessee that they will be found not to yield largely. The supply from all these sources, together with what we now have in the field, will exhaust the white race, and though it should greatly exceed expectations and put us on an equality with the enemy, or even give us temporary advantages, still we have no reserve to meet unexpected disaster or to supply a protracted struggle. Like past years, 1864 will diminish our ranks by the casualties of war, and what source of repair is there left us? We, therefore, see in the recommendations of the President only a temporary expedient, which at the best will leave us twelve months hence in the same predicament we are in now. The President attempts to meet only one of the depressing causes mentioned; for the other two he has proposed no remedy. They remain to generate lack of confidence in our final success, and to keep us moving down hill as heretofore.

Adequately to meet the causes which are now threatening ruin to our country, we propose, in addition to a modification of the President's plans, that we retain in service for the war all troops now in service, and that we immediately commence training a large reserve of the most courageous of our slaves; and further, that we guarantee freedom within a reasonable time to every slave in the South who shall remain true to the Confederacy in this war.

SLAVERY OR LOSS OF SLAVES.

As between the loss of independence and the loss of slavery, we assume that every patriot will freely give up the latter—give up the negro slave rather than be a slave himself. If we are correct in this assumption it only remains to show how this great national sacrifice is, in all human probabilities, to change the current of success and sweep the invader from our country, our country has already some friends in England and France, and there are strong motives to induce these na-tions to recognize and assist us but they cannot assist us without helping slavery, and to do this would be in conflict with their policy for the last quarter of a century. England has paid hundreds of millions to emancipate her West India slaves and break up the slave trade. Could she now consistently spend her treasure to rein-state slavery in this country? But this barrier once removed, the sympathy and the interests of these and other nations will accord with our own, and we may expect from them both moral support and material aid. One thing is certain, as soon as the great sacrifice to independence is made and known in foreign countries, there will be a complete change of front in our favor of the sympathies of the world.

This measure will deprive the North of the moral and material aid which it now derives from the bitter prejudices with which foreigners view the institution, and its war, if continued, will henceforth be so despicable in their eyes that this source of recruiting will be dried up. It will leave the enemy's negro army no motive to fight for, and will exhaust the source from which it has been recruited.

The idea that it is their special mission to war against slavery has held growing sway over the Northern people for many years, and has at length ripened into a bloody crusade against it. This baleful superstition has so far supplied them with a courage and constancy not their own. It is the most powerful and honestly entertained plank in their war platform. Knock this away, and what is left? A bloody ambition for more territory; a pretended veneration for the Union, which one of their own most distinguished orators (Dr. Beecher in his Liverpool speech), openly avowed was only used as a stimulous to stir up the anti-slavery crusade, and, lastly, the poisonous and selfish interests which are the fungus growth of the war itself. Mankind may fancy it a great duty to destroy slavery, but what interest can mankind have in upholding this remainder of the Northern war platform? Their interests and feelings will be diametrically opposed to it.

A STRONG MEASURE.

The measure we propose will strike dead all John Brown fanaticism, and will compel the enemy to draw off altogether, or, in the eyes of the world, to swallow the Declaration of Independence without the sauce and disguise of philanthropy. This delusion of fanaticism at an end, thousands of Northern people will have leisure to look at home and see the gulf of despotism into which they themselves are rushing. The measure will at one blow strip the enemy of foreign sympathy and assistance, and transfer them to the South; it will dry up two of his three sources of recruiting; it will take from his negro army the only motive it could have to fight against the South, and will probably cause much of it to desert over to us; it will deprive his cause of the powerful stimulous of fanaticism, and will enable him to see the rock on which his so-called friends are now piloting him. The immediate effect of the emancipation and enrollment of negroes on the military strength of the South would be to enable us to have armies numerically superior to those of the North, and a reserve of any size we might think necessary; to enable us to take the offensive, move forward, and forage on the enemy. It would open to us in prospective another and almost untouched source of supply, and furnish us with the means of preventing temporary disaster and carrying on a protracted struggle. It would instantly remove all the vulnerability, embarrassment, and inherent weakness which result from slavery. The approach of the enemy would no longer find every household surrounded by spies, the fear that sealed the master's lips, and the avarice that has in so many cases tempted him practically to desert us would alike be removed. There would be no recruits awaiting the enemy with open arms; no complete history of every neighborhood with ready guides; no fear of insurrection in the rear or anxieties for the fate of loved ones when our armies moved forward. The chronic irritation of hope deferred would be joyfully ended with the negro, and the sympathies of his whole race would be due to his native South. It would restore confidence in an early termination of the war with all its inspiring consequences; and even if, contrary to all expectations, the enemy should succeed in overrunning the South, instead of finding a cheap, ready-made means of holding it down, he would find a common hatred and thirst for vengeance which would break into acts at every favorable opportunity; would prevent him from settling on our lands, and render the South a very unprofitable conquest. It would remove forever all selfish taint from our cause and place independence above every question of property.

The very magnitude of the sacrifice itself, such as no nation has ever voluntarily made before, would appall our enemies, destroy his spirit and his finances, and fill our hearts with a pride and singleness of purpose which would clothe us with new strength in battle.

NEED FOR FIGHTING MEN.

Apart from all other aspects of the question, the necessity for more fighting men is upon us. We can only get a sufficiency by making the negro share the dangers and hardships of the war. If we arm and train him and make him fight for the country in her hour of dire distress, every consideration of principle and policy demand that we should set him and his whole race who side with us, free. It is a first principle with mankind that he who offers his life in defense of the State should receive from her in return his freedom and his happiness, and we believe in acknowledgment of this principle the constitutions of the Southern States have reserved to their respective governments the power to free slaves for meritorious services to the State. It is politic besides. For many years—ever since the agitation of the subject of slavery commenced—the negro has been dreaming of freedom, and his vivid imagination has surrounded that condition with so many gratifications that it has become the paradise of his hopes. To attain it he will tempt dangers and difficulties not exceeded by the bravest in the field. The hope of freedom is, perhaps, the only moral incentive that can be applied to him in his present condition. It would be preposterous, then, to expect him to fight against it with any degree of enthusiasm; therefore, we must bind him to our cause by no doubtful bonds; we must leave no possible loophole for treachery to creep in. The slaves are dangerous now, but armed, trained, and collected in an army they would be a thousandfold more dangerous. Therefore, when we make soldiers of them we must make freemen of them beyond all question, and thus enlist their sympathies also. We can do this more effectually than the North can now do, for we can give the negro not only his own freedom, but that of his wife and child, and can secure it to him in his old home. To do this we must immediately make his marriage and parental relations sacred in the eyes of the law and forbid their sale. The past legislation of the South concedes that a large free middle class of negro blood, between the master and slave, must sooner or later destroy the institution. If, then, we touch the institution at all, we would do best to make the most of it, and by emancipating the whole race upon reasonable terms, and within such reasontime as will prepare both races for the change, secure to ourselves all the advantages, and to our enemies all the disadvantages that can arise, both at home and abroad from such a sacrifice. Satisfy the negro that if he faithfully adheres to our standard during the war he shall receive his freedom and that of his race; give him as an earnest of our intentions such immediate immunities as will impress him with our sincerity and be in keeping with his new condition; enroll a portion of his class as soldiers of the Confederacy, and we change the race from a dread weakness to a position of strength.

THE SLAVES AS FIGHTERS.

Will the slaves fight? The helots of Sparta stood their masters good stead in battle. In the great sea fight of Lepanto, where the Christians checked forever the spread of Mohammedanism over Europe, the galley slaves of portions of the fleet were promised freedom, and called on to fight at a critical moment of the battle.

They fought well, and civilization owes much to those brave galley slaves. The negro slaves of St. Domingo, fighting for freedom, defeated their white masters and the French troops sent against them. The negro slaves of Jamaica revolted, and under the name of maroons held the mountains against their masters for 150 years; and the experience of this war has been so far that half-trained negroes have fought as bravely as many other half-trained Yankees. If, contrary to the training of a lifetime, they can be made to face and fight bravely against their former masters, how much more probable is it that with the allurement of a higher reward, and led by those masters, they would submit to discipline and face dangers?

ARGUMENTS AGAINST IT.

We will briefly notice a few arguments against this course: It is said republicanism cannot exist without the institution. Even were this true, we prefer any form of government of which the Southern people may have the moulding to one forced upon us by a conqueror.

It is said the white man cannot perform agricultural labor in the South. The experience of this army during the heat of summer from Bowling Green, Ky., to Tupelo, Miss., is that the white man is healthier when doing reasonable work in the open field than at any other time.

It is said an army of negroes cannot be spared from the fields. A sufficient number of slaves in now ministering to luxury alone to supply the place of all we need, and we believe it would be better to take half the able-bodied men off a plantation than to take the one master mind that economically regulated its operations. Leave some of the skill at home and take some of the muscle to fight with.

It is said slaves will not work after they are freed. We think necessity and a wise legislation will compel them to labor for a living.

It is said it will cause terrible excitement and some disaffection from our cause. Excitement is far preferable to the apathy which now exists, and disaffection will not be among the fighting men. It is said slavery is all we are fighting for, and if we give it up, we give up all. Even if this were true, which we deny, slavery is not all our enemies are fighting for. It is merely the pretence to establish sectional superiority and a more centralized form of government, and to deprive us of our rights and liberties.

We have now briefly proposed a plan which, we believe, will save our country. It may be imperfect, but, in all human probability, it would give us our independence. No objection ought to outweigh it which is not weightier than independence. If it is worthy of being put in practice, it ought to be moved quickly before the people, and urged earnestly by every man who believes in its efficacy. Negroes will require much training, training will require time, and there is danger that this concession to common sense may come too late.

P. R. CLEBURNE, Major-General Commanding Division;
D. C. GOVAN, Brigadier-General;
JOHN E. MURRAY, Colonel 5th Arkansas;
G. F. BAUCUM, Colonel 8th Arkansas;
PETER SNYDER, Lieut.-Col. Commanding 6th and 7th Arkansas;
E. WARFIELD, Lieutenant-Colonel 2d Arkansas;
M. P. LOWRY, Brigadier-General;
A. B. HARDCASTLE, Colonel 32d and 45th Mississippi;
F.A. ASHFORD, Major 16th Alabama;
JOHN W. COLQUITT, Colonel 1st Arkansas;
RICHARD J. PERSON, Major 3d and 5th Confederate;
G. L. DEAKINS, Major 35th and 8th Tennessee;
J. H. COLLETT, Captain, Commanding 7th Texas;
J. H. KELLY, Brig.-Gen., Commanding Cavalry Division.

Confederate Veterans Reunion at Valdosta 1933

The night before this picture was taken these veterans had enjoyed a banquet at the Valdosta Country Club. It was reported that all had a good time, which included a joyous and active cakewalk. (The Veterans are gathered for a meeting at First Methodist Church in downtown Valdosta, Georgia.)

Contributed by Col. Edmund N. Atkinson
Camp No. 680, SCV

GEORGIA MEMORIAL

A handsome memorial surrounded by a well maintained hedge and marked by a small Confederate battle flag is found in the Cedar Hill Cemetery, Dawson Georgia. The inscription on this unusual monument reads as follows:

Erected by Mary Brantley Chapter U.D.C. to mark the last resting place of slaves who died during the War Between the States in humble service. They were faithful to every trust.
February 1923.

Contributed by Mrs. E. B. Cobb and John B. Carroll, III.

AN ENCOUNTER WITH FORGOTTEN SOUTHERN HISTORY

Paul C. Pace, III of Gainesville, Florida, provides this account of his visit to the Cedar Hill Cemetery in southwest Georgia in 1990.

While passing thru Dawson, Georgia, I stopped at the City Cemetery to locate the grave of my Uncle P. T. Crawford who served as a Baptist missionary in China for 50 years during the time of the Civil War. I had visit the grave about 50 years ago with my father but still remembered about where it was.

Dr. Crawford became ill in China and my Aunt Martha Foster Crawford brought him back to the U.S. and was visiting our relatives, the Melton family in Dawson at the time of his death. She returned to China and worked with Lottie Moon continuing her missionary work where she died and was buried 8 years later.

As I drove into the cemetery I parked near some workers. A black man who appeared to be in charge of the caretaking activity greeted me and we located the grave I was looking for and I remarked to him how well I thought the cemetery looked.

At the time we were standing about the center of the cemetery. I noticed a large clear area with no grave markers and a flag pole in the center. As we walked across the clear area he proudly related this was where all the slaves who fought for the South were buried. He pointed out a large Georgia granite marker with a bronze plate attached located at the north end of the area. He told me, "They used to let us fly a flag on the flag pole but they won't now." I asked what kind of flag and he quickly and proudly said the Confederate flag.

We talked about the war and he said, "I wish folks would put all that behind them now but I guess they won't till we see these graves open up and people rising up to Heaven."

I left and proceeded on my way with a good feeling of mutual respect after a very moving experience. Both by grandfathers served the Confederacy.

Chapter II

Reports and Correspondence
from the Official Records

AN ACT for the payment of musicians in the Army not regularly enlisted.

The Congress of the Confederate States of America do enact, *That whenever colored persons are employed as musicians in any regiment or company, they shall be entitled to the same pay now allowed by law to musicians regularly enlisted: Provided, That no such persons shall be so employed except by the consent of the commanding officer of the brigade to which said regiments or companies may belong.*

Approved April 15, 1862.

Source: *The War of the Rebellion: A Compilation of the Official Records of the Union and Confederate Armies,* Series IV, Vol. 1, page 1059.

OFFICIAL RECORDS IN THE ARCHIVES

Gene C. Armistead

The National Archives and Records Administration maintains literally tons of actual, official records—both Union and Confederate—of the Civil War. These records are not readily accessible to most researchers and especially not to the casual student residing distant from Washington, DC. Fortunately, in most cases, such access is not necessary due to wider availability of published records, catalogs to records, and microfilm copies of other records.

THE "OR"

For the serious researcher of the Civil War or any of its aspects, including Black Confederates, the OFFICIAL RECORDS OF THE UNION AND CONFEDERATE ARMIES IN THE WAR OF THE REBELLION is indispensable. For the sake of brevity, this monumental work is most frequently referred to or cited as "O.R." or "OR." Actually, "OR-A" would be the more proper citation as there are two additional ORs of equal value to the historian. The idea for the collection and publication of official records of the war came from Maj. Gen. Henry W. Halleck in 1864 when he was the Chief-of-Staff of the U.S. Army. His initiative began the process, but collection, selection, compilation, and publication of OR-A continued until 1902. The OR-A consists of 128 volumes (the last a General Index) containing almost 140,000 pages. These volumes are supplemented by OR-M and OR-N. "OR-M" or "OR-Atlas" was begun in 1889 and completed in 1895 and contains 178 double-page plates of maps and of drawings of uniforms, flags, insignia, and equipment. Organized into four sections, and specifically designed to supplement OR-A, OR-N (or OFFICIAL RECORDS OF THE UNION AND CONFEDERATE NAVIES IN THE WAR OF THE REBELLION) was compiled and published between 1884 and 1922. Its twenty-two volumes include a large collection of Confederate diplomatic papers.

The three OR's are not a complete printing of all records of the Civil War. For one thing, not all Confederate records were captured by the Union; some were destroyed and others were scattered across the South in private possession. With the cooperation of various Southern leaders, compilers of the OR were able to obtain copies and transcripts of some of those not in possession of the U.S. government. Reports already collected and published—such as those of the U.S. Adjutant General, the U.S. Surgeon General, and the U.S. Quartermaster General— were not included. Routine letters, muster roles, discharges, contracts, and the like were purposely omitted. Also excluded were records and reports that were generated after the war.

Despite their essentiality for in-depth research, the OR are not particularly easy to utilize. The sheer magnitude of these works can be intimidating, and, to say the least, the OR are not well indexed. The General Index (vol. 128 of OR-A) lists not subjects, but only people, places and military units that are indexed only to a series and volume—not to a page number. From the General Index, the researcher has to proceed to "Book Indices," which do include subjects as well as people, places, and units. A Book Index will indicate a page number only for the beginning of a report mentioning the item indexed. This minimal referencing can be inconvenient when the published report is quite lengthy. Additionally, locations in the Trans-Mississippi area are incompletely indexed.

Despite the monumental nature, the omissions, and the poor indexing, the three OR are essential for any in-depth study of the Civil War. Frequent citations to OR are included in footnotes of books mentioning Black Confederates. The great value of OR references to these men is that such mentions are contemporary and "official" testimony of their service.

Although researching the OR may be somewhat laborious, copies are fairly accessible. Originally, over 11,000 complete sets were printed and distributed to executive departments of the government, to army officers, to members of Congress, and to libraries and organizations designated by congressmen and senators. Most major university and metropolitan libraries have a set of OR in some form—either reprint or microfilm.

CONFEDERATE GOVERNMENT "ARCHIVES"

Many Confederate Government records did not meet the criteria for inclusion in OR, nor are they included in the Compiled Service Records to be discussed later. Among these records applicable to Black Confederates are Acts of the Confederate Congress pertaining to the employment of Blacks on fortifications, in war plants, and in hospitals. Rolls listing free Blacks and slaves employed by the Confederate Army are also found in these archives. The various types of rolls can include name, period of service, name of owner, amount of pay, clothing issued, returns for work performed, occupation, age, or physical description. Because these records have been well indexed, researching them is not difficult. The index to these records also includes some additional records in various state archives and other libraries of the South.

Beers, Henry Putney. *GUIDE TO THE ARCHIVES OF THE GOVERNMENT OF THE CONFEDERATE STATES OF AMERICA*. Washington, DC: National Archives and Records Service, 1968.

Pages 493 ("Negroes") and 515 ("Slaves") of the book's index identify where to find a description of records—and record group number—pertaining to Black Confederates.

COMPILED SERVICE RECORDS

Many family researchers are familiar with the Compiled Service Records of Union and Confederate Soldiers held by the National Archives. These records were compiled in the late 1800s by the U.S. Army's Pension Office. They were compiled from muster rolls, hospital lists, prisoner of war records, parole lists, and similar records—most of which are not found in the OR. Black servant soldiers and the officially authorized Black cooks and musicians, though they drew their share of rations and were part and parcel of their units, were rarely included on a unit's official muster roll. Even when they were included, they may be difficult to identify as Black persons since the preparers of the Confederate muster rolls did not include any racial identifier for these integrated Confederate units. Where such an identifier is found, it most generally is because the source listing was a Union record (such as prisoner of war list). A sole given name and/or a military occupation such as "cook," "teamster," or "musician" may be the only clue that the listed soldier was a Black man.

Even though the names of most Black Confederate soldiers are not found in the Compiled Service Records, attempting to verify the existence of a such record is still always worthwhile—if a soldier's name is known. The search is easier if the unit is known, in which case a "NAT Form 80" can be submitted to the National Archives for a records check. In the case of Blacks, separate forms should be submitted for the given name, nickname, and full name. Another method is to peruse the *Consolidated Index to Compiled Service Records of Confederate Soldiers*. This microfilm publication (# M253) of 535 16mm rolls is strictly alphabetical and is available in many archive branches and some larger libraries. Although tedious, another method is to search the microfilm alphabetical indexes for each Confederate State and Territory. At least one group of Black Confederate soldiers is, however, more readily identifiable in the Compiled Service Records, members of the Louisiana Native Guards Militia Regiment of Infantry.

Compiled Service Records research is offered by a number of state archives and staff can supply names of genealogists who will perform this service for a fee.

Broadfoot Publishing Company (1907 Buena Vista Circle, Wilmington, NC 28411) also offers a "same day" search of Confederate records for a fee.

In *The War of the Rebellion: A Compilation of the Official Records of the Union and Confederate Armies* are recorded movements to bring into Confederate service men of color. In this volume, we have included examples of information that can be found.

Series IV-Volume III:

AN ACT to authorize the Governor to call into the State service free persons of color.

SECTION 1. *Be it enacted by the Senate and House of Representatives of the State of Louisiana in General Assembly convened,* That the Governor of this State be, and he is hereby, authorized to call into the service of the State all free men of color, resident in this State, between the ages of sixteen and fifty-five, not physically and mentally disabled, and to place them in such branches of the service as he may deem compatible with their civil status.

SEC. 2. *Be it further enacted, &c.,* That to effect this the Governor be authorized to adopt whatever system of enrollment he may deem most expedient.

SEC. 3. *Be it further enacted, &c.,* That when said free persons of color shall have been called into the service they shall be subjected to the same rules and regulations and shall receive the same compensation as other persons in the same branches of the service.

SEC. 4. *Be it further enacted, &c.,* That the Governor be, and he is hereby, authorized to transfer said persons of color to the Confederate Government whenever the enrollment of said persons shall have been completed: *Provided,* Said persons of color shall be exempt from said service by putting an able-bodied slave in his place.

SEC. 5. *Be it further enacted, &c.,* That this act shall take effect from and after its passage.

Approved February 11, 1864.

Volume XLV1/3 [S# 97]

CONFEDERATE CORRESPONDENCE, ORDERS, AND RETURNS RELATING TO OPERATIONS IN NORTHERN AND SOUTHEASTERN VIRGINIA, WEST VIRGINIA, MARYLAND, AND PENNSYLVANIA, FROM MARCH 16, 1865, TO JUNE 30, 1865.—#1

EXECUTIVE DEPARTMENT OF VIRGINIA,
Richmond, Va., March 16, 1865.

The PRESIDENT OF THE CONFEDERATE STATES:
SIR: I have the honor, by direction of the governor, to inclose herewith a copy of the joint resolution of the Virginia Legislature "in relation to the employment of

slaves and free negroes as soldiers, or otherwise, for the public defense," and to remain your very obedient servant,

BELL SMITH,

Aide-de-Camp.

Be it enacted by the General Assembly, That it shall be lawful for all free negroes and slaves, who may be organized as soldiers, now, or at any time hereafter by the State or the Confederate Government, for the public defense during the present war with the United States, to bear arms while in active military service, and carry ammunition as other soldiers in the Army.

2. All acts, and parts of acts, in conflict with the foregoing, are hereby repealed.

3. This shall be in force from its passage. A copy from the rolls (secret). Teste:

WILLIAM F. GORDON, JR.,

Clerk House of Delegates.

Passed March 6, 1865.

Series I—Volume XLVI/2 [S# 96]:

CONFEDERATE CORRESPONDENCE, ORDERS, AND RETURNS RELATING TO OPERATIONS IN NORTHERN AND SOUTHEASTERN VIRGINIA, NORTH CAROLINA (JANUARY 1-31), WEST VIRGINIA, MARYLAND, AND PENN-SYLVANIA, FROM JANUARY 1, 1865, TO MARCH 15, 1865.—#1

HEADQUARTERS,
Wilmington, January 4, 1865.

His Excellency Governor VANCE, Raleigh*:*

SIR: While our recollection of Christmas day and Fort Fisher is fresh, let me beg your aid and cooperation in getting immediately as large a force of free negroes as possible. I need labor always, now especially. We must not let our last place go for want of work; still less, because we have foiled the enemy's first effort, must we fold our arms and say enough has been done. In every department I need free laboring force. I am earnestly desirous of releasing all slaves, especially in view of the complaints I learn relative to clothing them. That is not my fault. I have done all in my power to provide clothing for negroes, even to overstepping the limits of my authority. It has been literally due to want of money and material. Still, the reports are greatly exaggerated, for many negroes have been sent here totally unprovided, in the first instance, by their masters. But at all times I am unwilling to impress. The act provides for the conscription of free negroes before impressing the slaves, and I hope, with your aid and that of your militia organization, to obtain a sufficient number of free negroes and to get back those that have deserted. An enrolled corps of 1,200 to 1,500 free negroes, properly organized into companies according to regulations, entitled to furlough at proper times, fed, clothed, paid, &c., retained in service, would relieve the people of the State of all use of their slaves for the defense here. With my works so well advanced I can preserve their condition and provide all I want of new construction with such a force. If we can get it in the State, I will guarantee the exemption of the slave labor, as far as we are concerned here. Please let me hear from you. I have written to Colonel Mallett.

Very respectfully,

W. H. C. WHITING,

Major-General.

Series IV-Volume III:

HEADQUARTERS VIRGINIA MILITARY INSTITUTE,
February 17, 1865.

Hon. J. C. BRECKINRIDGE, Secretary of War:

D<small>EAR</small> S<small>IR</small>: The present state of the country justifies any one in presenting for the consideration of the Government well-meant suggestions, even if they should appear crude to those who are better informed.

The tone of public sentiment and the tenor of present legislation indicate that the call of General Lee for negro troops will be responded to.
I suggest that the maximum number allowed to be raised should be half a million.

I do not suppose that so many are required or could be obtained. But to place the maximum at this figure would, I believe, inspire dread in the minds of our enemy, who exaggerates, through ignorance, our power in this particular; and further, to call for half a million would, by the effect upon the minds of owners and slaves, facilitate and insure the raising of 200,000.

The second suggestion I would make is, that in the event of the troops being raised you might command the services of our corps of cadets with their officers to perform the work of organization and drilling in the shortest time, and with the greatest efficiency.
In 1861, between the 20th of April and the 20th of June, the cadets drilled 15,000 men of the Army of Northern Virginia, and if a large camp of instruction were established at Camp Lee the same work could be done for all of the negro troops that would be sent there.

Allow me to say that these suggestions are the result of conversation among some of the officers of our school, and the last one is contained in a letter to me from General Smith, our superintendent, who is now absent at Lexington.

Very respectfully, general, your obedient servant,

J. T. L. PRESTON,

Acting Superintendent Virginia Military Institute.

Series 1—Volume L1/2 [S# 108]:

CONFEDERATE CORRESPONDENCE, ORDERS, AND RETURNS RELATING TO OPERATIONS IN MARYLAND, EASTERN NORTH CAROLINA, PENNSYL-VANIA, VIRGINIA (EXCEPT SOUTHWESTERN), AND WEST VIRGINIA.—#43

Joint resolutions in relation to the employment of slaves and free negroes as soldiers or otherwise for the public defense.

Resolved, That the General Assembly of Virginia do hereby authorize the Confederate authorities to call upon Virginia, through the Governor of the Commonwealth, for all her able bodied male free negroes between the ages of eighteen and forty-five, and as many of her able-bodied male slaves between the ages aforesaid, as may be deemed necessary for the public defense, not exceeding twenty-five per centum of said slaves, to be called for on the requisition of the General-in-Chief of the Confederate Armies, as he may deem most expedient for the public service.

Resolved, That whenever such call is made it shall be properly apportioned among the different counties and corporations of the Commonwealth, according to the number of male slaves between the ages of eighteen and forty-five in said counties and corporations, so that not more than one slave in every four between the ages indicated shall be taken from any one owner.

Resolved, That our senators are hereby instructed and our representatives requested to vote for the passage of a law to place at the disposal of the Confederate authorities as many of the male slaves and free negroes in the Confederate States of America between the ages of eighteen and forty-five, not exceeding twenty-five per centum of such slaves, as are necessary for the public defense, to be called for on the requisition of the President, or General-in-Chief of our armies, in such numbers as he shall deem best for the public service, each State furnishing its proper quota according to its slave population. But nothing in the foregoing resolutions shall be construed into a restriction upon the President or General-in-Chief of the Confederate army, or a prohibition to the employment of the slaves and free negroes for the public defense in such manner, as soldiers or otherwise, as the General-in-Chief may deem most expedient.

A copy from the rolls.
Adopted March 4, 1865.
WM. F. GORDON,
Clerk House of Delegates.

Series IV-Vol III:

AN ACT to increase the efficiency of the Army by the employment of free negroes and slaves in certain capacities.

Whereas, the efficiency of the Army is greatly diminished by the withdrawal from the ranks of able-bodied soldiers to act as teamsters, and in various other capacities in which free negroes and slaves might be advantageously employed: Therefore,

The Congress of the Confederate States of America do enact, That all male free negroes and other free persons of color, not including those who are free under the treaty of Paris of eighteen hundred and three, or under the treaty with Spain of eighteen hundred and nineteen, resident in the Confederate States, between the ages of eighteen and fifty years, shall be held liable to perform such duties with the Army, or in connection with the military defenses of the country, in the way of work upon fortifications or in Government works for the production or preparation of material of war, or in military hospitals, as The Secretary of War or the commanding general of the Trans-Mississippi Department may, from time to time, prescribe, and while engaged in the performance of such duties shall receive rations and clothing and compensation at the rate of eleven dollars a month, under such rules and regulations as the said Secretary may establish: *Provided*, That the Secretary of War or the commanding general of the Trans-Mississippi Department, with the approval of the President, may exempt from the operations of this act such free negroes as the interests of the country may require should be exempted, or such as he may think proper to exempt, on grounds of justice, equity or necessity.

SEC. 2. That the Secretary of War is hereby authorized to employ for duties similar to those indicated in the preceding section of this act, as many male negro slaves, not to exceed twenty thousand, as in his judgment, the wants of the service may require, furnishing them, while so employed, with proper rations and clothing, under rules and regulations to be established by him, and, paying to the owners of said slaves such wages as may be agreed upon with said owners for their use and service, and in the event of the loss of any slaves while so employed, by the act of the enemy, or by escape to the enemy, or by death inflicted by the enemy, or by disease contracted while in any service required of said slaves, then the owners of the same shall be entitled to receive the full value of such slaves, to be ascertained by agreement or by appraisement, under the law regulating impressments, to be paid under such rules and regulations as the Secretary of War may establish.

SEC. 3. That when the Secretary of War shall be unable to procure the service of slaves in any military department in sufficient numbers for the necessities of the Department, upon the terms and conditions set forth in the preceding section, then he is hereby authorized to impress the services of as many male slaves, not to exceed twenty thousand, as may be required, from time to time, to discharge the duties indicated in the first section of this act, according to laws regulating the impressment of slaves in other cases: *Provided*, That slaves so impressed shall, while employed, receive the same rations and clothing, in kind and quantity, as slaves regularly hired from their owners; and, in the event of their loss, shall be paid for in the same manner and under the same rules established by the said impressment laws: *Provided*, That if the owner have but one male slave between the age of eighteen and fifty, he shall not be impressed against the will of said owner: *Provided further*, That free negroes shall be first impressed, and if there should be a deficiency, it shall be supplied by the impressment of slaves according to the foregoing provisions: *Provided further*, That in making the impressment, not more than one of every five male slaves between the ages of eighteen and forty-five shall be taken from any owner, care being taken to allow in each case a credit for all slaves who may have been already impressed under this act, and who are still in service, or have died or been lost while in service. And all impressments under this act shall be taken in equal ratio from all owners in the same locality, city, county or district.

THOMAS S. BOCOCK,
Speaker House of Representatives.
R. M. T. HUNTER,
President pro tem of the Senate.

Approved February 17, 1864.

JEFFERSON DAVIS.

Series I - Volume XLII/2 [S# 88]:

CONFEDERATE CORRESPONDENCE, ORDERS, AND RETURNS, RELATING TO OPERATIONS IN SOUTHEASTERN VIRGINIA AND NORTH CAROLINA, FROM AUGUST 1, 1864, TO SEPTEMBER 30, 1864.—#5

WAR DEPARTMENT, C. S. A.,
Richmond, Va., September 22, 1864.

General R. E. LEE,
Commanding Army of Northern Virginia:

GENERAL: I have the honor to acknowledge your letter of the 20th instant and to thank you for the full expression of your views relative to the impressment and supply of slaves for service with the armies. Concurring in your general views, I shall proceed at once to impress and collect, to the number of 20,000, as authorized by the act of Congress, for employment with the armies. I propose likewise to have all free negroes of the age for service enrolled and organized thoroughly, to be employed mainly in localities most exposed and where there is the greatest danger of slaves running away. I think these negroes, whether free or slave, had better be arranged and organized into something like companies, battalions, and regiments, after the plan adopted by the English, with reference to what they call navies, or laborers, with superintendents and overseers in lieu of officers. From these organizations appropriate details may be made, singly or by squads, companies, or the like, for the various duties in which they are intended to be employed. Many advantages, I think, would result from this system in enabling us to preserve better order and exercise more care and supervision over the negroes so employed. The requisite number deemed necessary might be sent to the armies in organized bodies and the requisite details made by commanding officers. Orders will be promptly issued, and as little delay as possible be allowed in their execution. I hope these views may have the concurrence of your judgment.

Very respectfully, your obedient servant,
JAMES A. SEDDON,

Secretary of War.

SERIES IV—VOLUME III:

CORRESPONDENCE, ORDERS, REPORTS, AND RETURNS OF THE CONFEDERATE AUTHORITIES FROM JANUARY 1, 1864, TO THE END.—#34

HEADQUARTERS ARMY OF NORTHERN VIRGINIA,
Petersburg, November 21, 1864.

Maj. Gen. J. F. GILMER, *Chief of Engineer Bureau:*

GENERAL: Your letter of the 19th instant with regard to the organization of the negro laborers to be attached to the armies of the Confederacy under the act of Congress of 17th of February, 1864, has been received. Upon the examination of your plan in all its details I think that it is perhaps the best which can be adopted. I do not know that three overseers will be necessary in addition to one manager for each "gang" of 100 men. Would not two be enough? When the negroes arrive in the army and are temporarily attached, as recommended, to the working parties already organized, I think they should be organized into a gang as soon as they reach 100 in number, instead of waiting until 800 are collected, as is suggested. Too much care cannot be taken in the selection of the directors, superintendents, and managers. They should be men of probity, energy, and intelligence. Every precaution should be taken to insure proper and kind treatment of the negroes and to render them contented in the service. The code of punishments should be distinctly defined, and the graver punishments should not be left in the hands of the managers and overseers without due reference to the directors and superintendents. There should be a system of rewards, too, for good conduct and industry, these rewards to be paid to the meritorious over and above the hire paid to their masters. Most of the negroes are accustomed to something of this sort on the plantations. Foremen could be selected from among those who exhibit the best qualifications and character, who would correspond to non-commissioned officers in our military organizations. These would aid materially in promoting the efficiency of the organization and might receive extra wages as a reward and encouragement.

I would respectfully recommend to the Honorable Secretary of War that he urge upon the chief of Bureau of Conscription the importance of carrying forward as rapidly as possible the impressment of the 20,000 slaves authorized by law and heretofore ordered to be impressed; that the same be sent in convenient gangs under proper guards to the armies in the field, to be attached temporarily to the engineer troops serving with the same, and to the harbors of Wilmington, Charleston, Savannah, and Mobile, to be employed on the coast defenses, strict care being taken as to preserving accurate records, as suggested in my letter to General Lee.

J. F. GILMER,

Major-General and Chief Engineer of Bureau.

[Second indorsement.]

Series I--Volume XLII/2 {S#88}:

CONFEDERATE CORRESPONDENCE, ORDERS, AND RETURNS, RELATING TO OPERATIONS IN SOUTHEASTERN VIRGINIA AND NORTH CAROLINA, FROM AUGUST 1, 1864, TO SEPTEMBER 30, 1864.—#6

HEADQUARTERS,

Wilmington, September 24, 1864.

General R. E. LEE,

Commanding Army of Northern Virginia, Petersburg:

GENERAL: I have received your letter, handed me by General Beauregard, this morning. As to labor, I have used every exertion for the past year to procure sufficient, but with very indifferent success; four precious months in the spring were lost by the whole of my small force of negroes being taken away. I succeeded at last in procuring orders for all free negroes to be enrolled. At present only 800 have been received. Owing to desertions daily and sickness the force at work is short of 600. I have work for 2,000 and upward, and it is very pressing. The Conscript Bureau was ordered to enroll the free negroes, and if the number proved insufficient to impress the slaves. An order to those officers would, perhaps, stir them up. Our need is very great. Provision ought to be made to clothe and pay these negroes. The quartermaster and engineer departments are six months in arrears here. The first to the amount of $2,500,000, the latter to $500,000. I have been compelled to address the Secretary of the Treasury directly on the subject. This occasions great distress among the free negroes and their families, and is no doubt the cause of their continual desertions. With regard to the new lines proposed, the works about the city can only be taken in hand by a largely increased force of negroes. Those for the positions of supports at Sugar Loaf, near Fort Fisher, and Piney Point and Lockwood's Folly should be put up only by the troops in position at those points, and to construct them and have them unoccupied would be dangerous and troops should be there now. Every available man at present is employed in finishing the forts and strengthening them, and in putting up the additional guns which have arrived. The city garrison is on guard every night. . . .

W.H.C. WHITING,

Major-General.

HEADQUARTERS,
Wilmington, N. C, September 24, 1864.

His Excellency Governor VANCE, *Raleigh:*
   SIR: Can you do anything for Wilmington in the way of labor? I have most important work to do on Bald Head and at Caswell—work that is essential to the safety of this place. In the spring all negroes—the whole of the very small force sent here—were taken away and four months of precious time were lost. Of the free negroes ordered to be enrolled, I have been able to get but 800, and many of these have deserted and many are down in sickness. If you can do anything to aid in this matter, I beg you will do it quickly. There is another sort of help wanted; we must have troops here; all the labor and all the fortifications and all the engineering skill in the country will not be able to save this place without an adequate force. At no time since the war began has the force to defend Wilmington been so small as it is now; at no time has it been in greater danger. . . .
                                 W.H.C. WHITING,
                                                          Major-General.
Series I--Volume XV [S# 21]:

SEPTEMBER 7-8, 1862.— Expedition from Carrollton to vicinity of Saint Charles Court-House, La, and skirmish.
No. 2.—Report of Maj. Frederick Frye, Ninth Connecticut Infantry.

CAMP PARAPET, LA., *September 12, 1862.*

   GENERAL: I have the honor of inclosing to you my report of an expedition against the enemy in the neighborhood of Saint Charles Court House, on the opposite side of the river.

   The expedition, accompanied by the armed steamer Mississippi, was under command of Actg. Brig. Gen. H. E. Paine, and was composed of the Fourth Wisconsin and Sixth Michigan Regiments and a section of the First Maine Battery in one division, and the Ninth Connecticut and Fourteenth Maine Regiments, with another section of the same battery, in another division.

   Word had been received that the enemy were establishing a camp and had already concentrated a force of 2,000 infantry, a full battery of light artillery, and about 500 cavalry. In accordance with orders, the Ninth Connecticut, about 550 strong, embarked at Carrollton on the transport Morning Light, with a section of battery, at 11 o'clock on the night of September 7, and landed at daylight at a point above Carrollton on the opposite side of the river, with the Fourteenth Maine, the other division landing 5 or 6 miles above, all to converge to a common center, proper signals having been arranged. After moving forward about a mile signal was made from the mast-head of the Mississippi, "Enemy approaching." The artillery shelled the woods, but failing to dislodge the enemy, the Ninth Connecticut were thrown forward as skirmishers. After moving forward several miles through woods, swamps, bayous, and canebrakes, everywhere finding traces of a flying enemy, abandoned haversacks, blankets, bundles, papers, &c., it was found that the enemy, mostly cavalry, attempting to break through in this direction, had been driven back, and, abandoning their horses, saddles, and equipments, had fled into an almost impenetrable swamp, but being surrounded on all sides our troops killed and wounded 8, taking about 40 prisoners and bringing in upwards of 200 horses ready equipped. This was accomplished without loss on our side. A lot of sutler's and other stores were also recaptured, which had been taken by the enemy from the steamer Whiteman, sunk by collision after the battle of Baton Rouge.

The regiments were re-embarked at about 6 o'clock p.m., the Wisconsin and Michigan regiments, with their section of battery and the captured booty, returning to Carrollton, while the Connecticut and Maine regiments and the other section of battery proceeded up the river to cut off the enemy's retreat. Pickets were thrown out that night, and Captain Hennessy, Company E, of the Ninth Connecticut, having been sent out with his company, captured a colored rebel scout, well mounted, who had been sent out to watch our movements. It being ascertained that the enemy had proceeded in another direction, we re-embarked and returned to our encampment, arriving at 6 p.m., September 9.

The men deserve great credit for their energy and determination, for though not recovered from the effects of the Vicksburg and Baton Rouge expeditions, not a man lagged.

Very respectfully, your obedient servant,
FREDERICK FRYE,
Major, Comdg. Ninth Regiment Connecticut Volunteers.
J. D. WILLIAMS,
Adjutant-General, State of Connecticut.

Series I-Volume XXVI/2 [S# 42]:

Confederate Correspondence, Orders, And Returns Relating To Operation's In West Florida, Southern Alabama, Southern Mississippi, Louisiana, Texas, And New Mexico, From May 14 To December 31, 1863.—#21

ENGINEER'S OFFICE, DEPARTMENT OF THE GULF,
Mobile, Ala., December 13, 1863.

Governor [T. H.] WATTS:
GOVERNOR: In soliciting Your Excellency's cordial co-operation with the Engineer Department of the Confederate States, it is at the same time my duty to explain

to you the reasons which render the continued and urgent calls for laborers on the Mobile defenses an absolute necessity.

Two forts (constructed at a period when neither the penetration of a 200-pounder or 300-pounder Parrott shell nor the resistance offered to solid shot by an iron-clad vessel were known to the engineers), a few wooden gunboats, and several rows of piles, not reaching across the whole distance of 3 miles, form as yet the only defense of the main entrance to Mobile Bay. Any Ironsides or Dictator can, at any hour, pass the forts, cut them off from all supplies, and render herself undisputed mistress of Mobile Bay.

The undersigned urges the construction of a strong battery between Forts Morgan and Gaines, as well as the obstruction of the main channel by a system of sawyers, ropes, and torpedoes.

His plans have been approved by the major-general commanding, by Admiral Buchanan, and by the best engineers in the service, Generals Beauregard and Gilmer included; but their execution, though it would require comparatively only a short time, has had to be postponed for want of the necessary labor and transportation, and most precious time is thus being lost irreparably.

Fort Powell (Grant's Island), with a battery projected for Cedar Point, will render Grant's Pass safe against any attack by water. Unfortunately, Fort Powell is not completed; the new battery not commenced yet, for want of labor and transportation.

The two most important batteries—Mcintosh, formerly Spanish River, and Gladden, formerly Pinto,—are being reconstructed entirely.

Your Excellency may form an idea of the difficulties in our way from the fact that over 120,000 cubic yards of earth are required for the construction of the parapets, bomb-proof traverses, &c.; that the earth has to be brought from a point over 10 miles distant from the batteries, and that the engineer department has only their small flats and one steamboat at its disposal to do all this work; yet excellent progress is being made by pushing on the work day and night.

Batteries Huger and Tracey (which serve as protection to the Appalachee and Tensas Rivers) will equally require some additional work before they can be considered efficient works.

Much progress has been made toward the completion of the city intrenchments, but much labor is required to render Mobile safe against a land attack. The construction of the heavy new works would require at least 3,500 hands for three months. The engineer department had yesterday only 530 hands at work on Redoubts A and B, the only ones of the nine new redoubts that could be commenced.

Recapitulation of work to be done yet:

1. Citadel of Fort Morgan to be changed into a wide, covered bomb-proof.
2. A new battery to be built the west bank of the channel between Forts Morgan and Gaines.
3. Obstructions to be placed in the main channel.
4. Fort Powell to be completed.
5. A new battery on Cedar Point to be built.
6. Batteries Mcintosh and Gladden to be completed.
7. Batteries Huger and Tracey to be strengthened.
8. The inner line of redoubts to be completed.
9. Redoubts A and B to be completed.
10. Seven new re-doubts to be built.
11. A citadel—very heavy work—to be built.

It remains with Your Excellency to decide whether any engineer, however able, active, and patriotic he may be, can, with the small force at work now, complete works of such magnitude before the expected attack will be made.

The engineer department will use all possible exertion to push the work as vigorously as its limited means will allow. It is willing to assume all responsibility for carrying out the proposed plans promptly, if furnished with the laborers and transportation it has asked for, but it will most positively decline all responsibility of a certain failure if the very people for the immediate protection of whom these works have been planned decline to give the asked-for assistance.

With 4,000 negroes, 500 of whom to be axmen, and 100 4-mule wagons, the whole work can be completed in three months, and the work shall not only stand a most minute criticism, but, what is better, shall stand any siege.

Permit me now to call your attention to the complaints made by planters against the engineer department:

1. Negroes are retained beyond the sixty days for which they were impressed. I am fully aware of the fact that if the planter, on the one side, has promptly responded to the call for slave labor made on him by the Government, good faith itself will demand that the Government, on the other side, should retain no negro beyond the term for which he was impressed. I have gone even further, by ordering that the time required for coming to and returning from Mobile shall form part of these sixty days, and be paid for as such. Yet the call made on the planters on the 19th of November has not been responded to yet, while the engineer department, anxious to act with every consideration for the planter's interest, his, by prompt discharges, reduced its working force from over 3,100 hands to 1,597. (See report of December 12, No.____.)

Any further reduction of the working force would be equivalent to a total suspension of operations. Who is to blame? Is it the engineer department, which is willing to discharge every negro on the very day his time expires, and give him even three, four, and five days to return home, or is it the planter who does not respond to the call that is made on him nearly one month before his negro is wanted here? In my humble opinion, it is the planter who is to blame.

2. The treatment of negroes employed on the public works.

I would respectfully refer you to the two inclosed orders,____Nos. I and 2. Abuses have existed, and, unfortunately, are existing yet. The overseers sent here by the planters in charge of their impressed hands are not always men who deserve the confidence of their employers, and who, when reprimanded by any employee of this department, seek for and find retaliation in misrepresenting facts altogether. The engineer department would be very thankful to any gentleman of standing who would come here and lend his assistance in this matter.

The presses, serving as quarters for the negroes, have all been planked in, and chimneys have been and are being built in every camp...

The engineer department is making payments for impressed slave labor through General Green, quartermaster-general of the State, to whom the necessary funds are turned over every month. Finally, permit me to call Your Excellency's attention to a plan by which continued impressments and all grievances in their sequel could be avoided easily. Why not raise a corps of 5,000 negro laborers to serve during the war, and to be paid, clothed, and subsisted alike with our common soldiers? The advantages of such an organization are too obvious for me to venture to tire Your Excellency with their recapitulation.

I have the honor to be, Governor, &c.,
VON SHELIHA,
Lieutenant- Colonel, and Chief Engineer

Series IV-Vol. I:

HDQRS. VOL. AND CONSCRIPT BUREAU, ARMY OF TENN.,
Huntsville, March 6, 1863.
The PLANTERS OF LAUDERDALE, LAWRENCE, AND FRANKLIN COUNTIES:

Your position is much endangered by the raids of the enemy's cavalry. Wherever they go they seize all the negroes they can find. Our army has 2,000 veteran soldiers driving teams. We want to hire negro teamsters to relieve these soldiers and restore them to the ranks, thus greatly strengthening the army. All the negroes you hire to the army will be thus saved to their owners, while at the same time the army is more able to defend and protect the country. I have made a like requirement of the slave owners of Maury, Giles, and Lincoln Counties, Tenn., and of Madison, Limestone, and Morgan Counties, Ala., and I now call upon you. The above counties have responded with patriotic promptitude. In meeting this want of the army and Government you are performing a patriotic duty, and advancing your own interest by preserving your property and siding the army to protect the homes and property of the owner. If owners shall fail or refuse to comply with this request, they need not -complain of the Government if they should be robbed of their negro property. I send Captain McIver, assistant quartermaster, with contracts signed and complete to carry out this order. His official acts will be binding upon the Government. The terms of the contract, you will see, are liberal, and in everything protect your rights.

GID. J. PILLOW,
Brigadier General, C. S. Army, and Chief of Bureau.

SERIES I—VOLUME 14 [S# 14]:

CORRESPONDENCE, ORDERS, AND RETURNS RELATING TO THE PENINSU-LAR CAMPAIGN, VIRGINIA, FROM MARCH 17 TO SEPTEMBER 2,1862. CONFEDERATE CORRESPONDENCE, ETC.-45

HEADQUARTERS RIGHT WING OF ARMY,
Lee's Farm, April 29, 1862.

Hon. GEORGE W. RANDOLPH,
Secretary of War, Richmond, Va.:

SIR: I have learned that complaints have been made to you of the treatment of the slaves employed in this army.

It is quite true that much hardship has been endured by the negroes in the recent prosecution of the defensive works on our lines; but this has been unavoidable, owing to the constant and long-continued wet weather. Every precaution has been adopted to secure their health and safety as far as circumstances would allow. The soldiers, however, have been more exposed and have suffered far more than the slaves. The latter have always slept under cover and have had fires to make them comfortable, whilst the men have been working in the rain, have stood in the trenches and rifle pits in mud and water almost knee-deep, without shelter, fire, or sufficient food. There has been sickness among the soldiers and the slaves, but far more among the former than the latter.

I write this for your information, supposing that you might not know the facts.

Very respectfully, your obedient servant,

J. BANKHEAD MAGRUDER,

Major-General, Commanding Right Wing, Army of Virginia.

SERIES I—VOLUME IV [S# 4] CHAPTER XIII:

AUGUST 7, 1861.—The burning of Hampton, Va.
　No. 3.—Reports of Brig. Gen. John B. Magruder, C. S. Army.

HEADQUARTERS, Bethel, August 9, 1861.

SIR: As soon as I learned the result of the battle of Manassas, I ordered about 2,000 men, under Colonel Johnston, of the cavalry, to proceed to the immediate vicinity of Hampton and Newport News, to make reconnaissance of those places, and to be guided by the results. I directed him also to scour the country up to the enemy's pickets, and to capture and send up to the works at Williamsburg all the negroes to be found below a certain line. These duties were well performed by Colonel Johnston, and some 150 negroes were captured and delivered at Williamsburg. As soon as he appeared before Hampton a large balloon was sent up. Our force was reconnoitered, and a hasty evacuation of Hampton took place. The enemy kept close to their lines, and our troops returned to Yorktown and Williamsburg on the 29th and 30th July. As soon as these troops were rested, I ordered, at Young's Mill, in Warwick County, the junction of a part of the troops from Williamsburg with a part of the garrison from Yorktown—in all about 4,000 infantry, 400 cavalry, and two batteries of the howitzer battalion, under Major Randolph. Having established a depot of supplies at Warwick Court-House, 2 miles in rear of Young's Mill, I marched this force to Bethel Church, leaving a commissioned officer and one man from each company to guard the camps and supplies at Young's Mill and the Court-House.

On the 6th instant, in the afternoon, I took post with my whole force at Whitney's farm, within a mile of New Market Bridge, which I had rebuilt, the enemy having destroyed it. My force was then placed between the troops at and around Fort Monroe and those in garrison at Newport News.

In order to gain exact information of the force and movements of the enemy at Newport News, I had ordered Capt. Jefferson C. Phillips, of the Old Dominion Dragoons, to make a close reconnaissance of the place, which was done by him in his usual gallant and skillful manner. He succeeded in reaching a point far within the inmost pickets of the enemy, and at a distance of about 300 yards from the works, where he remained until daybreak, an hour before which time troops were embarked in a steamer which came to the fort during the same night, but a large number remained behind. He could not ascertain whether this steamer brought troops or not. He, however, induced one of our farmers to visit the fort next day on business, and learned the departure of a Vermont regiment and the arrival of another, Colonel Phelps, of the Vermont regiment, late of the Regular Army, remaining behind in command. Sent also Private Joseph Phillips to reconnoiter the shipping and another part of the work, which he successfully did. He represented two war steamers and a ship so disposed as to take the approaches to the works, which were extremely strong, and garrisoned with twenty-five guns. The next morning I displayed my force within a mile and a half of (Newport News) the work, with the hope of drawing the enemy out, but he remained close within his intrenchments. Disappointed in my expectations that the enemy would give me battle, I moved the left flank to within a mile of Hampton, and there a late copy of a Northern paper, the *Tribune*, containing an official report of General Butler, commanding at Old Point, to the Federal Secretary of War, was placed in my hands. I have not the report with me, but will forward it by the next mail. In it General Butler announces what his intentions are with respect to Hampton, about one-third of which, however, had been burned by the enemy when they evacuated it. He states in substance that this evacuation was the consequence of the withdrawal of 4,000 of his best troops to go to Washington; that he intended to fortify and make it so strong as to be easily defended by a small number of troops; that he did not know what to do with the many negroes in his possession unless he possessed Hampton; that they were still coming in rapidly; that as their masters had deserted their homes and slaves, he should consider the latter free, and would colonize them at Hampton, the home of most of their owners, where the women could support themselves by attending to the clothes of the soldiers, and the men by working on the fortifications of the town.

Having known for some time past that Hampton was the harbor of runaway slaves and traitors, and being under the guns of Fort Monroe, it could not be held by us even if taken, I was decidedly under the impression that it should have been destroyed before; and when I found from the above report its extreme importance to the enemy, and that the town itself would lend great strength to whatever fortifications they might erect around it, I determined to bum it at once.

****

The sickness among the troops in the Peninsula is grave, both in extent and character, all diseases taking more or less a typhoid character, and many deaths occurring—at Yorktown about two a day. Some idea may be formed of its effects when I state that the Fifth North Carolina Regiment, composed of twelve companies and over 1,000 strong, is now less than 400 for duty. Every precaution has been taken and every arrangement will be made to prevent the disease and alleviate its effects, and the health of the troops now is reported as improving. Large numbers of the troops here have been sent across the York River to Gloucester, private families kindly offering to take charge of many of the patients. One or two regiments in Yorktown have remained healthy. They will be permitted to remain in their present encampments, and the rest should be encamped some miles from the works, but toward the enemy, at places supposed to be more healthy. The sickliest season has not yet arrived, and as this is by far the most unhealthy portion of the seat of war, I cannot too earnestly impress upon the authorities the necessity of attending promptly to the requisitions and suggestions of the medical officers as regards the sanitary condition of the troops in this Peninsula. Two hundred barrels of potatoes have arrived and been issued, and also a very seasonable supply of medicines; but as, in addition to the measles, ague and fever, bilious and typhoid fever, symptoms of scurvy are apparent throughout the command, a continued supply of potatoes and other vegetables, which I understand are abundant and very cheap farther South, is essential. Typhoid has been so prevalent and fatal at Jamestown Island as to make the withdrawal of the men from that post necessary. They will be encamped in the immediate vicinity on one of Mr. William Allen's farms, supposed to be more healthy.

****

I have called out a large force of negroes, at considerable expense to the Government, to complete the fortifications upon which our troops have been so laboriously working. The troops can no longer do this work, and I respectfully request that the Quartermaster-General be directed to furnish to the assistant quartermaster-general of this department, Captain Bloomfield, the funds necessary for the payment of the laborers without delay, as a great many of them are free negroes, who have families, who must starve if they are not paid, and to all I promised prompt payment. There are, perhaps, 1,000 now at work on the Peninsula.

THE BLACK CONFEDERATES OF
HENRY COUNTY, TENNESSEE

A History of Henry County Commands Which Served in the Confederate States Army, published in 1904, provides information and photographs of black veterans from the Paris, Tennessee area. Here we find "the colored cooks" described as "an important adjunct." of the Fifth Tennessee rEginent, CSA. Books of this nature are excellent sources for genealogical and military unit research

Chapter III

Veteran Accounts

Here is a strange fact. We find that the Confederates themselves first armed and mustered the Negro as a soldier in the late war. General Butler says: "While I was waiting at Ship Island the Rebel authorities in New Orleans had organized two regiments from the free negroes, calling them 'National Guards, Colored.' When General Lovell, Confederate commander, ran away from the city with his troops on the approach of union forces, these colored soldiers remained." Their organization was complete; the line officers were colored men, and the field officers white.

Captain Dan Matson, U. S. Volunteers

From *War Sketches and Incidents As Related by the Companions of the Iowa Commander, Military Order of the Loyal Legion of the United States,* Volume 11, 1898.

The writings of Civil War veterans run the gamut from aged, barely legible notes stored in archival collections to the newly reprinted, professionally produced volumes available for sale in larger bookstores. Numbers of articles, narratives, and reminiscences written by Civil War veterans contain accounts of the service of slaves and freedmen to the war effort of the South. Some sources, such as the *Confederate Veteran Magazine* published by S. A. Cunningham of Nashville, Tennessee, from 1893-1932, are filled with articles that pay tribute to men and women of color. Other Civil War publications, however, contain only brief mention of African American activities; but, when pieces of information are juxtaposed, the contributions of Black Confederates begin to take on a greater meaning.

A Union Account of a Confederate Sharpshooter

A number of Union reports provide information about the marksmanship of Black Confederate skirmishers and sharpshooters. The following occurred in April of 1862 during the siege of Yorktown, Virginia and it was reported by Captain C. A. Stevens in Berdan's United States Sharpshooters in the Army of the Potomac, 1861-1865 *(Reprint:* The Press of Morningside Bookshop, *Dayton, Ohio, 1972)*

For a considerable time during the siege the enemy had a Negro rifle shooter in their front who kept up a close fire on our men, and, although the distance was great, yet he caused more or less annoyance by his persistent shooting. On one occasion while at the advanced posts with a detail, the writer with his squad had an opportunity to note the skill of this determined darky with his well-aimed rifle. Being stationed at a pit on the edge of a wood fronting the treeless stretch of ground around the opposing works, with sand bags piled up for cover, during the forenoon this rebellious black made his appearance by the side of an officer and under his direction commenced firing at us. For a long time this chance shooting was kept up, the black standing out in plain view and coolly drawing bead, but failed to elicit any response, our orders being to lie quiet and not be seen. So the Negro had the shooting all to himself, his pop, pop, against the sand bags on the edge of the pit often occurring, while other close shots among the trees showed plainly that he was a good shot at long range. He became pretty well known among the scouts and pickets, and had established quite a reputation for marksmanship, before he came to grief. Emboldened by his having pretty much all this promiscuous shooting unopposed, the pickets rarely firing at him, he began to work at shorter distance, taking advantage of the ground and scattering trees. This was what our men wanted, to get him within more reasonable range, not caring to waste ammunition trying to cripple him at the long distance he had at first been showing himself. They wanted to make sure of him. In the meantime our boys would when opportunity offered, without being seen, posted a man forward to await in concealment for the adventurous darkey. The scheme succeeded and his fate was sealed. The result was finally announced in the "latest from the front," one morning in camp, that "a scouting party having cornered the nigger in a chimney top a quarter of a mile distant, where he had been concealed, finally brought him down," and thus ended his sport with his life. It was said that Sergt. Andrews of Company

E; (afterwards captain) discovered the fellow in the second story of the old chimney,—standing monument of destruction, of which there were many along this Peninsula route,—and with the aid of his fine telescope, found him firing through a hole in the back of the fireplace.

Negro Rifleman Brought Down at Yorktown

An 1866 publication, The Pictoral Book of Anecdotes and Incidents of the War of the Rebellion, *provides another account of a Confederate rifleman downed by Union troops.*

One of the best morning's work done at Yorktown was that of reducing to a state of perfect inutility in this mundane sphere, a rebel negro rifleman, who, through his skill as a marksman, had done more injury to our men than any dozen of his white compeers, in the attempted labor of trimming off the complement of Union sharpshooters. The latter had known him a long time, had kept an eye on him, and lain in wait to pick him off. His habit was to perch himself in a big tree, and, keeping himself hid behind the body, annoy the Union men by firing upon them. He climbed the tree as usual one morning, but in advance of the others coming out, and, smuggling himself into his position, was anticipating his usual day of quietude. The Union men might have killed him as he came out, but avoided shooting, so as not to alarm the others. His tree was about twenty rods from one of the Union pits. When our men fired on the advancing rebel pickets, he of course saw the fix he was in—that he was indeed and decidedly up a tree.

"I say, big nigger," called out one of the Union soldiers, "you better come down from there."

"What for? " returned the big nigger.

"I want you as prisoner."

''Not as this chile knows of," replied the concealed Ethiop.

"Just as you say," replied our sharpshooter.

In about an hour the darkey poked his head out. Our man was on the lookout for him; he had his rifle on the bead-line ready—pulled the trigger—whiz-z went the bullet, down came the negro. He was shot through the head.

Confederate States Negro Troops

John C. Stiles, Brunswick, Georgia from the Confederate Veteran. Vol. XIII, 1905.

On account of the South's being practically drained of fighting men by the middle of the year 1863, the question of using male slaves to reinforce the army was agitated. Various sources offer a few opinions on the subject.

As early as September 9, a gentleman from Augusta, Ga., signing himself a "Native Georgian," wrote to the department thus: "The idea may have been presented to you of employing the negroes as soldiers. They can certainly fight as well for us as against us. Let the negro fight negro, and he will show much more courage than when opposed to whites. Promise freedom when the war is over and colonize them either in Mexico or Central America."

On December 21 the Hon. J. P. Benjamin, Secretary of State, expressed himself as follows: "It appears to me enough to say that the negro will certainly fight against us if not used for our defense. There is no other means of swelling our armies than that of arming the slaves and using them as an auxiliary force. I further admit that if they fight for our freedom they are entitled to their own."

Gen. Howell Cobb, an unbeliever in this expedient, wrote from Macon, Ga., January 8, 1865:

I think that the proposition is the most pernicious idea that has been suggested since the war began. You cannot make soldiers of slaves or slaves of soldiers. The moment you resort to this your white soldiers are lost to you, and one reason why this proposition is received with favor by some portions of the army is because they hope that when the negro comes in they can retire. You cannot keep white and black troops together, and you cannot trust negroes alone. They won't make soldiers, as they are wanting in every qualification necessary to make one. [Note General Lee on the negro as a soldier.] Better by far to yield to the demands of England and France and abolish slavery and thereby purchase their aid than to resort to this policy, which would lead to certain ruin and subjugation.

Samuel Clayton, Esq., of Cuthbert, Ga., wrote on January 10, 1865:

All of our male population between sixteen and sixty is in the army. We cannot get men from any other source; they must come from our slaves. Some say that negroes will not fight, but they fought us at Ocean Pond, Honey Hill, and other places. The government takes all of our men and exposes them to death. Why can't they take our property? He who values his property more than independence is a poor, sordid wretch.

General Lee, who clearly saw the inevitable unless his forces were strengthened, wrote on January 11:

I should prefer to rely on our white population; but in view of the preparation of our enemy it is our duty to provide for a continuous war, which, I fear, we cannot accomplish with our present resources. It is the avowed intention of the enemy to convert the able-bodied negro into soldiers and emancipate all. His progress will thus add to his numbers and at the same time destroy slavery in a most pernicious manner to the welfare of our people. Whatever may be the effect of our employing negro troops, it cannot be as mischievous as this. If it ends in subverting slavery, it will be accomplished by ourselves, and we can devise the means of alleviating the evil consequences to both races. I think, therefore, that we must decide whether slavery shall be extinguished by our enemies and the slaves used against us or use them ourselves at the risk of the effects which may be produced upon our soldiers' social institutions. My own opinion is that we should employ them without delay. I believe that with proper regulations they can be made efficient soldiers. They possess the physical qualifications in an eminent degree. Long habits of obedience and subordination, coupled with the moral influence which in our country the white man possesses over the black, furnish an excellent foundation for that discipline which is the best guarantee of military efficiency. We can give them an interest by allowing immediate freedom to all who enlist and freedom at the end of the war to their families. We should not expect slaves to fight for prospective freedom when they can secure it at once by going to the enemy, in whose service they will incur no greater risk than in ours. In conclusion, I can only say that whatever is to be done must be attended to at once.

President Davis on February 21 expressed himself as follows:

It is now becoming daily more evident to all reflecting persons that we are reduced to choosing whether the negroes shall fight for or against us and that all the arguments as to the positive advantage or disadvantage of employing them are beside the question, which is simply one of relative advantage between having their fighting element in our ranks or those of the enemy.

The question was argued and thrashed over in Congress, and on March 23, 1865, the following order was issued from the adjutant and inspector general's office in Richmond:

The Congress of the Confederate States of America do enact that, in order to provide additional forces to repel invasion, maintain the rightful possessions of the Confederate States, secure their independence, and preserve their institutions, the President be and he is hereby authorized to ask for and accept from the owners of slaves the services of such numbers of able-bodied negro men as he may deem expedient for and during the war to perform military service in whatever capacity he may direct. * * * That while employed in the service the said troops shall receive the same ration, clothing, and compensation as allowed other troops in the same branch of the service. * * * No slave will be accepted unless with his own consent and the approbation of his master by a written instrument conferring as far as he may the rights of a freedman. * * * The enlistment will be for the war.

On March 28 the following order was issued to various parties: "You are hereby authorized to raise a —— of negro troops under the provision of Congress, and you are allowed sixty days' absence and will be detached from your command for that purpose."

If there were any such troops enlisted, there is no official record of same. For two reasons the act was never accomplished: First, the experiment was tried too late in the game; second, the owners of the slaves were so reluctant to part with their property that the following letter was brought forth on the subject:

RICHMOND, VA., April 2, 1865.

I have delayed writing in order to give you some information on the negro question. * * * If the people of the South only knew and appreciated General Lee's solicitude on this subject, they would no longer hold back their slaves. * * * Their wives, daughters, and the negroes are the only elements left us to recruit from. And it does seem that our people would rather send the former to face death than give up the latter.

In my opinion, if this method had been adopted earlier in the war, it certainly would have made a material difference in its duration ; but I am not prepared to say that I think it would have changed the final result. I feel, however, that the negro would have fought as well for us as against us, and when they were properly officered the records show that they put up a pretty good opposition. Since that time the negro in the United States army has always given satisfaction as a fighter, as the records of our Indian and Spanish-American Wars will show, and also the records show that thirty-two of these people are holders of medals of honor given for personal gallantry on the field of battle.

A TERRY TEXAS RANGER'S ACCOUNT

H. W. Graber provides an account of a wartime episode involving a loyal slave's kindness to Confederate soldiers in spite of a master who may have been a Union man. (From A Terry Texas Ranger: The Life Record Of H.W. Graber, a facsimile reproduction of the original published by State House Press, Austin, Texas, 1987).

We were soon ordered back to Middle Tennessee, under General Forrest, where we operated around McMinnville, Manchester and along the railroad. After an attack on the outskirts of Manchester one morning, which Colonel Forrest decided was too strong for us, we withdrew further down the railroad, where we charged a block-house, the first we ever attempted to capture and the first we had ever seen. But, although some of our men got right up to the house, we were unable to force them to surrender, and were forced to give it up as a bad job. While engaged in this venture, a large force of infantry, cavalry and artillery had moved out on the road from McMinnville and were about to cut off our line of retreat. When we got in sight of this force, hurrying to get out of this corner, they raised a shout, which I must say made me feel very uncomfortable, knowing that they outnumbered us perhaps five to one, but we succeeded in dashing across the main road, where we wheeled and charged their advance column, bringing them to a halt, permitting others of the command to cross, that were virtually cut off, but they did capture a large fine looking Negro man, who was the servant of General Forrest. His name was Napoleon, and he was devotedly attached to General Forrest. In connection with his capture they also captured two fine horses belonging to the general. They carried this negro to Louisville prison and did their best to persuade him to take the oath of allegiance and join them, but he steadfastly refused, as he was devotedly attached to General Forrest and was finally, through some special arrangement, exchanged and returned to the general. The last I knew of him I heard of him in Louisville prison, when he was sent around for exchange.

After operating a while longer in Middle Tennessee without any important captures, we got information that General Bragg had crossed the Tennessee River at Chattanooga and was moving across Cumberland Mountain, driving the Federal Army before him and we were instructed to harass the enemy as much as possible. In accordance there only one steamboat, and Harrison's Brigade was ordered to cross last, necessitating our camping in the river bottom for several days, during which time details were sent out of our brigade to collect provisions, as we were without commissary. I had charge the second day of a small detail, and after riding about twenty miles, we scattered out, each man to bring in as much as possible. On my return to camp that evening late, without having succeeded in securing anything, only a piece of cornbread and a slice of bacon for myself, I was feeling disgusted. When about a mile from our camp, following a well-beaten path, I spied a negro man on another path crossing the one I was on and when within a few yards of me, I stopped him and asked if he couldn't tell me where there was something to eat, telling him that I had ridden all day long, trying to get something for our command and had signally failed.

The country through which we had passed for several days is the greatest sweet potato country perhaps in the South; large fields all over the country had been devoted to sweet potatoes, which had fallen a ready prey to Sherman's army and the whole country seemed to be eaten out. I told this negro, after he told me where he lived, about a half mile from there, that I was satisfied he knew where there were sweet potatoes and where there was corn for our horses. He assured me he did not and said that the Federals had taken everything that his old master had and didn't leave him anything. I continued to talk with him, trying to arouse his sympathy, told him of our poor fellows not having had anything to eat for several days and I had been riding all day long without securing anything, thereby working on his sympathy. Finally he broke down and said, "Young Marster, if I were to tell you where there are sweet potatoes, old marster would kill me." I told him that his old master never would know anything about it, and he finally said he didn't think it was right, that his old master had given these Yankees everything they wanted, had plenty of potatoes left and refused to give our own folks anything at all. "Now," he said, "if you will strike across this way," pointing in the direction of his house, entering a lane leading to the house, "about a hundred and fifty yards this side of the house, on the left across the fence, you will find some haystack poles standing, with a lot of shattered hay in the lot and if you will dig down about two feet you will strike more potatoes than you will need for several days. Up the river, in the bottom, about two miles, you will find a couple of pens of corn, enough to feed your horses for several days." He had just finished telling me, when I noticed an old man, who proved to be his master, coming our way, and as soon as the negro saw him he said, "Fo' Gawd, marster; there he is now; he'll kill me; he'll kill me." "No," I said "he will not; he never will know that you told me; you stand perfectly still and don't get scared." I jerked out my pistol and threw it down on him, telling him within hearing of his old master, that if he didn't tell me where there was something to eat, I would kill him, and the old man called, "Let that man alone; he don't know where there is anything to eat; there is nothing on the place, the Federals just took everything I had." I still insisted on killing the negro if he didn't tell me where there was something to eat, and finally let him off, satisfying the old man that he hadn't told me anything.

As soon as I reached camp I told Colonel Harrison to get out a detail of fifty men, with sacks to carry potatoes in, when he ordered Major Pearrie, our commissary, to get out the detail and follow my instructions. I told Pearrie that I was satisfied the people at the house about a half mile from there had plenty of potatoes, but did not tell him the source of my information, determined not to tell anybody. When we moved up the lane near the house, Major Pearrie halted us, went to the house to talk to the old man and negotiate for the potatoes, when the old man satisfied him there were no potatoes on the place. In the meantime I had no trouble in finding the lot just as the negro had described to me and when the major returned and ordered us, "About face; move back to camp; there is nothing to be had," I dismounted, crossed the fence into the lot and commenced digging with my hands and in about two feet, struck potatoes, then called to the men to come over with their sacks, which, it is hardly necessary to say, we filled up to the top. We thought we left potatoes enough to last the old man and his family for another year, and perhaps more. We then sent up the river bottom and found the corn, on which we fed our horses. Here is another instance of the attachment of the negro to our own people, his sympathy for us controlling his actions, and I always regretted not taking this negro along with us, fearing perhaps that his old master might have suspected him of giving us information about these potatoes and corn.

A LIFE IS SAVED

Many Confederate soldiers were ably assisted by servants during battles. Per-haps the most poignant (and most recorded) accounts involved faithful slaves who recovered their masters' bodies from battlefields and transported them back home. In many instances, even after the original master had been killed, loyal servants continued to serve with Confederate armies.

The following account is not unusual except that the soldier being assisted, Private Jason G. Guice, was rescued by a Black Confederate who was not his body servant but a stranger. The Roster of Confederate Soldiers of Georgia, 1861-1865, compiled by Miss Lillian Henderson, reports that Private Guice was "wounded in arm, necessitating amputation, at Wilderness, Virginia, May 6, 1864. Captured in Richmond, Virginia hospital April 3, 1865, and left said hospital May 21, 1865." He died at Eufaula, Alabama, on July 6, 1903.

This excerpt is from the Confederate Military History, *copyright 1890 by the Confederate Publishing Company and reprinted in 1987 by the Broadfoot Pub-lishing Company of Wilmington, North Carolina, in a 17 volume set, written by Confederate veterans, and edited by General Clement A. Evans of Georgia. This particular selection is taken from Volume VIII (Alabama), pages 595-598, vol-ume edited by General Joseph Wheeler.*

Please note that the officer rank mentioned in the first paragraph for Guice is his postwar United Confederate Veteran rank (honorary).

Jason G. Guice, of Eufaula, major on the staff of Gen. Geo. P. Harrison, command-ing the Alabama division, United Confederate veterans, and brigadier-general of State troops, Third division of Alabama, under Governor Oates, was born in Talbert county, Ga., November 19, 1841, was reared from infancy to boyhood at Columbus, Ga., and educated in Barbour county, Ala., whither his parents removed when he was ten years of age. In this county he aided in the organization of a military company in 1860 and was made lieutenant. When the war began this company made various unsuccessful attempts to get into the service, and became a part of a regiment formed by Colonel Jones, president of a military school at Glenville, Ala., which rendezvoused at Union Springs. But at that time there was a hesitancy in accepting volunteers for lack of arms, and the command was disbanded. A regiment was then assembling at Columbus, Ga., and about a fourth of Jones' unaccepted regiment joined it, one company, the Mitchell Guards, of Glenville, going in entire as Company C, under Captain Griffiths. Company K, of this Georgia regiment, from Terrell county, Ga., called the Bartow Avengers, had already seen arduous service with Wise's legion in West Virginia, and spent the winter of 1861-62 there, and in the company in service it had lost its officers in West Virginia, and was numbered as Company K. Lieutenant Guice joined this veteran company as a private. The regiment was numbered as the Thirty-first Georgia, and at the reorganization in April, 1862, Maj. Clement A. Evans, whose gentlemanly bearing had made him very popular with the men, was elected colonel almost unanimously. Applying for service in Virginia, then the scene of activity, the regiment was ordered to join Stonewall Jackson in the Virginia valley, and reached Staunton, Va., about the time that Jackson had won the victory of Cross Keys and Port Republic. Joining Jackson's command there, the Thirty-first was from that time a part of the old Stonewall division. A corps of sharpshooters was formed, composed of ten men from each company, and Mr. Guice was one of those thus detailed, but retaining his company membership. This was his line of duty throughout the war, and it involved a multitude of skirmishes in addition to the great battles of the army. His first battle was Gaines' Mill, in the Seven Days' campaign before Richmond, and though he was wounded there, he remained on duty until McClellan was driven to the James river. Then Jackson marched to meet Gen. John Pope, beyond the Rappahannock, and after various skirmishes and maneuvers they made the famous flank movement to Bristoe Station and Manassas junction, where the Thirty-first Georgia burned the quartermaster and commissary stores of the Federal army. That night they marched to Centerville, and the next day to the old Manassas battlefield, and on Thursday night this brigade (Lawton's) and Trimble's, of Ewell's division, opened the battle of Second Manassas. At this time, where the lines of the Thirty-first Georgia and Fifteenth Alabama lapped, General Ewell fell severely wounded, and Guice and others of the two regiments caught him as he fell from his horse. As they started to carry the general to the rear he objected, crying out: "Put me down, and give them hell. I'm no better than any other wounded soldier, to stay on the field." The next day (August 30) and on the 31st, the regiment was in battle, and on the latter day Mr. Guice was severely wounded in the left foot, and while being taken to Rapidan Station he was given up to die, but the devotion of a negro teamster, a stranger, who sat up all night caring for him, saved his life. He was not able to return to the field until just before the battle of Fredericksburg, in which he took part, also, in the battles of Chancellorsville and Gettysburg. At the battle of the Wilderness, May 5, 1864, he was wounded in the arm in the famous charge of Gordon's Georgia brigade which made John B. Gordon a major-general and Colonel Evans a brigadier-general. Returning home on furlough on account of this wound, when recovered he started on his return to the army, and had reached Macon, Ga., when General Sherman approached that city in his raid during the siege of Atlanta, and burned the bridge at Walnut creek. About three hundred furloughed and disabled men from Lee's army volunteered to meet Stoneman, and Private Guice was chosen to lead them. Gen. Howell Cobb, in command of the State troops, directed Mr. Guice to advance, and he proceeded to Woolfolk's hill, and encountered the enemy in a cornfield. Deploying his men as skirmishers, he attacked the Federal line, charging with the "Rebel yell," and drove them across Walnut creek. In this gallant action he was again wounded, severely, in the right ankle. Nevertheless, on the expiration of his furlough, he reported to Staunton, Va., where he was put in a hospital, and after a few days again furloughed. He returned to his regiment in time to take part in the famous battle of

Cedar Creek, in the Shenandoah valley, with the sharpshooters of Evans' brigade opening the morning attack. After various fighting in the valley, they were transferred to the Petersburg lines, in January, 1865, where he fought at Hatcher's Run, February 6 and 7, and in March took position in front of Petersburg. In the attack on Fort Stedman, night of March 25 or morning of 26, 1864, he was one of the three hundred men of Gordon's division and of Evans' brigade who made the first rush early in the morning of the 26th with empty guns, and captured the fort and turned the guns upon the enemy. After the line of battle had reached this position, Guice, with a detachment of sharpshooters from his own brigade and Hays' Louisiana brigade, pushed on to Grant's military railroad, and captured a battery. While in this advanced position several trainloads of Federal reinforcements arrived, and the Federal general, mistaking the Confederate sharpshooters for Federal skirmishers, rode near Guice and his comrades to encourage them in the fight and was promptly hauled in and pulled from his horse and made a prisoner. On account of the courteous treatment accorded him he presented Mr. Guice his buckskin gauntlets. Returning to Fort Stedman the sharpshooters took part in the repulse of several Federal charges on Evans' brigade, and finally the Confederates retired under a destructive fire to their own lines. In so doing, a grapeshot from Fort New York struck Mr. Guice's left wrist and knocked out the bone, leaving nothing but shreds of flesh. Amputation was immediately made below the elbow. After a few days spent by him in the hospital at Richmond, the Confederate capital was abandoned to the Federals. Then learning that he was to be sent to the prison camp at Point Lookout, he escaped to the mountains, where he was cared for by a lady of that region until he was informed that all of Lee's soldiers would be paroled on surrendering. Going to Richmond he received his parole papers in May, 1865, and then started for home, walking most of the way, and arrived home June, 1865, with nothing save the bloody clothes he wore. His wound was still bleeding and painful. In 1866 he engaged in farming, but soon abandoned this occupation, and, removing to Eufaula, in October, 1866, embarked in the cotton trade, in which he was engaged with much success for thirty years. He is now retired from active business but retains his position as vice-president of the East Alabama national bank. In 1873 he was married to Stella Drewry, who is now vice-president of the Barbour county chapter of the United Daughters of the Confederacy. It is worthy of note at the close of this sketch of a Confederate who suffered so much for the cause, to state that he was in most of the battles fought by the army of Northern Virginia, was wounded severely five times in different battles, and that he was one of five brothers who fought with equal devotion. James M. Guice served with the Georgia troops and died from disease in the army. William H., of the Twelfth Georgia, was killed at the battle of McDowell in May, 1862. John G., a lieutenant in the Fourth Alabama, was severely wounded at First Manassas and at Second Manassas lost a leg. George W., of Hilliard's legion, was wounded at Chickamauga, participated in the battles in front of Petersburg and of the Crater, and surrendered at Appomattox.

ACCOUNTS OF SERVANTS IN PRISON

As recorded in the Confederate Veteran, *Vol. XIII, 1905, Capt. A. O. P. Nicholson, Columbia, Tenn., writes:*

"In the interesting article of De Gourney's Battalion of Artillery in the January *VETERAN* the writer speaks of Capt. Hewett's servant as 'Bill.' His name was Dick, and he was faithful and loyal to his master to the end. The Federal officers at Johnson's Island offered all kinds of inducements to get Dick to leave Capt. Hewett and take service with them, but he stoutly declined, preferring to remain in prison and share the hardships with his master. They refused to issue him any rations, but each of us divided our own meager supply, which gave him a portion equal to ours. Dick was exchanged with his master only a short time before the surrender, and Capt. Hewett died soon after reaching Dixie.

"There was another faithful slave in Johnson's Island named John, who belonged to Capt. J. R. Wilson, now living in Florence, Ala. He also went through the hardships of prison with his master rather than accept his freedom and remunerative service from the Federals. John went out on exchange with his master, and lived for some years after the war, until his death, on the plantation of Capt. Wilson, in Mississippi. It is needless to say that John never wanted for anything his master could supply."

Lt. General Richard Taylor's Account of Captured Negro Troops

Richard Taylor, the son of President Zachary Taylor, served as colonel of the Ninth Louisiana Brigade in Ewell's Division and participated in the campaigns of Stonewall Jackson. In later years Taylor served with distinction in the Western theaters and at the close of the war was placed in command of the Department of Alabama, Mississippi, and East Carolina. A gifted writer and scholar, General Taylor was the author of one of the most enduring postwar narratives, Destruction and Reconstruction, *from which this selection is taken**

The Confederate Congress had enacted that negro troops, captured, should be restored to their owners. We had several hundreds of such, taken by Forrest in Tennessee, whose owners could not be reached; and they were put to work on the fortifications at Mobile, rather for the purpose of giving them healthy employment than for the value of the work. I made it a point to visit their camps and inspect the quantity and quality of their food, always found to be satisfactory. On one occasion, while so engaged, a fine-looking negro who seemed to be leader among his fine comrades, approached me and said: "Thank you, Massa General, they give us plenty of good victuals; but how you like our work?" I replied that they had worked very well. "If you will give us guns we will fight for these works, too. We would rather fight for our own white folks than for strangers." And, doubtless, this was true. In their dealings with the negro the white men of the South should ever remember that no instance of outrage occurred during the war. Their wives and little ones remained safe at home, surrounded by thousands of faithful slaves, who worked quietly in the fields until removed by the Federals. This is the highest testimony to the kindness of the master and the gentleness of the servant; and all the dramatic talent prostituted to the dissemination of falsehood in "Uncle Tom's Cabin" and similar productions can not rebut it.

*Contributed by Scott Buie of Ft. Worth, Texas.

South Carolina Body Servants

Source: <u>A Sketch of the War Record of the Edisto Rifles, 1861-1865</u>, *by William Valmore Izlar Company "A," 1st Regimernt S.C.V. Infantry Colonel Johnson Hagood Provisional Army of the Confederate States 1861-1862 Company "G," 25th Regiment S.C.V. Infantry Colonel Charles H. Simonton Confederate States Army 1862-1865.*

In the rolls of the Edisto Rifles, and of the other companies from Orangeburg District, records which will be valued more and more every year, Mr. Izlar has perpetuated in two paragraphs; "Caesar," "Anthony," "Sam," Cudjo," "Pierce," "Peter," "Sephas," "Derril," "Wash," "Toney," "Issac" and "Jim," the names of twelve body-servants of as many gentlemen. "Many of the young members of the Edisto Rifles," he says, "took with them to the army their negro servants, who not only waited on their young masters faithfully, but cooked their meals also. When in Virginia, these servants stayed in the rear with the wagon train, but would bring meals to the front every day. These servants were regularly rationed by the government the same as enlisted men," This detail is interesting, and, so far as I know, unique among the South Carolina company and regimental histories. "Bull Run" Russell, correspondent of the *London Times*, writing from Charleston, after the bombardment of Fort Sumter by the Confederate and state authorities, makes mention of the many negro body-servants who had accompanied their masters to Charleston; and Russell, or some other correspondent, reported that their function was not only to wait on their masters, but to do any disagreeable work, such as digging trenches, throwing up breast-works, etc. Of course, such roseate ideas of soldier life were soon dispelled. It would be interesting if Mr. Izlar had told how long those Edisto Riflemen found it possible to retain their body-servants; certainly not in the trenches around Petersburg.

"What do you think of arming the Negroes?"

Source: Contributed by Gregory C. White, historical researcher and descendant of Private Azariah Bostwick. White is the author of This Most Bloody & Cruel Drama: A History of the 31st Georgia Volunteer Infantry, *published by Butternut and Blue, Baltimore, Maryland in 1997.*

February 23, 1865, letter by Azariah Bostwick, Co.D, 31st GA

"What do the people think of arming the Negroes? I am one who thinks it ought to be done & that immediately. I don't see why the Negro will not make as good a Soldier for us as for the Yankees. Every Negro between the ages of 18 & 45 will be put in service just as soon as they can be got out (the sooner the better). He is no better to fight for his country than I am, my home is his. The army are all high up for it. There have already been five thousand Negroes volunteered in Richmond, Va., they all seem high up for it."

Master and His Faithful Slave

By Samuel Coleman, Sixth Alabama Cavalry
From the Confederate Veteran, *Vol. XX, 1912.*

This contribution records a deed done during the war by one in the humblest walks of life, as heroic in character as any ever performed by the men who to-day proudly wear the victor's cross of honor. The facts were brought more vividly to mind by an accidental meeting with one of the actors recently. In the lobby of a hotel in Houston I noticed a tall, heavily built man wearing the cross of honor. I spoke to him as a comrade, and learned that he was a member of the staff of Brig. Gen. James H. Clanton, of Alabama. I then recognized him as Baxter Smith, ordnance officer of the command, now a practicing physician of Bay City, Tex.

Well, to the story. On the morning of July 14, 1864, a detachment of the 6th Alabama Cavalry, about one hundred and fifteen men, under the command of General Clanton, encountered a largely superior force of the Rousseau raiders at Greensport Ferry, on the Coosa River. Colonel Livingstone, with about two hundred and fifty men, was holding back the enemy's main body at Ten Island Ford. It was imperative for us to hold the road until reinforcements could reach us; otherwise the Oxford Iron Works, upon which the Confederate foundries at Selma, Ala., depended, would be destroyed.

The men had been well posted behind trees and rocks on the slope of a thickly wooded hill, and the road extended along the river bluff. The firing on both sides was spirited. The enemy, in spite of superior numbers, could not drive our boys from their position; but they seemed determined to gain possession of the road, and they formed a heavy column with which they could pass our thin line and clear the road before them. General Clanton and two of his staff officers, Capt. R. A. Abercrombie and "Bat" Smith, also Tommy Judkins, were standing in the middle of the road dismounted. A few feet away on the side of the road were five or six young fellows attached to headquarters and eight or ten boys of the 6th Alabama Cavalry, also dismounted. I was behind a large tree, a few feet in advance of the General, and had a good view of everything in front. A heavy column of the enemy on foot was coming around the curve of the road, about two hundred yards distant. Suddenly just behind me I hear a loud, fierce yell, and the two staff officers, followed by the headquarters' boys and the small squad of the 6th Alabama Cavalry, dashed at the enemy, who quickly poured a deadly fire upon them and then halted.

Abercrombie and Tommy Judkins were killed. Bat Smith and the handful of boys close behind him kept on. In a few seconds, Smith fell headlong upon his face and then turned over on his back. The effect of the enemy's fire was appalling. Not one of that gallant little band was left standing. The charge was reckless in the extreme, but it illustrated the spirit and high courage of our soldiers. That feat of daring was followed by another of the lowliest and humblest man there present. A tall, strapping, young negro named Griffin approached General Clanton and asked: "General, where is Marse Bat?" The General pointed down the road and said: "There near the enemy's line dead." Griffin at once started down the road. He was called back, but did not heed. He sped on in the face of that heavy fire, took up the wounded young officer and carried him in his arms from the field. He came up the road for a few yards, then stepped into the woods and came out again on the road just where the General was standing. "Is he dead, Griffin?" asked General Clanton. "I don't know, sir," he replied. "Mammy was his nurse and I am the older. I promised mammy to take care of him and to bring him back to her, and I am going to carry him home."

Simple words, but how much do they convey! An untutored negro slave carrying out his mother's commands in behalf of her nursling at the risk of his own life! I have often thought of that day, and the scene is vivid. I can see the deadly pale face of the unconscious and sorely wounded young officer as he was being carried to safety in the arms of his faithful slave.

If some of our Northern neighbors could have witnessed this scene, they might form some conception of the devotion existing in the old days South between master and servant.

"A New Member is Received Into the Camp"

The minutes of United Confederate Veterans camps contain the names of men of color. The following minutes are from the Zeb Vance Camp, UCV, of Hazelhurst, Georgia; Gilbert Baird is received into membership. Contributed by Judge Ken W. Smith of Hazelhurst, Georgia.

May Meeting

The May meeting of Zeb Vance Camp of United Confederate Veterans, held in Confederate Hall of the County Court House on the 30 instance, was attended by an unusually large number of members, on account of plans then formulated for the general reunion to be held in Biloxi, Mississippi, June 3-6 inclusive.

The meeting was presided over as usual by Dr. R. H. Reeves the commander, and was opened with the singing, by the assemblage of the verses of "How Firm a Foundation." Rev. Samuel Hilliard, the chaplain, read a short passage of scripture, and offered the invocation.

Following the reading of the minutes of the previous meeting, the Adjutant gave certificates to fifteen members of Zeb Vance Camp who expressed their intention of attending the reunion. They were instructed to meet at the Southern Ticket Office on the following Monday morning to sign up in the presence of the agent there, and receive round trip tickets for this trip. R. L. Fitzpatrick and R. T. Underwood appointed delegates to convention. L.L. Froneberger with an assistant came to bring absentee ballots to the veterans who did not expect to return from Biloxi in time to vote in the primary.

A new member received into the Camp was Gilbert Baird a faithful colored man who served the Confederacy during the War Between the States.

A resolution as follows was presented by Maj. P. R. Young following a statement to that effect made by the Adjutant:

"Whereas the constitution of Zeb Vance Camp U.C.V. does not include in the list of officers of this camp, that of custodian of any room or rooms, be it declared that the office of custodian of the Trophy Room is null and void." By unanimous vote of the members of Zeb Vance Camp, in regular monthly session on May 30, 1930 this fact was recognized and an agreement entered into that a statement of it should be addressed to Mrs. Maude E. Truitt, this statement bearing the name of Sr. R. H. Reeves Commander and by Members of Zeb Vance Camp U.C.V., Eliza W. H. Underwood, (Mrs. R. T. Underwood) Adjutant.

The Adjutant went personally to the members just before the vote was cast to inquire if all then in the hall heard and understood the measure before the house.

Dinner was served by Mrs. Margaret Harwood chairman, assisted by Mrs. J.W. Dillon, Mrs. H. C. Thompson and other members of Fanny Patton Chapter of

United Daughters of the Confederacy. Several members of Thomas Johnston Camp S.C.V. had luncheon at this time.

Respectfully submitted
Eliza W. H. Underwood
(Mrs. R. T. Underwood)
Adjutant Zeb Vance Camp, U.C.V.

Southern Humor

The humor of Southerners is legendary. This account is from the Confederate Veteran *Vol. II, 1894 and is entitled "He Borrowed Trousers From a Negro."*

Rising generations should have some idea of the straitened circumstances of a Confederate soldier. I was wounded near Atlanta, July 22, 1864, and sent to a hospital in the woods, in tents near Forsythe. On arriving at the hospital, I was divested of all my wearing apparel, and the hospital authorities gave me a receipt for my wardrobe, consisting of pants, one roundabout coat, hat, shoes and shirt and drawers. I was taken from this hospital of tents in the woods to the college hospital at Forsythe, where I remained several months and endured three courses of gangrene. From the college I was sent to Macon and from there to a "college" hospital, the Cuthbert. After several months at Cuthbert, when I had gotten almost well, the nurse brought me a pair of crutches and would come to my room occasionally to practice me in learning how to use them, so he concluded after awhile that I had learned enough about them to risk myself out on the ground. So he brought in my knapsack; but lo! to my surprise and sorrow, on opening it I found I was entirely destitute of pants. Some good fellow, in the rounds I had taken had confiscated the only trousers that I possessed in the world. I didn't have a cent, and I couldn't draw any. What was I to do? The little town we were in had some fifteen hundred wounded and disabled soldiers then, but I could learn of none who had more that one pair of pants, and I couldn't get out to beg the good citizens, and what should I do? For about nine months I had been confined to my bunk and room, and now I was physically unable to paddle my own canoe. I was almost heart-sick, and had well-nigh given up ever getting another pair, when a negro boy named Byrd, serving his young master, Ridley Jackson, in an open-hearted way, proposed to lend me a pair until I could do better. I gladly accepted, put the negro's pants on, and felt as big as a king. I was soon out on the ground, down in town, at the depot, at the Alhambra, and around generally.

But alas! my joy was soon ended. After I had worn the pants five or six days, my benefactor came to me one morning just after I had donned his trousers, and said to me that he had just received orders to go to the front, and unless I could pay him three dollars and twenty cents for his pants he would have to ask me to vacate and turn them over to him. With a heavy and sorrowful heart I gave them up and stretched myself out on my bunk, where I mused over the trials and tribulations of a Confederate soldier.

Black Confederates: Gen. Robert E. Lee's Perspective

The following letters reveal thoughts of General Robert E. Lee on the recruitment of Negroes for service in the Confederate Army

Hd Qs CS Armies
27th March 1865
Lt Gen RS Ewell
Commdg General,

General Lee directs me to acknowledge the receipt of your letter of the 25th inst: and to say that he much regrets the unwillingness of owners to permit their slaves to enter the service. If the state authorities can do nothing to get those negroes who are willing to join the army, but whose masters refuse their consent, there is no authority to do it at all. What benefit they expect their negroes to be to them, if the enemy occupies the country, it is impossible to say. He hopes you will endeavor to get the assistance of citizens who favor the measure, and bring every influence you can to bear. When a negro is willing, and his master objects, there would be less objection to compulsion, if the state has the authority. It is however of primary importance that the negroes should know that the service is voluntary on their part. As to the name of the troops, the general thinks you cannot do better than consult the men themselves. His only objection to calling them colored troops was that the enemy had selected that designation for theirs. But this has no weight against the choice of the troops and he recommends that they be called colored or if they prefer, they can be called simply Confederate troops or volunteers. Everything should be done to impress them with the responsibility and character of their position, and while of course due respect and subordination should be exacted, they should be treated as to feel that their obligations are those of any other soldier and their rights and privileges dependent in law & order as obligations upon others as upon theirselves. Harshness and contemptuous or offensive language or conduct to them must be forbidden and they should be made to forget as soon as possible that they were regarded as menials. You will readily understand however how to conciliate their good will & elevate the tone and character of the men. . . .

Very respy.
Your obt. servt.
Charles Marshall

Lt. Col & AAG
Hd. Qts. CS Armies

30th March 1865
Lt Gen RS Ewell
Commdg General,

General Lee directs me to acknowledge the receipt of your letter of the 29th inst: and to say that he regrets very much to learn that owners refuse to allow their slaves to enlist. He deems it of great moment that some of this force should be put in the field as soon as possible, believing that they will remove all doubts as to the expediency of the measure. He regrets it the more in the case of the owners about Richmond, inasmuch as the example would be extremely valuable, and the present posture of military affairs renders it almost certain that if we do not get these men, they will soon be in arms against us, and perhaps relieving white Federal soldiers from guard duty in Richmond. He desires you to press this view upon the owners.

He says that he regards it as very important that immediate steps be taken to put the recruiting in operation, and has so advised the department. He desires to have you placed in general charge of it, if agreeable to you, as he thinks nothing can be accomplished without energetic and intelligent effort by someone who fully appreciates the vital importance of the duty. . . .

Very respy
Your obt servt
Charles Marshall
Lt Col. & AAG

Letter from Isaac Calhoun, Captain of the Cooking Department

Source: The Southern Confederacy *newspaper introduces a letter written by Black Confederate Isaac Calhoun. This article is found on microfilm in the Georgia Department of Archives and History, Atlanta.*

A Negro's Letter.

We have been furnished with the following letter written by a negro belonging to Col. J.L. Calhoun, and addressed to his young mistress—the daughter of the Colonel—at Newnan. The negro went to the war along with his young master who is a member of the Newnan Guards.

This is a specimen of the down-trodden African for whom the Yankees sympathise so much.

The reader will be careful to observe the official standing and position of the darkey, and his censure on the officers in the retreat from Laurel Hill.

We will add that the letter is here inserted exactly as the negro wrote it, without any alterations or corrections. It is written at Camp McDowell, Virginia.

Camp at McDowels.

Young Miss After my best Respects I drop you a few lines, and would of done so before now, but I lost your Letter while we war on the retreat. You must give my respects to all Misses Kate & Eugene and also Aunt Lucy & Mary, I wish to know of Uncle Wallace Berry how my Little Girl is getting on. I am not well this morning but think I will be well in a day or two as I feel better this morning than I have in a day or too—

I wish you would drop a few Lines to Marter & Let him know that we have lost all of our clothing & so on.

Remember me to Uncle Kato & tell him to give my respects to all of my inquiring Friends in Neunan.

Tell Brother Simmon that I send him a book, witch I think will be of a great deal of importance to him, let me know how his family is getting on tell him to please write me word—

If my health still improves I shall want to remain in the Army, but if it does not I shall return home soon—Tell Brother to remember me in his Prares—I hope you will excuse a short letter this time the coach leavs in a few moments.

It is by the Providence of God that we are save, not by the good general ship of our officers, so with my best respecs I say good by hoping you will write again soon.

ISAAC CALHOUN
Capt. of Cooking Department

An Incident Worthy of Record....

Source: This selection is drawn from a column entitled "Confederate Veteran's Association's Annual Meeting," <u>Savannah Morning News</u>. *April 27, 1901.*

An incident worthy of record was brought to the attention of the meeting by Mr. Jacob Gardner. Mr. Gardner said he had been at Laurel Grove during the morning and that while there he had seen Col. John H. Deveaux, collector of the port of Savannah, a colored man, looking after the grave of Lieut. Thomas Pelot, of the Confederate navy, who led the attack which resulted in the capture of the Water Witch. In that attack Lieut. Pelot lost his gallant life. The man who cared for his grave yesterday was with him on the expedition and was only prevent from boarding the vessel by the peremptory command of Lieut. Pelot. It was a striking illustration of the relations that existed between the races in the olden time and of the fact that bonds so tightly forged as these cannot be severed, even by death

New York Soldier Writes . . .

Source: Greg C. White, a historical researcher, writes: A fellow researcher tipped me off to a Civil War collection at Navarro College in Corsicana, Texas. I wrote them and requested an inventory of the "Pearce Civil War Documents Collection". I spotted something that may be of interest to your project. See the attached descriptions.

Bailey, Frank
Autographed letter signed, by a New York soldier, four pages, octavo, dated May 12, 1862 and addressed to *"Dear Brother,"* a Mr. A.E. Bailey of "Middleville, Herkimer Co, NY." In this letter, Bailey, serving with the 34th New York Volunteer Infantry, describes rumors he has heard of the exploitation of blacks by the Confederate Army in 1862. Bailey also dispels the idea that blacks are not serving in the Confederate army *"there is no mistake but the rebels have black soldiers for I have seen them brought in as prisoners of war, I saw one who had the stripes of a orderly sergeant on his coat."* Signed *"I am as ever your, Brother Frank."*

N. B. Forrest Camp, Number 4
United Confederate Veterans

HENRY J. STEWART, TREASURER
HAMILTON NAT'L BANK BUILDING
W. M. NIXON, SERGEANT-MAJOR
& ASSISTANT ADJUTANT
1026 JAMES BUILDING

CAPT. E. G. ROBERTS, COMMANDER
B. L. GOULDING, CAPTAIN & ADJUTANT
CONFEDERATE MEMORIAL HALL
401 GEORGIA AVENUE
PHONE MAIN 1323

Chattanooga, Tennessee
December 5th, 1927.

Commander or
    Adjutant
        Camp of Confederate Veterans,
            Talbotton, Upson Co., Ga.

Dear Comrade,
            Some two weeks ago an old darkey Shadrick Searcy 82
years of age , claiming to have served four years in the Confederate
Army as the servant of Dr. John Searcy, but unable to give name of
Capt. or other officers of the Company, nor the number of the regiment further than the "Lighthorse Cavalry, applied for help in an application for Tennessee negro Confederate Pension.
            If his command can be established and some evidence
obtained that he did this service he is entitled to this pension
of $10.00 per month balance of his life. I wrote Mrs. Victoria Parker
of your section who he said is a daughter of his old master and
could give the information desired and would gladly assist him.
Also sent a copy of my letter to your Camp hoping you can locate
some member of the company and knowing about its organization and
old uncle Shadricks service in the army. But have no reply from any
one, and old uncle Shadrick is needy, very needy, unable to work, and
is of course interested in securing this help, and we want to help
him, are unable to do so unless you or some of you can give the
information necessary, in fact essential. Kindly let us hear
from you as soon as possible to secure the required information

Copy to
Mrs. Victoria Parker
                            Yours Respectfully   Srgt.Major.

United Confederate Veterans attempt to help
Black Confederate, 1927

Source: copy of original letter dated December 5, 1927 from W. M. Nixon, Sergeant-
Major of N. B. Forrest Camp, Number 4, United Confederate Veterans, Chatta-
nooga, Tennessee addressed to "Camp of Confederate Veterans, U. C. V., Upson
County, Georgia. Searcy, the Black Confederate, received his pension.

Chapter IV

Confederate Pension Applications and Compiled Service Records

A good source for African American military service is the Confederate pension applications and records that are found in southern state archives, county court-houses, historical societies, and in a variety of other locations. Often times the preserved affidavits of compatriots, friends, and family members give evidence of Confederate service that is found nowhere else. For example, in a 1919 South Carolina pension application for Thomas Tobi, we find M. M. Buford of the 5th South Carolina Cavalry stating, under oath, that Tobi, a Confederate pension applicant, was "a free Negro who volunteered in this company and served to the end of the war." This man's time of service, from August 1, 1861 to April 26, 1865, is remarkable. (This document was discovered in the probate office of Newberry, South Carolina by Glenda Bundrick.)

Confederate pensions were issued by the veterans' state of residence and were not easy to obtain. Aside from probing creditable service, soldiers and widows had to provide witnesses who would testify that the applicant was disabled or indigent. Because of these strict requirements, most Confederate soldiers and their wives never applied for -- or received -- state pensions.

One of the best sources for tracking Confederate soldiers is the Complied Service Records found on microfilm at National Archives branch locations and in departments of archives and history in the southern states. The names of most Black Confederates, however, will be missing because most of these men were never officially enrolled as regular soldiers

Compiled service records do exist, however, for some black soldiers, especially for those listed as musicians, freemen, or prisoner of war. Moreover, the names of thousands of white soldiers who served in state militia and local guard units are also missing. And there are "regular" troops whose names are not included because pages of some Confederate muster rolls are now missing or were destroyed.

PENSIONS TO NEGROES FAITHFUL TO SOUTH
The Chattanooga Times 1923

COLUMBIA, S.C., March 7.---- Faithful negroes who stood by their masters during the Civil war today were voted pensions by the South Carolina legislature. The house this afternoon passed the Johnstone bill providing such pensions which already had passed the senate by a vote of 67 to 34. The bill provides that slaves who served the state and their masters in the Confederate army during the war shall be granted pensions under virtually the same conditions as those now paid to Confederate veterans.

Source: *The Chattanooga Times*, 1923

A FAMILY STORY IS VERIFIED WITH ARCHIVAL DOCU-MENTS

As important as oral history is, in many cases, verification is never done. In this instance, however, researcher Shirley Craig Fiser of Panama City, Florida searched for archival records to substantiate family stories about a loyal servant named Frank Hogins. Mrs. Fiser writes:

Not long ago a friend from my home town, Russellville, Arkansas sent a copy of the enclosed news article -- a reprinting of an item in a 1915 issue. There are some errors in the article: Reece Bowen Hogins, my great grandfather was 16 when he went to war, not 18; and Frank could not have been more that four when the family came from Dickson County, Tennessee in 1841.

I knew that Reece was wounded in battle and that Frank carried him for miles on his back trying to get him to safety. In spite of Frank's valiant efforts, he was taken prisoner, and instead of running away, Frank returned to the company and served until the end of the war.

Enclosed are documents obtained from the Arkansas History Commission regarding the pension for Frank Hogins. Notice the petition was rejected in 1915 "because he was not a regular soldier," but was granted in 1917. Also note that it was stated that he was as valuable to the company as any enlisted man.

Frank remained with the Family after the death of Reece Hogins. My Uncle, Ben Hogins, remembers knowing Frank; and says he had his own little table in the dining room, and at big family dinners he was urged to sit at the big table with the others, but he always said, "No, it isn't proper!" No one ever had a more loyal friend, or was held in higher regard by a family.

Reece Bowen Hogins was a grand nephew of the Reece Bowen of Virginia who died at the Battle of Kings Mountain in the American Revolution. (See Kings Mountain Men, White; and Kings Mountain and Its Heroes, Draper.)

In the documents, the J. F. Hogins signature is that of the oldest son of Reece, John Floyd Hogins, and my grandfather. The J. W. Russell is another branch of the family and son of Dr. Thomas Russell for whom the town of Russellville is named.

Reece Hogins was one of the leaders in the terrible reconstruction era when men of prominence had to literally fight or be killed in the Pope County Militia War. Later he was sheriff of the county and Warden of the State Penitentiary.

This article about Frank Hogins was reprinted in the *Courier Democrat*,
Russellville, Arkansas, Sunday, January 26, 1992.

August 12, 1915

At the solicitation of friends among the white folks,
among whom he has many, "Uncle Frank" Hogins made
application for a Confederate pension. Uncle Frank is
an ex-slave 78 years old, and is a well known character in Russellville and Pope County. He was reared in
Tennessee by the mother of the late Col. Reece B.
Hogins and came with her to Pope County. Being a
Pickaninny of some twelve or thirteen years at the time
of Col. Hogin's birth, a great deal of the care of the
"Young Marse" fell upon him, and when Mr. Hogins
went to war at the age of 18, Uncle Frank went with
him as was the case with many slaves. He was with
him constantly through the War and at the battle of Pilot Knob and Mars Hill, Mr. Hogins being shot through
the thigh while charging the fort in the battle Pilot Knob.
After the war instead of seeking his freedom, Uncle
Frank continued to make his home with the Hogins
family, where he is still a trusted servant. One of the
pathetic scenes at the funeral of Col. Hogins was the
grief of Uncle Frank, for whom a seat had been reserved near the bier in the M.E. Church, South, and
outside the immediate family there was no more sincere mourner at the funeral.

For Original Applicants

PROOF OF SERVICE

(By Comrades if possible)

STATE OF ARKANSAS,

County of _Pope_ }

On this day personally came before the under-

signed, a _Notary Public_ within and for the County of

Pope and State of _Ark_

citizens of _Dover Pope Co. Ark_ whom I certify to be credible per-

sons and worthy of confidence, who, being duly sworn, state that they are each, personally,

well acquainted with applicant _Frank Hogins Colored_

and have known him _60_ years, respectively.

with the army in
That he was a Confederate ~~soldier~~, ~~belonging to~~ Company _A Hill Regiment_

~~Regiment of~~ _Cabels Brigade_ That as such soldier he served from

_1862_ to _End of Nov 1865_ That he was ~~honorably dis-~~

help to the Confederate Cause as much as any enlisted
~~charged (paroled or released) from such service and did not desert the same.~~ That we have
Soldier

no interest in this claim.

W H Poynters

Jo. L. Lee

Subscribed and sworn to before me this _26_ day of _July_ 191_5_

S L Coynts n.p

DEMOCRAT P. & L. CO. LITTLE ROCK.

my Commission Expires July, 2, 1918,

A 1927 NORTH CAROLINA PENSION APPLICATION

This page is extracted from a Confederate pension application for Shadrack Skeeter who served with the 4th South Carolina Regiment, State Troops. The state of North Carolina approved this man's pension even though he served with a South Carolina unit. Confederate pensions were not based on whether a soldier served with a unit from his state of residence, but rather on whether it could be documented that he served with any bona fide Confederate unit (in-state or out-of-state) and whether disability and indigence criteria were met.

Submitted by Hunter Edwards of Garner, North Carolina

A PARTIAL LISTING OF BLACK MEN AND WOMEN WHO APPEAR ON ROLLS OF GEORGIA INFANTRY COMPANIES.

The foremost source for the names of Confederate soldiers in Georgia is Miss Lillian Henderson's *ROSTER OF THE CONFEDERATE SOLDIERS OF GEORGIA* published in 6 volumes from 1959-1964. Unfortunately, this set includes only the names of those who served in regular infantry units; it does not include the names of soldiers who served in Confederate artillery, cavalry, or state militia units and legions. Most Black Confederate would not be included since they were not regularly enrolled; but, some who served in infantry units (to include black women) are found in Miss Henderson's *ROSTER*. Apparently, some army cooks, musicians, and nurses were carried on muster rolls as shown in these excerpts.

MUSTER ROLL OF CO. A, 1st REGIMENT
GEORGIA VOLUNTEER INFANTRY (OLMSTEADS'S),
ARMY OF TENNESSEE C.S.A.,
CHATHAM COUNTY, GEORGIA

DeLyon, Charles Henry (colored) - Musician Aug. 10, 1861. Transferred to Co. D, 63rd Regt. Ga. Inf. Aug. 1, 1863; Co. B, Oct. 31, 1863. No later record.

MUSTER ROLL OF COMPANY *C, 1st REGIMENT
GEORGIA VOLUNTEER INFANTRY (OLMSTEAD'S)
ARMY OF TENNESSEE C.S.A.
CHATHAM COUNTY, GEORGIA
("1st REPUBLICAN BLUES")

*Originally Capt. George A. Gordon's Company (Phoenix Riflemen), 1st Regt. Ga. Inf. (Olmstead's), Apr. 26, 1862. Enlistment for May 30, 1861 must have been originally in some other command. This company was not organized until Aug. 30, 1861. Was reorganized Apr. 26, 1862 and formed into a battalion of three companies, which subsequently became companies B, F, and K, 63d Regt. Ga. Inf.

Davidson, William (Colored) - Drummer May 30, 1861. See Davenport's Independent Company Cavalry, Ga. State Troops.

80   Confederate Pension Applications and Compiled Service Records

Harris, Alexander (Colored) - See Musician 2d Republican Blues.
Miller, Joseph (Colored) - See 2d Republican Blues
Waters, William (Colored) - Musician May 30, 1861. "Colored man, not mustered in but in service." Absent with leave Dec. 31, 1861. No later record.

MUSTER ROLL OF COMPANY *M, 26th REGIMENT
GEORGIA VOLUNTEER INFANTRY,
ARMY NORTHERN VIRGINIA C.S.A.
McINTOSH COUNTY, GEORGIA
McINTOSH COUNTY GUARDS

Green, Charles (Colored) - Musician Aug. 13, 1861. Reported "absent without pay" on roll dated Feb. 28, 1862. NO later record.
Savally, Henry (Colored) - Musician Aug. 13, 1861. Appears last on roll for Oct. 31, 1861.

MUSTER ROLL OF COMPANY H, 14th REGIMENT
GEORGIA VOLUNTEER INFANTRY
ARMY NORTHERN VIRGINIA C.S.A.
LAURENS COUNTY, GEORGIA
("BLACKSHEAR GUARDS")

Topp, Bill (Colored) - Drummer July 9, 1861. Surrendered, Appomattox, Va. Apr. 9, 1865.

MUSTER ROLL OF *COMPANY A 63rd REGIMENT
GEORGIA VOLUNTEER INFANTRY
ARMY OF TENNESSEE C. S. A.
RICHMOND COUNTY, GA.
OGLETHORPE LIGHT ARTILLERY

*This company was organized as (1st) Co. A, 12th Battn. Ga. Light Artillery in Apr. 1862, and was composed of a good many men who had previously served in the 1st (Ramsey's) Regt. Ga Vol. Inf. which was disbanded at the end of its one year enlistment in Mar. 1862. It was transferred to the 13th Battn. Ga. Inf. about Nov. or Dec. 1862. This battn. was increased to regimental size in Dec. 1862, and became known as Gordon's Regt. Later the designation was changed to the 63rd Regt. Ga. Vol. Inf.

Fox, Joe (Colored) - Nurse, Enlisted Apr. 1, 1863, by consent of owner.

Jones, Nelson (Colored) - Enlisted as a nurse Feb. 1, 1864, for a period of one month by consent of owner.
Morgan, Eliza (Colored) - Nurse, Enlisted as a nurse and laundress Apr. 1, 1863.
Morris, Ellen (Colored) - Nurse. Enlisted as a nurse Apr. 1, 1863.
Dawson, Hannah (Colored) - Cook. See private Co. H.
Dawson, Catharine (Colored) - Cook. See private Co. H.

MUSTER ROLL OF COMPANY D, 30th REGIMENT
GEORGIA VOLUNTEER INFANTRY
ARMY OF TENNESSEE C. S. A.
BIBB COUNTY, GEORGIA
HUGUENIN RIFLES

Riley, David (Colored) - Musician Oct. 20, 1862. Discharged in Bibb County, Ga. Nov. 20, 1862.

MUSTER ROLL OF *COMPANY D, 63rd REGIMENT
GEORGIA VOLUNTEER INFANTRY C. S. A.
MISCELLANEOUS COUNTIES

Burroughs, Lydia (Colored) - Enlisted as a cook May 6, 1863.

MUSTER ROLL OF COMPANY A, 2nd BATTALION
GEORGIA VOLUNTEER INFANTRY
ARMY OF NORTHERN VIRGINIA
WRIGHT'S BRIGADE C. S. A.
MUSCOGEE COUNTY, GEORGIA
"CITY LIGHT GUARDS"

Harris, Peter (Colored) - Musician Apr. 20, 1861.
Schley, Wesley (Colored - Musician Apr. 20, 1861. Discharged May 20, 1862

APPROVED PENSION APPLICATION FOR WARREN PEARSON OF SUMTER, SOUTH CAROLINA

The application of Warren Pearson, body servant of James B. Fort, includes an affidavit provided by Joseph Brown (a first cousin to Fort) to validate Confederate military service. Notations describe Mr. Pearson as "a good Loyal and Faithful Body Servant and Cook" who "served with us until the end of the war."

Contributed by Allen D. Thigpen

State of South Carolina,

County of _Sumter_

SUMTER COUNTY GENEALOGICAL SOCIETY
SUMTER, S.C.

TO THE COUNTY PENSION BOARD:

The undersigned applies for enrollment under the Act of 1923. I served the State of South Carolina in the War between the States, as _Body Servant_ under _James B. Ford_ who was in Company .... Regiment .... Captain .... I went in the service .... 18......., and served continuously until _the end of the war_ 18_65_, remaining faithful to the Confederacy throughout the said war, and my conduct since the war has been such that I am entitled to a pension under the aboveAct. I reside at _Hoyt Heights_ in _Sumter, Sumter_ County, S. C.

Harry Doyt

Sworn to and Subscribed before me this ..._12_...day
of _June_ 192_3_
Wm. E. Richardson

his
Warren X Pearson
mark
Give name in full.

STATE OF SOUTH CAROLINA,

County of ....

SUMTER COUNTY GENEALOGICAL SOCIETY
SUMTER, S.C.

Personally appeared before me .... and .... and being duly sworn, each of them deposes and says that they know .... who is an applicant for a pension, and they have read the said application; that they know of their own knowledge that the applicant served the State of South Carolina for more than six (6) months during the War between the States under.............. and remained faithful to the Confederacy during the said war and that his conduct since then has been such that will entitle him to a pension under the Act of 1923; that the applicant is a resident of the State and resides in .... County, S. C.

Sworn to before me this .... day
of ...., 192.........

.... ,

Approved by ..._E. S. Carson_..Chairman Board of Honor, ...
County, this .... day of ...., 192........

Application under Act of 1923

OF

Warren Pearson

POST OFFICE

Sumter R. 1

COUNTY OF

APPROVED BY

Chairman County Board of Honor.

SOUTH CAROLINA PENSION CHECKS FOR BLACK CONFEDERATES.

Service and pension records of Confederate soldiers are not always preserved for posterity. Allen D. Thigpen, President of the Sumter County (South Carolina) Historical Society, contributes these samples of South Carolina pension checks issued by the Office of Judge of Probate in Sumter, South Carolina to black veterans.

The inscription on each check identifies the payees as "an old and faithful Negro." In 1924, as today, the common perception could have been that all Confederate pensioners were white so the qualifying statements might have been added so that the bank would readily cash the check for the black recipient.

MISSISSIPPI SERVANTS RECEIVING PENSIONS

Bobby Mitchell of Holly Springs, Mississippi writes:

This summer in researching the Marshall County (MS) court house I found old Confederate pension application lists. On a recent business trip to Jackson, applications on file were copied concerning these Black Confederates. I am sending copies of the applications found...the quality of the reproductions was not good, and the Mississippi applications do not give as much detail as some states' records.

I am enclosing a copy of our (SCV) Camp Newsletter, *"The Gray Ghost,"* (Vol. X, No. 50 Sept. - Oct. 1991), which has a compilation of those blacks who received a pension in this county, although not all were from this county during the war.

In the last issue of this Newsletter we announced that Compatriot Mitchell had recently discovered a listing of Confederate pensioners in the Marshall County Courthouse. Upon analysis of the list, it was found that several servants of soldiers had applied for and received Confederate pensions. To date, we have found that 42 applied and 28 received pensions. Below are listed those who receive pensions in Marshall county, Mississippi..

Pud Arnold	Byhalia	William Joyner	Mt. Pleas.
Ben Boggan	Byhalia	Richard Lay	Waterford
Henry Bowen	----------	Martin Leggett	----------
Jim Brunson	Byhalia	Coleman Lester	Holly S.
Adam Bryon	----------	Manuel Matthews	Victoria
Edward Burton	Holly S.	Norwood McKissack	----------
Ben Dean	Chulahoma	Alfred Peal	----------
Tom Dockery	----------	Fletcher Phillips	Chulahoma
Ben Duncan	Holly S.	Adam Pryor	Laws Hill
Hardy Garrett	Holly S.	Jas. Smith	Byhalia
David Hill	Waterford	George Spears	Holly S.
Monroe Hill	Holly S.	Robert Walker	Holly S.
Tobe Howell	----------	Wyatt N. White	----------
Tony Ingram	Byhalia	Joe Wilson	Holly S.

BLACK CONFEDERATES AS PRISONERS OF WAR

Archival records reveal that Black Confederates were imprisoned in Northern prisoner of war camps. The compiled service records shown here are for Henry Marshall of Co. B, 14th Kentucky Cavalry. This brave soldier was captured and sent to Camp Chase, Ohio and Camp Douglas, Illinois. (Courtesy of Walter J. Bowman, Archivist, Kentucky Dept. of Military Affairs, Records and Research Branch, Lexington.)

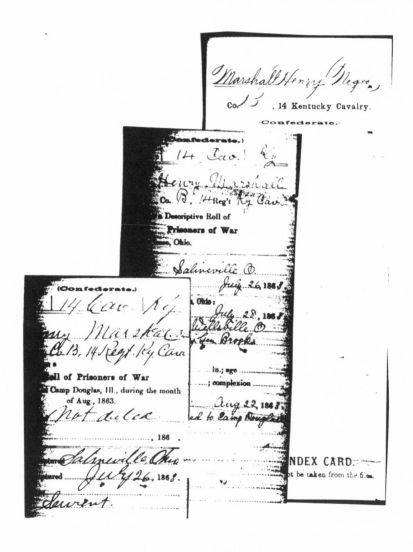

UNCLE CHARLES RICHARDSON, VETERAN OF THE CONFEDERATE ARMY

The *Arkansas Democrat* reported in its April 24, 1929 edition that "Funeral service for Uncle Charles Richardson, 95, negro slave and veteran of the Confederate army, will be held Thursday afternoon at 3 o'clock from the colored Methodist church." The article which appeared on page six went on to say, "He drew a Confederate pension, having fought through the war with his young master who was killed, and later supplied money to take his second master, a Confederate officer and himself to St. Louis." An official document from his pension record group is found in the Arkansas State Archives and show here. Contributed by Edwin Lee Chaney of Bald Knob, Arkansas.

SOME WHO RODE WITH GENERAL JOHN HUNT MORGAN OF KENTUCKY

By   John Britton Wells, III
           Genealogist-in-chief
           Sons of Confederate Veterans

The slave company listed below appears to have been composed of the personal slaves of the staff of the 8th Kentucky Cavalry, C.S.A., along with the personal slaves of several members of Company A of the 8th. Most of the owners were from the Athens area in Fayette County, Kentucky, just a few miles southeast of Lexington. This roll was made many years after the war, judging form the stationary, and seems to have been an early war list. The 8th Kentucky Cavalry was formed in September 1862, and was a part of the famous cavalry command of Gen. John Hunt Morgan. Thomas Foster the regimental surgeon, was disabled and discharged on December 7, 1862, and most of the other owners were captured on the Ohio Raid in July 1863. It is probable that this "company" had been dissolved by that date.

Colored Troops	Co.? [Q or L]
	[OWNER]
Col. Cluke's Jim	[Col. Roy S. Cluke, 8th KY Cav.]
Col. Coleman's Dave	[Lt. Col. Cicero Coleman, "]
Maj. Bullock's Jo	[Maj. Robert S. Bullock, "]
Dr. Foster's crooked leg Negro	[Thomas Foster, Surgeon "]
Capt. McCaine's Dave	[Capt. Thos. W. McCann, So. A, 8th]
Lt. Surr's Sol	[Lt. Richard A. Spurr, " "]
Lt. Prewitt's Negro man	[Lt. David Prewitt, " "]
Cliff Estill's Conley	[Pvt. C. F. Estill, " "]
T. E. Eastin's Richard the 3rd	[Thos. E. Eastin, Adjt., 8th KY]
Guss Eastin's Anthony	[Pvt. Preston (?) Eastin, Co. A, 8th]
Albert Dudley's Sanford	[Pvt. Albert Dudley, " "]
Capt. Curry's John	[W. E. Currey, AQM, 8th KY Cav.]
Sam Downing's John	[Pvt. Sam Downing, Co. A, 8th KY]
Larry Thompson's Cuffy	[Pvt. Lawrence Thompson, " "]
John & Jim Gesses Lewis	[Pvt. James W. Gess, Co. A, 8th KY]
	[Pvt. John W. Gess, " "]

TEXAS WIDOW SEEKS PENSION

The widow of George H. Hampton attempts to qualify as beneficiary for her late husband's Confederate pension. The county judge, J. J. Bolton, is not aware that blacks served in Confederate armies and is seeking a ruling from the Texas Comptroller of Pensions in this 1932 letter.

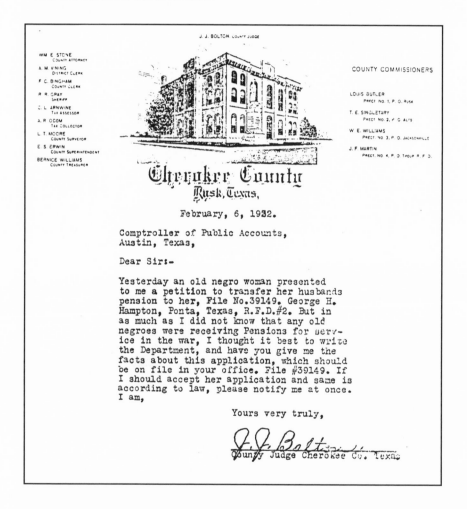

J. J. BOLTON. COUNTY JUDGE

WM. E. STONE
    COUNTY ATTORNEY
A. M. VINING
    DISTRICT CLERK
F. C. BINGHAM
    COUNTY CLERK
R. R. GRAY
    SHERIFF
C. L. ARNWINE
    TAX ASSESSOR
A. R. ODOM
    TAX COLLECTOR
L. T. MOORE
    COUNTY SURVEYOR
E. S. ERWIN
    COUNTY SUPERINTENDENT
BERNICE WILLIAMS
    COUNTY TREASURER

COUNTY COMMISSIONERS

LOUIS BUTLER
    PRECT. NO. 1, P. O. RUSK
T. E. SINGLETARY
    PRECT. NO. 2, P. O. ALTO
W. E. WILLIAMS
    PRECT. NO. 3, P. O. JACKSONVILLE
J. F. MARTIN
    PRECT. NO. 4, P. O. TROUP. R. F. D.

Cherokee County
Rusk, Texas,

February, 6, 1932.

Comptroller of Public Accounts,
Austin, Texas,

Dear Sir:-

Yesterday an old negro woman presented
to me a petition to transfer her husbands
pension to her, File No.39149. George H.
Hampton, Ponta, Texas, R.F.D.#2. But in
as much as I did not know that any old
negroes were receiving Pensions for service in the war, I thought it best to write
the Department, and have you give me the
facts about this application, which should
be on file in your office. File #39149. If
I should accept her application and same is
according to law, please notify me at once.
I am,

Yours very truly,

J. J. Bolton
County Judge Cherokee Co. Texas

Note: George Hampton's original pension application is on file in the Texas Confederate Pension Records and shows that he was approved on April 7, 1913 for a payment of $300 a year. Hampton states that he was in service "two years, six months" herding cattle and horses for "the Texas Confederate soldiers." Also, written on the application is the statement that this man was "Discharged and Freed."

A BLACK CONFEDERATE IS DISCHARGED FROM SERVICE AT APPOMATTOX

The handwriting on archival documents is not always easy to read. On this 1919 South Carolina pension application, M. M. Buford of Company 5, 5th South Carolina Cavalry attests to the Confederate service of Thomas Tobi who was (from the application) "a free Negro who volunteered in this Co. and served to the end of the War." This time in service is extraordinary - August 1, 1861 to April 26, 1865. This document was found in the local probate office of Newberry, South Carolina by Glenda Bundrick.

THE APPOMATTOX PAROLES
April 9-15, 1865

The Virginia Civil War Battles and Leaders Series 3rd Edition
William G. Nine and Ronald G. Wilson

Published by H. E. Howard, Inc., Lynchburg, Virginia, 1989
Addendum:
Miscellaneous Units Paroled at Appomattox Court House

BLACKS WITH THE ARMY OF NORTHERN VIRGINIA

Ordnance Train	16	(45)
servants w/Donaldsville Artillery (LA)	4	(63)
musicians w/ 18th GA Battalion	4	(226)
cooks w/ 18th GA Battalion	4	(226)
Quartermaster Dept., Gary's Cavalry Brig.	8	(487)
TOTAL	36	

*Note: The numbers in parentheses are the corresponding page numbers in Vol. 15 of the *Southern Historical Society Papers.*

"..ALL SEND LOVE TO THE 'OLD REBEL NEGRO.' "

This article appeared in the *Mobile* (Alabama) *Register*, 1906, and is contributed by Lewis D. Brasell of Mobile.

COLORED CONFEDERATE

Who has applied to legislature for pension and whom sons and veterans are aiding, pending the issue. *(New Orleans Picayune.)*

Robert Shropshire, the old negro Confederate Veteran, was born at Nashville, Tenn., and is now about 73 years old. He was a member of Company A. Fifth Texas Cavalry or Second Regiment, Sibley's Brigade. He served as teamster and was sworn in and paid monthly in the Confederate army. Robert belonged to Major John Shropshire, who was killed in a battle at Glorietta, out near the Texas line. After the death of his master Robert belonged to Mrs. Robert Shropshire, who is living and gives Robert the best of recommendations. Robert continued to serve in the army as teamster with the brother of his former master, Captain Ben Shropshire, until the end of the war. He then went with Captain Shropshire to Holly Spring, Miss., and was there wounded by a piece of a shell, which cut him in the head, and he was disabled for a long time. At the close of the war he worked on steamboats.

Previous to this he went to Columbus, Texas, to his mistress, Mrs. Robert Shropshire, where he remained a few months.

Although 73 years old Robert is as loyal to the Confederate cause as ever. He is very feeble, and has made application for a pension from - the state, and is perhaps the only colored man in the state entitled to a pension. He is a familiar figure at all the reunions, the last one he attended being held at Baton Rouge, Aug. 9.

The following extract - from a letter written by a well known gentleman of this city to a prominent member of the last Legislature shows the feeling existing among the old soldiers for Bob. He said: "As a Confederate soldier and one who appreciates the services rendered during the four years of untold hardships, I would request of you that you introduce a bill in the House granting a pension to the old and faithful colored man, Robert Shropshire. From personal observations I know that Roberts was true and faithful and bears the marks of a wound which nearly resulted in a fatally, obtained at Holly Springs, Miss. It will be a very small matter for the great State of Louisiana to recognize the services of this poor old negro in his old age."

What could be more sincere than the sentiments expressed in a letter received by Bob a few days since from a white comrade in Texas. He addresses Bob as "Dear Bob and comrade," and says:

"You did not say if you took part in the reunion at New Orleans. I wanted to come just to see you, but could not leave home. I wrote you about Charley Shropshire's death, also Mr. Dick died some time back. Only a few of our old boys are living. Bob, I will enclose you a one dollar bill and want you to acknowledge receipt of it and tell me if you had a good time at the reunion. Bob, I will never forget you and our trip home in 1862 through the mountains of New Mexico, when you had the smallpox and no one would go near you in the wagon but myself. And, afterwards when you had gotten well and I had the measles, you stayed by me as I had you. On our trip alone from San Antonio you stuck to me when I was so sick. And this trip, Bob, is heart bound one white man and one negro together. You had lost your master in the battle of Glorietta, I had lost my health, but to each other we stood true, and are today enjoying the blessings that were bestowed on but few of those old boys. Long life Bob. Nora and the boys all send love to the 'Old Rebel Negro.' Write soon to your old comrade and friend."

It is the hope of many that Bob's services will be recognized. He can not live much longer, and when he passes to the Great Beyond it should be with the feeling that his white comrades appreciated the bravery and devotion and suffering of old Bob, and that it was also recognized by the state.

During the past week the Army of Tennessee and Camp Beauregard, Sons of Veterans, each appropriated $2.50 a month for Bob's relief.

A NORTH CAROLINA PENSION IS AWARDED

Frank Hunter of Lincoln County, North Carolina appears on the rolls of Confederate pensioners in that state. He entered service "on or about the 22nd of 1861" with the 23rd Regiment, Co. K, State Troops and was the servant of Stanhope Hunter and "built barracks and breast works." Another member of the unit, James Nixon, provided this letter to support the pension application.

(Contributed by William Hunter Edwards of Garner, North Carolina)

North Carolina,
Lincoln County.

James Nixon of Lincoln County,State ofnNorth Carolina,a duly
enrolled Confederate Vetran,having served with Company K,23rd.Regiment,
North Carolina State Troops,being duly sworn,states,that to his certain
knowledge one Frank Hunter,a servant of Stanhope Hunter,a member of
Company K,23rd Regiment,North Carolina Troops,served with said Stanhope
Hunter in the Confederate amry for alperiod of about two years.

He further states that to his certain knowledge that the said
Frank Hunter built *** barracks and breast works.

James Nixon

Subscribed and sworn to before me,this the 1st day of July,1927.

M. T. Leatherman

Clerk Superior Court.

BLACK CONFEDERATE IN CHIMBORAZO HOSPITAL

Compiled Service Records of Private F. Presley with the notation col'd (interpreted as "colored") of Co. E. 23rd Georgia Infantry. This soldier was admitted to Chimborazo Hospital in Richmond, Virginia, on April 21, 1862 and returned to duty on May 20, 1862.

A FREE PERSON OF COLOR SEEKS
AGRICULTURAL EXEMPTION.

(Courtesy of Grover Criswell.)

> Tugalo Academy. Apr 18ᵗʰ 1864.
>
> Mr. Jas E Hagood:
>   Dear Friend; Stephen Ladd —
> a Free Person of color — for whom I am Guardian.
> is going to your place to morrow to report to the Enrolling
> officer, in accordance with orders from Head quarters.
> He will also make application for exemption on the
> grounds of being a Farmer and more useful to the
> Country at home than in other service. Will you
> so kind as to examine his papers, and if consistent with
> your feelings, direct him how to do and give him your
> influence for his good.   Your Friend confidently
>   C. L. Collingsworth

DISAPPROVED CONFEDERATE PENSION FOR FREE NE-GRO

Source: Indigent Pension Application (1904 for James Clark of Emanuel County, Georgia, A free negro who served as a volunteer fifer for Co. K, 28th Georgia Infantry.

Swainsboro, GA. Oct 13, 1904

Hon. J. W. Linsey, coms [commissioner] of pensions
Atlanta, Ga.

Dear col [colonel] I have had a talk with 2 or 3 of the members of the company that James Clark col [colored] the Free Negro was in; and they say that he was not mustered in to service he just went in with co [company] on his own account and was payed by the company for his services as a fifer and he left command on his own account.

He was not compelled to stay so I inclose you his application for you to pass upon.

Yours truly

John E. Youmans ordy [Ordinary]

DISAPPROVED

NAME: Clark, James (free negro)   Year 1904   COUNTY Emanuel

•

WHEN AND WHERE BORN? 1804 - Burke County, Georgia

ENLISTED WHEN AND WHERE? 1861 - Emanuel County, Georgia

RANK.

COMPANY AND REGIMENT?   Company K, 28th Ga. Regt.

NAME OF CAPTAIN AND COLONEL?

WOUNDED?

CAPTURED, WHEN, AND WHERE?

RELEASED.

WHEN AND WHERE SURRENDERED?
                Discharged as fifer and sent home (date not given)

IF NOT PRESENT AT SURRENDER, WHERE WERE YOU?

DIED, WHEN AND WHERE?

BURIED.

WITNESSES. J. R. Martin - same command -- No data

1w

George Briggs, Confederate pensioner from Union South Carolina
(Born March 13, 1852; died March 11, 1944)

Chapter V

Historical Accounts

One may get the idea from what I have said, that there was bitter feeling toward the white people on the part of my race, because of the fact that most of the white population was away fighting in a war which would result in keeping the Negro in slavery if the South was successful. In the case of slaves on our place this was not true, and it was not true of any large portion of the slave population in the South where the Negro was treated with anything like decency.

Booker T. Washington
Up From Slavery

Although absent from most official records, the names of African Americans who supported the Confederacy can be found in the holdings of southern state archives, local libraries, genealogical societies, and various historical organizations. Personal letters and diaries, family histories, and veterans' narratives provide an unvarnished view of the black experience in Southern history. In addition, regional history books and society journals are filled with information that is genealogical in scope and valuable for those who are tracking the military service of local men.

County histories are also an excellent source for locating the names of Black Confederates. In this example, from *The Echo of the Black Horn* (a history of Jones County, Mississippi), Ethel Knight writes: "Among the volunteers who were ready to throw down their lives for their white friends were faithful slaves who hated the Yankees as much as the Johnny Rebs. Contrary to general belief, Southern Negroes did the Confederacy great service, and although it is said that no slaves were taken into the army, below is a copy of an old record of an ex-slave, who was born Willis Edmund. . ." [Mrs. Knight goes on to provide details about the military experiences of this soldier and others as well.]

Researchers will stumble upon passages that provide information about the military service of men and women of color. From *The Battle of Griswoldville* by Charles F. Wells we find that "Professor E. M. Coulter [an eminent Georgia scholar] said Jeff Davis's simplicity of manner and kindness was shone when he shook hands with forty negro workmen from a pistol factory in Griswold, Georgia." [In this little known battle in central Georgia, young boys and old men filled the ranks of state militia units who fought an ill-fated encounter with Sherman's veteran troops. There are reports that blacks fought alongside the state troops at Griswoldville, but supporting documentation is scarce or nonexistent.]

Intriguing discourse can be found in the personal papers of notable military and governmental leaders. In a letter written on July 19, 1895 by Confederate General Henry Heth to Major C. J. Green, we find these comments: "Mr. Kirkley informed me he had some twenty or thirty letters in his possession recommending Confederates as suitable persons to raise colored regiments; he examined all such papers on file but failed to find the one recommending you for so employment, so I presume the letter you refer to was destroyed. It certainly never came in possession of the Rebellion Record office." [Source: the private papers of General Henry Heth held at the Virginia Historical Society.]

The selections in this chapter are a sampling of accounts that can be found in county histories, genealogical publications, family papers, historical journals, Confederate veteran magazines, and published books.

An Account Penned by a Confederate Heroine

Mary A. H. Gay of Decatur, Georgia, risked her life to deliver military papers through Union lines during the Battle of Atlanta. She also aided Confederate armies by concealing large stores of uniforms and ammunition from Sherman's troops. Local newspapers hailed the young Miss Gay as a "Confederate hero-ine" and "one of the most indomitable characters of the Old South." In later years, she authored a popular book entitled <u>Life in Dixie During the War</u> and from this selection we learn about a faithful servant named Toby.

The excitement incident to the morning and evening of yesterday left my mother and myself in no frame of mind for repose, and we spent the night in suspense and painful apprehension of trouble yet to come greater and more dreadful than that through which we had passed. The medicine left for Toby by the physician sum-moned last night was faithfully administered according to direction, and the morn-ing found him better, though able to sit up only for a short while at a time. Measles had developed, and we felt hopeful that it would prove to be a very slight attack ; and such it might have been could we have controlled him properly, but the excite-ment and ever-varying scenes in the yard, and as far as vision extended, were so new and strange to him that, when unobserved, he spent much of his time at a window commanding the best view of the scene, and, thus exposed to a current of air, the disease ceased to appear on the surface and a troublesome cough ensued.

Having been without food since the preceding morning, our thoughts turned to the usual preparation for breakfast, but alas, those preparations had to be dis-pensed of, as we had nothing to prepare. This state of affairs furnished food for at least serious reflection, and the inquiry, "What are we to do ?" found audible expression. The inexorable demands of hunger could not be stifled, and we knew that the sick boy needed hot tea and the nourishment which food alone could give, and yet we had nothing for ourselves or for him-so complete had been the robbery of the "advance guards" of the Grand Army of the Republic that not a thing, animate or inanimate, remained with which to appease our hunger. "What are we to do?" Was iterated and reiterated, and no solution of the question presented itself. Even then appetizing odors from the campfires were diffusing themselves upon the air and entering our house, but aliens were preparing the food and we had no part in it. We debated this question, and finally resolved not to expose ourselves to the jeers and insults of the enemy by an act of ours that would seem to ask for food ; but that we would go to our Southern citizens in the war-stricken and almost deserted town, and, if he were not completely robbed, ask them to share their supplies with us until we could procure aid from outside of the lines so arbitrarily drawn.

In this dilemma an unexpected relief came to us, and convinced us that there was good even in Nazareth. A large tray, evidently well-filled, and covered with a snow-white cloth, was brought in by an Irishman, who handed a card to my mother containing these words "To Mrs. Stokes and daughter, Miss Gay, with compliments of (MAJOR) CAMPBELL. "Please accept this small testimonial of regard and respectful sympathy."

The latter part of the brief message was the same that secured acceptance of this offering, and my mother and myself jointly acknowledged it with sincere thanks, and again we thought of Elijah and the ravens. The contents of the tray-coffee, sugar, and tea, sliced ham and a variety of canned relishes, butter, potatoes, and oatmeal and bread, were removed and the tray returned. That tray on its humane mission, having found its way into our house, more than once opportunely reappeared. We enjoyed the repast thus furnished, although briny tears were mingled with it.

The day passed without any immediate adventure. Great activity prevailed in army ranks. The coming and going of cavalry ; the clatter of sabre and spur ; the constant booming of cannon and report of musketry, all convinced us that the surrender of Atlanta by the Confederates was quite a matter of time. A few thousand men, however brave and gallant, could not cope successfully with "three hundred thousand" who ignored every usage of civilized warfare, and fought only for conquest.

I cannot say how long this state of affairs lasted before Wheeler's Cavalry, supported by Confederate infantry, stole a march upon the Yankees and put them to flight. Garrard and his staff officers were in our parlor-their parlor pro tem.-holding a council; the teamsters and army followers were lounging about promiscuously, cursing and swearing and playing cards, and seeming not to notice the approaching artillery until their attention was called to it, and then they contended that it was their men firing off blank cartridges. I intuitively felt that a conflict was on hand. Ma and I held whispered conversations and went from one window to another, and finally rushed into the yard. Men in the camps observed our excitement and said, "Don't be alarmed, it is only our men firing off their blank cartridges."

The irony of fate was never more signally illustrated than on this occasion. I would have laid down my life, yea, a thousand breathing, pulsing lives of my own, to have witnessed the overthrow of the Yankee army, and yet, I may have been the means of saving a large portion of it on that occasion. Dreading for my mother's sake and for the sake of the deaf girl and the sick boy, an attack upon the forces which covered our grounds, I ran to one of the parlor doors and knocked heavily and excitedly. An officer unlocked the door and opening it said

"What is it?"

"Our men must be nearly here," I replied.

"Impossible," he said, and yet, with a bound he was in the yard, followed in quick succession by each member of the conclave.

A signal, long, loud, and shrill, awakened the drowsy, and scattered to the four winds of heaven cards, books and papers; and, in a few minutes, horses and mules were hitched to wagons, and the mules, wagons and men were fairly flying from the approach of the Confederates. Women and children came pouring in from every direction, and the house was soon filled. Before Garrard's wagon train was three hundred yards away, our yard was full of our men--our own dear "Johnnie Rebs." Oothcaloga Valley boys, whom I had known from babyhood, kissed, in passing, the hand that waved the handkerchief. An officer, ah, how grand he looked in gray uniform, came dashing up and said

"Go in your cellar and lie down; the Federals are forming a line of battle, and we, too, will form one that will reach across the grounds, and your house will be between the two lines. Go at once."

My mother ran and got Toby's shoes and put them on for him, and told him to get up and come with her, and as he went out of the house, tottering, I threw a blanket over him, and he and Telitha went with ma to our near neighbor, Mrs. Williams, her cellar being considered safer than ours. I remained in our house for the twofold purpose of taking care of it, if possible, and of protecting, to the best of my ability, the precious women and children who had fled to us for protection. Without thought of myself I got them all into the room that I thought would be safest, and urged them to lie down upon the floor and not to move during the battle. Shot and shell flew in every direction, and the shingles on the roof were following suit, and the leaves, and the limbs, and the bark of the trees were descending in showers so heavy as almost to obscure the view of the contending forces. The roaring of cannon and the sound of musketry blended in harmony so full and so grand, and the scene was so absorbing, that I thought not of personal danger, and more than once found myself outside of the portals ready to rush into the conflict for was not I a soldier, enlisted for the war ? Nor was I the only restless, intrepid person in the house on that occasion. An old lady, in whose veins flowed the blood of the Washingtons, was there, and it was with the greatest difficulty that I restrained her from going out into the arena of warfare. The traditions of her ancestors were so interwoven with her life, that, at an age bordering on four score years and ten, they could not relax their hold upon her ; and she and I might have gone in opposite directions had we fled to the ranks of the contending armies.

Mine was, no doubt, the only feminine eye that witnessed the complete rout of the Federals on that occasion. At first I could not realize what they were doing, and feared some strategic movement; but the "rebel yell" and the flying blue-coats brought me to a full realization of the situation, and I too joined in the loud acclaim of victory. And the women and children, until now panic-stricken and silent as death, joined in the rejoicing. All the discouragement of the past few weeks fled from me, and hope revived, and I was happy, oh, so happy 1 I had seen a splendidly equipped army, Schofield's division, I think, ignominiously flee from a little band of lean, lank, hungry, poorly-clad Confederate soldiers, and I doubted not an overruling Providence would lead us to final victory.

When the smoke of the battle cleared away, my mother and her ebony charge returned home. Toby quickly sought his pallet, and burning fever soon rendered him delirious the greater part of the time. In one of his lucid intervals, he asked me to read the Bible to him, and he told me what he wanted me to read about, and said

"Miss Missouri used to read it to me, and I thought it was so pretty." And I read to him the story of the cross-of Jesus' dying love, and he listened and believed. I said to him

"My boy, do you think you are going to die ?"
"Yes'm, I think I am."
I bowed my head close to him and wept, oh, how bitterly.
"Miss Mary, don't you think I'll go to heaven ?" he anxiously asked.
"Toby, my boy, there is one thing I want to tell you; can you listen to me ?"
"Yes'm."

"I have not always been just to you. I have often accused you of doing things that I afterwards found you did not do, and then I was not good enough to acknowledge that I had done wrong. And when you did wrong, I was not forgiving enough; and more than once I have punished you for little sins, when I, with all the light before me, was committing greater ones every day, and going unpunished, save by a guilty conscience. And now, my boy, I ask you to forgive me. Can you do it ?"

"Oh, yes'm"

"Are you certain that you do ? Are you sure that there is no unforgiving spirit in you towards your poor Miss Mary, who is sorry for all she has ever done that was wrong towards you."

"Oh, yes'm"

"Then, my boy, ask the Lord to forgive you for your sins just as I have asked you to forgive me, and He will do it for the sake of Jesus, who died, on the cross that sinners might be redeemed from their sins and live with Him in heaven."

I can never forget the ineffable love, and faith, and gratitude, depicted in that poor boy's face, while I live; and as I held his soft black hand in mine, I thought of its willing service to "our boys," and wept to think I could do no more for him, and that his young life was going out before he knew the result of the cruel war that was waged by the Abolitionists! He noticed my grief, and begged me not to feel so badly, and added that he was willing to die.

I arose from my position by his bed and asked him if there was anything in the world I could do for him. In reply he said

"I would like to have a drink of water from the Floyd spring."

"You shall have it, my boy, just as soon as I can go there and back," and I took a pitcher and ran to the spring and filled and refilled it several times, that it might be perfectly cool, and went back with it as quickly as possible. I'll drank a goblet full of this delicious water and said it was "so good," and then added

"You drink some, too, Miss Mary, and give Miss Polly some."

I did so, and he was pleased. He coughed less and complained less than he had done since the change for the worse, and I deluded myself into the hope that he might yet recover. In a short while he went to sleep, and his breathing became very hard and his temperature indicated a high degree of fever. I urged my mother to lie down, and assured her that if I thought she could do anything for Toby at any time during the night I would call her.

I sat there alone by that dying boy. Not a movement on his part betrayed pain. His breathing was hard and at intervals spasmodic. With tender hands I changed the position of his head, and for a little while he seemed to breathe easier. But it was only for a little while, and then it was evident that soon he would cease to breathe at all. I went to my mother and waked her gently and told her I thought the end was near with Toby, and hurried back to him. I thought him dead even then; but, after an interval, he breathed again and again, and all was over. The life had gone back to the God who gave it, and I doubt not but that it will live with Him forever. The pathos of the scene can never be understood by those who have not witnessed one similar to it in all its details, and I will not attempt to describe it. No timepiece marked the hour, but it was about midnight, I ween, when death set the spirit of that youthful negro free. Not a kindred being nor a member of his own race was near to lay loving hand upon him, or prepare his little body for burial. We stood and gazed upon him as he lay in death in that desolated house, and thought of his fidelity and loving interest in our cause and its defenders, and of his faithful service in our efforts to save something from vandal hands; and the fountain of tears was broken up and we wept with a peculiar grief over that lifeless form.

My mother was the first to become calm, and she came very near me and said, as if afraid to trust her voice, "Wouldn't it be well to ask Eliza Williams and others to come and 'lay him out?'"

Before acting on this suggestion I went into another room and waked Telitha and took her into the chamber of death. A dim and glimmering light prevented her from taking in the full import of the scene at first; but I took her near the couch, and, pointing to him, I said, "Dead!-Dead!"

She repeated interrogatively, and, when she fully realized that such was the case, her cries were pitiable, oh, so pitiable.

I sank down upon the floor and waited for the paroxysm of grief to subside, and then went to her and made her understand that I was going out and that she must stay with her mistress until I returned. An hour later, under the manipulation of good "Eliza Williams"-- known throughout Decatur as Mrs. Ammi Williams' faithful servant-and one or two others whom she brought with her, Toby was robed in a nice white suit of clothes prepared for the occasion by the faithful hands of his "Miss Polly," whom he had loved well and who had cared for him in his orphanage.

We had had intimation that the Federals would again occupy Decatur, and as soon as day dawned I went to see Mr. Robert Jones, Sen., and got him to make a coffin for Toby, and I then asked "Uncle Mack," and "Henry" - now known as Decatur's Henry Oliver - to dig the grave. Indeed, these two men agreed to attend to the matter of his burial. After consultation with my mother, it was agreed that that should take place as soon as all things were in readiness. Mr. Jones made a pretty, well-shaped coffin out of good heart pine, and the two faithful negro men already mentioned prepared with care the grave. When all was in readiness, the dead boy was placed in the coffin and borne to the grave by very gentle hands.

Next to the pallbearers my mother and myself and Telitha fell in line, and then followed the few negroes yet remaining in the town, and that funeral cortege was complete.

At the grave an unexpected and most welcome stranger appeared. "Uncle Mack" told me he was a minister, and would perform the funeral service-and grandly did he do it. The very soul of prayer seemed embodied in this negro preacher's invocation; nor did he forget Toby's "nurses," and every consolation and blessing was besought for them. And thus our Toby received a Christian burial.

Loyal slave is put to death by Sherman's troops.

This account is from Goodly Heritage *by Anne P. Collins and is courtesy of the author. Contributed by Max Dorsey of Chester, South Carolina.*

BURREL HEMPHILL STORY

A poignant account of how a Chester County - slave, Burrel Hemphill, was cruelly put to death by Sherman's soldiers rather than to betray the trust of his master has been handed down through the generations in Blackstock.

History records that the Federal Army left Columbia and marched north to the vicinity of Blackstock. There they made a right turn and moved toward Cheraw. Raiding parties called "bummers" fanned out in every direction from the line of march to pillage and plunder for food and booty.

Such a group came one day to the home of Robert Hemphill, three miles northeast of Blackstock. Hemphill was a planter of considerable wealth and prestige, owning scores of slaves who worked the 2,200 acres of the estate. A bachelor, he was widely known for his kindly attitude toward his slaves.

Upon the approach of the soldiers, Hemphill fled to North Carolina, leaving Burrel to talk to the raiders. According to "Uncle" Charles Hemphill, a grandson of Burrel who was a 12-year-old witness to the happening, the soldiers were convinced that Burrel knew the hiding place of the family silverware and other valuables, and also the hiding place where a considerable amount of money had been buried by Robert Hemphill before he fled.

Sources say that Burrel knew only where the silverware was, for the master had carried away what money there was on the premises. Though cruelly tortured, tied to a horse and dragged half a mile from the Hemphill home to Hopewell Church, Burrel would give no information. Soldiers then carried him into the woods near the Hemphill house where he was hanged on a limb from a blackgum tree and his body riddled with bullets. As a final gesture of violence, the frustrated soldiers burned the nearby cotton house to the ground—and, with it, 300 bales of cotton.

In later years, members of the Hopewell community chipped in and erected a granite marker with this inscription: "In Memory of Burrel Hemphill Killed by Union Soldiers February,' 1865. Although a Slave He Gave His Life Rather Than Betray a Trust, He Was a Member of Hopewell."

Two Black Republicans Were Confederate Vets.

Contributed by Mrs. Isabel R. Vandervelde, Chief Researcher, Aiken County Historical Museum, Aiken, South Carlona.

Aiken County South Carolina was the only county in the state actually founded during Reconstruction days in 1871. Among the African-Americans taking political power during the push for voting rights in the area were Samuel Jones Lee of Abbeville County and Charles Doughterty Hayne of Charleston.

Lee was active politically in old Edgefield District and Hayne in old Barnwell District. Both men were free before the war, Lee as part of the black family of General Samuel Jones McGowan and Hayne as a member of a family of wealthy free blacks in the low-country. Both were proud to have served in the Confederate Armies.

Hayne, a free black born in 1842, was conscripted and went into the Confederate Army as a private in Company B, Thirty-second Georgia Infantry Regiment under Colonel George P. Harrison. He participated in active service all around Charleston at Fort Sumter, Mount Pleasant, James Island, John's Island, Pocataligo, Florida, and finally in North Carolina until Johnston's surrender at Greensboro.

His regiment served first at Mount Pleasant. Hayne was then among those sent to Fort Sumter where he remained during three months of bombardment. He served in Florida five months, engaging in the battle of Olustee. When federal troops landed in force and marched on Charleston, his regiment marched with Rhett's regiment up to North Carolina where they took part in the final battles at Hillsboro, Bentonville, and Greensboro where they surrendered and were paroled.

Hayne then started his walk home, going through Georgia by way of Atlanta, then to Augusta, and by steamboat downriver to Savannah and then Charleston. He took up his peacetime trade, that of tailoring, moving his office first to Augusta, Georgia, and then across the river to Aiken, South Carolina, where he was elected to the state legislature in 1868, and in 1871 was chosen the first state senator from the new county.

He became disillusioned with the Republicans and came out for Wade Hampton in the crucial 1876 election. After the return to power of the democrats he moved back to Charleston where he was active in many charitable organizations and a member of the Charleston Hook and Ladder Company, which was also a unit of black Confederate veterans.

Samual Lee, born in 1844, was the son of General Samuel J. McGowan of Abbeville. As a child he lived with his mulatto mother and his siblings in Diamond

Hill, a town of freed slaves who worked the McGowan plantation. He was 16 when McGowan, a prominent lawyer and veteran of the Mexican War, organized an Abbeville militia unit consisting of the 100 wealthiest planters of the county. Each man was to provide all equipment for himself and a companion, a black man assigned as his squire, in fill uniform and armed, with horse and equipment.

McGowan chose Lee to serve in this capacity in the 14th South Carolina Regiment. Lee was always proud to have ridden everywhere beside the General. Lee was wounded first at Second Manassas, clipped in the ear by a Minie ball while riding along with McGowan on the battlefield. He was again wounded by a ball in the thigh near Hanover Junction in the retreat to Richmond in 1864. After the surrender he returned to Abbeville. He then moved to Edgefield County where he was appointed as an assistant revenue commissioner until being appointed a registrar of the county. He was elected a member of the state house of representatives, meanwhile reading law and passing the South Carolina bar examination, and was among the first legislators from the new Aiken County. He was immediately chosen Speaker of the House.

After the Red Shirt overthrow of Republicans he moved to Charleston to set up a successful law office. Under Wade Hampton,, Lee was Brigadier General of the black national guard units in all of the low-country.

Information is found for Jeff Mabry, A Texan
Reputed to be 110 Years Old.

While conducting local research, Wilbur Thomas Myers of Sulphur Springs, Texas discovered information about Jeff Mabry, a veteran from Hopkins County, Texas. Researcher Myers used census rolls, local county histories, vital records, the recorded minutes of the Mat Ashcroft Camp #170, United Confederate Veterans, and old newspaper files in order to learn about Mabry's military service. The UCV camp records listed this Black Confederate as "Uncle Jeff, Colored, Body Servant to Col H. P. Mabry." The camp members attempted to secure a state pension for Uncle Jeff and the minutes of the regular meeting of November 3, 1923 state: Verbal report of committee to investigate whether Jeff Mabry could collect a pension and it was shown that there was no available funds for colored men in Texas. On motion, report was received and committee discharged. Mr. Myers provides his research findings in this narrative:

On the seventh of June, 1929 when Jeff Mabry died at the home of Mr & Mrs William G. Murray he was reputed to be 110 years and was recognized as the only black man to have actively served with the Confederate Army from Hopkins County, Texas. Uncle Jeff, as he was affectionately referred by all that knew him, was 101 years old when he married Sarah Jeter, a long time employee of the Murray family, on 26 March 1920 and moved to the Murray residence to live out the rest of his life.

According to the 1920 census for Hopkins County he stated that he was 101 years old at the time and had been born in the State of Georgia. Little or nothing is known about Jeff Mabry between the time of his birth in 1819 and 1861 when he was living in the household of Hinche Parham Mabry, born on 27 October 1829 in North Carolina and was a member of the legal profession in Jefferson with T. J. and J. H. Rogers at the time Texas seceded from the Union.

Hinche Parham Mabry answered the call to colors on 13 June 1861 and Jeff Mabry joined right along with him and both were assigned to Company "G" 3rd Texas Cavalry. Both served the entire war with their -unit until it surrendered in May 1865. Jeff Mabry took great delight as being known as the "Head Chicken Thief of the 3rd Texas Cavalry".

After the end of the war in 1865 Col H. P. Mabry returned to Jefferson, Texas to resume his legal practice and at that time Jeff Mabry elected to remain in Hopkins County among his many former comrades.

Uncle Jeff was well cared for by former Confederate soldiers and was provided with a place to live, food to eat and medical attention when needed. He attended the monthly meetings of the Mat Ascroft Camp #170, U.C.V. in Sulphur Springs and was able to make all of the Confederate reunions up until a year before he died.

He died while the Confederate convention was being held in Charlotte in 1929. The Confederate veterans that were able attended his funeral and Camp #170 sent a large floral arrangement adorned with red and gray ribbons.

Uncle Jeff Mabry and his wife Sarah and are both buried in unmarked graves at the Mel Haven cemetery in Sulphur Springs, Texas. They did not have any children or other relatives living in the area.

Uncle Jeff was proud of his service to the South and proudly wore his many convention medals when attending camp meetings.

Identification of a Missouri Black Confederate

A 1993 publication entitled *Branded as Rebels* by Joanne Chiles Eakin and Donald R. Hale provides a listing of Missouri men who served in Confederate units. A number of soldiers with the surname Noland are shown and one veteran, Frank Noland, is black. Most likely, this soldier was a manservant who took his master's surname and -- like the "white" Nolands listed -- may have served under the Confederate guerilla leader, Quantrill.

Black Soldier of the Confederacy -- Peter Vertrees

Rev. Peter Vertrees is the subject of several articles by Kenneth C. Thomson of Bowling Green, Kentucky. Mr. Thomson writes, "Years have passed since his death but the enduring legacy of Peter Vertrees, a Baptist minister and Confederate soldier [of the Seventh Kentucky Cavalry] lives in the lives of those he touched. He organized numerous churches in middle Tennessee, and with the help of the Rosenwald Foundation, many schools were built. His example as a humanitarian was his greatest contribution."

This prominent gentleman served with the famed "Orphan Brigade, " and dedicated an autobiography to his wife Diora. He mentions his experiences as a servant and bodyguard in the many campaigns of the Army of Tennessee and his ministry of over sixty years to the people of his adopted state of Tennessee. Scott E. Sallee's article entitled "Black Soldier of the Confederacy: The Life and Legacy of Peter Vertrees, a Kentucky Orphan" appeared in the June 1990 (Vol. VIII, No. 5) issue of the *Blue & Gray Magazine*. The following excerpt is courtesy of Mr. Sallee.

In summing up his four years of service in the Confederate army, Peter wrote:

Those days of conflict made a very great change in me at first but proved helpful to me in the end. . . The many, many things which I learned in the service helped me in after years to know how to deport myself and bring credit to myself and those with whom 1 am cast ....[They] gave me a vision of the future which I could not have gotten otherwise. My heart was touched with divine love and my life was inspired for nobler things. Those days of bitter conflict made lasting impressions on my mind. Never can I forget Shiloh and Vicksburg.

Though he was never on the firing line, Peter Vertrees suffered the same deprivations that all soldiers felt. He recalled that, "Sometimes I was hungry, sometimes cold, sometimes drenched with rain, sometimes tired and footsore from walking; but I stayed at my post until the end."

For his service in the Confederate army, Peter Vertrees was awarded a pension by the state of Tennessee in 1921, which he drew until his death on January 18, 1926. He was buried at Gallatin, and in 1986 a bronze military marker was placed on his grave site through the efforts of Stephen Lynn King of Bowling Green, Kentucky, who is a member of the Joseph E. Johnston Chapter of the Sons of Confederate Veterans in Nashville. The marker reads, "PETER VERTREES/6 KY INF/CSA/ DEC 16 1840-JAN 18, 1926." He was indeed an honored member of the famed Kentucky Orphans.

Note: Reverend Vertrees was the father of eight children; a son, Peter, was killed in action in the South Pacific during World War II; and three daughters currently live in Nashville.

Two companies of blacks saw action in the trenches at Petersburg

Source: *The Virginia Home Guards* (*The Virginia Regimental Histories Series*) by Jefferey C. Weaver; published by H. E. Howard, Inc. of Lynchburg, Virginia, 1996.

Medical Battalions

Jackson Battalion
Scott's Battalion Local Defense Troops.

Jackson's Battalion, also known as Scott's Battalion Local Defense Troops, was organized on March 5, 1865, from detailed men, assistants, and convalescents at the Jackson Hospital in Richmond. Major Henry C. Scott was Acting Assistant Surgeon of the 3rd Division of that facility. Scott wrote on March 11, after his men were sent to the front, "my men acted with the utmost 'promptness and good will."

One of the three companies composing this battalion was made up of black men. Part of this company was transferred to Major Jackson Chambliss' Negro Battalion. Chambliss' 'two-company battalion was organized under an act of the Confederate Congress dated March 5, 1865, as part of a Negro brigade being raised by Majors James W. Pegram and Thomas P. Turner.

Members of Scott's Battalion were from various states in the Southern Confederacy. There is a limited amount of information available on these men. Most of the information comes from hospital slips where the men were readmitted to the Jackson Hospital in late March 1865. The three companies of this battalion were:

Company A, Captain T. R. Colvin's Company. Colvin was assisted by 1st Lieutenant D. Foley and 2nd Lieutenant M. Connell.
Company B, Captain William M. Orr's Company. Orr's subalterns were W.M. Baxley, F. A. Foster, and J. H. Smith.
Company C, Captain A. Lockett's Company. Lieutenants in this unit were C. C. Hayslett, A. P. Drake, and C. A. Crow.

Two additional companies were composed of blacks employed at Jackson Hospital. On March 11, 1865 these two companies of blacks and the three companies of whites saw action in the Petersburg trenches. Major Scott reported:

I ordered my battalion... to the front on Saturday night at 12 o'clock and reported by order of Maj. Pegrarn to Col. Ship ...I have great pleasure in stating that my men acted with the utmost promptness and good will. I had the pleasure of turning over to Major Chambliss a portion of my negro company to be attached to his negro command. Allow me to state Sir that they behaved in an extraordinary acceptable manner.

The next mention of this organization was that the African-American company paraded in capital square on March 22, 1865. The demonstration they gave of the manual of arms surprised many white onlookers standing around for the display.

Roster

ANDREWS, T. G.: 4th Sgt. In Jackson Hosp., Richmond on 3/17/65.

BAXLEY, W. M.: 1st Lt., Co. B. Previously served in Co. A, 1st SC Inf.

COLVIN. T. R.: Capt., Co. A. Previously served in Co. K, 2nd LA Inf.   CROW, C. A.: 3rd Lt., Co. C, In-Jackson Hosp., Richmond on 3/17/65.

DRAKE, A. P.: 2nd Lt., Co. C.

EDGE, G. H.: Previously served in Co. H, 2nd SC Inf. In Jackson Hosp., R i c h - mond on 3/17/65.

FOLEY, D.: 1st Lt., Co. A. Previously served in Co. A, 2nd Battn. GA Inf.

FOSTER, F. A.: 2nd Lt., Co. B. Conscript.

FOSTER, 2. T.: In Jackson Hosp., Richmond on 3/17/65.

HAYSLET, C. C.: 1 st Lt., Co. C. In Jackson Hosp., Richmond on 3/17/65.

LOCKETT. A.: Capt., Co. C, In Jackson Hosp., Richmond on 3/17/65.

NEELY, D. F.: 3rd Sgt. In Jackson Hosp., Richmond on 3/17/65.

ORR, WILLIAM M.: Capt., Co. B. Previously served in Co. I, 16th GA Inf.

REEVES, 3rd Sgt. In Jackson Hosp., Richmond on 3/17/65.

SCOTT, HENRY C.: Major, F&S. Also assigned as Acting Assistant Surgeon at Jackson Hosp., Division 85, Richmond.

SMITH, I.: 3rd Lt., Co. 7. In Jackson Hosp., Richmond on 3/17/65.

SMITH, J. H.: 2nd Lt., Co. B. Previously served in Co. K, 48th GA Inf.

TAYLOR, WASHINGTON: Adjutant, Scott's Battn. VA LDT. B. 2/22/1828 D. 2/6/ 1904. Buried in the Elmwood Cem., Norfolk, VA

VANOY, A. M.: 3rd Corp. In Jackson Hosp., Richmond on 3/17/65.

Some Accounts of Black Musicians in
Confederate Units

Richard A. Kelly of Phoenix-City, Alabama writes:
I am currently involved in a project researching the history of the Columbus Guards. Dr. LeBron Matthews of Columbus and I hope to one day be able to publish a book on the history of this proud company. Two of the curiosities that we have discovered that you might be interested in are:

The March, 1919 issue of *The Georgia Historical Quarterly* (Vol. III, Number 1) has the following description of rite musicians during a parade of the Columbus Guards just prior to the war. "At the two bass drums were Peter De Votie and Lymus Jones, and at the fifes were Tom Rhodes and Tom Hicks and the Kettle drums were handled by Peter Harris and Henry Harris. All these were colored except the last named. In addition, the Columbus Guards Roster dated March 1, 1861 list three musicians: R.M. Harris, Thomas Rhodes and Jesse Howell. The roster had the designation of "colored" by the names of Mr. Rhodes and Mr. Howell.

Robert M. Howard was a private in the Columbus Guards before transferring to Nelson's Independent Company of Georgia Calvary in June of 1862. Then is a notation in the *Gray Book of Georgia-Confederate Regiments* that Howard "Applied for authority to raise a company of colored troops, April 1, 1865."

In a recent interview with the *Columbus Ledger-Enquirer,* (the local newspaper) Dr. Matthews and I mentioned the black musicians that were part of the Columbus Guards. Of course, the reporter was fascinated by the subject and immediately challenged us to write an article for inclusion in the newspaper during Black History month. A casual investigation has demonstrated how little literature there is concerning the subject of black Confederates.

A Family Account

From Richard Alan Young of Harrison, Arkansas:

My great-grandfather was Benjamin Franklin Young of Giles County, Tennessee, who served in one or more Tennessee infantries. We are unable to piece together his complete war record, but when he participated in the founding of the Hillsboro, Texas, chapter of the United Confederate Veterans, he listed his service as in Brown's Brigade, Breckenridge's Division.

When he came to live with my grandfather, John Morgan Young (named for John Hunt Morgan), in about 1910, he told several stories to my father, Morgan Martin Young, who was born in 1902.

In one story he told of "stealing horses from the Federals for the Confederacy,"which leads us to believe he saw service in Nixon's Cavalry, and a B. F. Young is listed as having served thus (but specific records of Nixon's Cavalry have been lost). The problem is compounded by the fact that there was more than one B. F. Young living in Tennessee at the time, including one who served in the Federal army.

The story he told that stands out most in my memory, as told to me by my late father, was this one simple statement:

Benjamin Franklin Young of the 32nd Tennessee Infantry only fought in one battle (probably Lookout Mountain), and he told his grandson in about 1910, that as he fought, a young black man of the same age fought beside him for the Confederacy. The Youngs never owned slaves, being sharecroppers themselves, and no mention was made of the young black man, the same age as B. F. Young - about 20 at the time - being the body servant of anyone else in the brigade. This leads me to believe that the young black man was a volunteer who had gone along, as many did, within the camaraderie of the other young men going off to defend their country. Most of them didn't really know why the war was being fought; they only understood that land their families had lived on for decades was being invaded by soldiers, and they sprang to the defense of their homeland.

African-American Confederate in York County

by Sam Thomas - Historical Center of York County

(This article was originally printed in The Quarterly of the York County Genealogical and Historical Society)

On August 6 and 7, 1891 one of the largest gatherings in York County, South Carolina's history took place in the town of Yorkville. Not for another 100 years would so many people meet in one spot in the county for one purpose. The occasion was the annual Survivor's Reunion of Confederate Veterans organized by William H. McCorkle, the former Captain of the Palmer Guards, Company A, 12th South Carolina Volunteers and, at the time of the reunion, Probate Judge of York County. On these two days nearly 600 veterans and over 5,000 friends and family members were on hand for the festivities.

Included in the activities of the second day was a parade of the veterans south, down Congress Street to the York County Courthouse, and continuing on Congress onto Jefferson Street to their camping grounds at the Yorkville Graded School. Thousands of people lined Jefferson and Congress Streets as the procession passed with Confederate flags and the "stars and stripes" waving side-by-side to the sounds of "Dixie." One thing which might have seemed out of place to a spectator of today about the procession, but was not unusual at that time, was that not all of the veterans in their faded gray uniforms were white. Among the 600 veterans on that historic day in York were Afro-Americans.

Information and sources on black Confederates is scant at best. No mentions are made in the history books of slaves or freed blacks following or even "supporting" their masters and former masters. Many of the sources in which we find these accounts today are publications written around the turn of the century. Furthermore, these were publications written primarily for and by Confederate veterans. As such, they are often discredited as to their content by many historians. At the same time, arguments are put forth that there was no voluntary service by blacks in the cause of the South, that the slaves in the Confederate armies were forced to serve, and who, when given the slightest chance, ran away to Union lines. There is no doubt that this was the case in many instances, but there were some Afro-Americans who not only resisted the temptation to run away, but actually voluntarily stayed and served the Confederate Cause either out of a sense of loyalty or patriotism or both.

Following the War Between the States, the Federal government began issuing pensions to all veterans of the Union armies. All those who had served in the Confederate armies had their pension applications turned down. In order to assist the Confederate veterans, the southern states, which were already experiencing tremendous financial difficulties, awarded state pensions to these veterans. In 1902 two organizations, the United Confederate Veterans and the Sons of Confederate Veterans recommended to the southern states that they also accept applications for pensions from blacks who served with Confederate forces. In South Carolina, the Act of 1923 did just that. Blacks in Confederate service for periods of not less than six months were awarded state pensions beginning in that year. The York County Confederate pension rolls for 1923 list the names of 15 blacks receiving pensions from the state, and the names of those whites whom they served under.

NAME	SERVED UNDER
Samuel W. Agurs	Capt. Culp
George Bird	J. C. Chambers
Harvey Barron	Commander, Fort Sumter
Adam Guy	Capt. Roberson
Sam Leech	Commander, Fort Sumter
Alvin Bratton Smith	D. J. Smith
Henry White	J. W. White
Heyward Marshall	Dr. J. Rufus Bratton
Anthony Barnett	Commander, Sullivan's Island
Noah Banks	William Avery
Anderson Chambers	Commander, Fort Sumter
James Harris	William Crosby
George Melton	Samuel Melton
Peter Crawford	William Crawford
Jeff Mackey	Dr. J. F. Mackey

On August 12, 1891 the Yorkville Enquirer gave front page coverage of the Survivor's Reunion and included a listing of veterans in attendance by company and regiment. Within this roster of attendees are the names of 5 "persons of color" listed with their companies and regiments.

Name	Company, Regt.
J. Han. Beatty	Co. B, 18th SCV
George Bird	Co. A, 12th SCV
Thad Archer	Reserves
Erwin Watson	Co. B, 5th SCV
Dan Witherspoon	Co. A, 12th SCV

Having the names, we are left with two questions. Did any of these men volunteer for service? Did any of them remain with the companies they served for the duration of the war?

Information found on two of the men: George Bird and James Harris (This is not the same James Harris whose name is listed on the Catawba Indian monument at Confederate Park in Fort Mill) might tend to shed some light. George Bird, from Sandersville, is listed in the 1860 free (meaning that he was a free person and not a slave) census.

Although this does not prove that he was not coerced into service to the Confederacy, it seems unlikely that if he had been coerced he would be taking part in the Reunion parade in 1891. Bird enlisted as cook in the Palmer Guards, Co. A, 12th regiment in 1861 and served the regiment until the end of the war in 1865.

In 1861 William Crosby, the son of Dennis Crosby of the Bullock Creek area, Joined Co. E, 5th South Carolina Volunteers and soon went to Virginia. At the battle of 2nd Manassas, William was wounded so severely that he could not return home. Dennis then sent one of his slaves, James Harris, to care for the boy. Sometime within the next two months the young man died of his wounds. James Harris, however, did not return home or run away to the Union lines. Instead, he served William's company as cook until the surrender at Appomattox in 1865.

Although there was no organized movement to actually put armed southern blacks into the army until the last days of the war, Afro-Americans played an important part in the defense of their homes and the Confederacy. York County is proud of all of its "Sons of the Confederacy."

A Virginia Boy In The Sixties

By Henry Clinton Sydnor, from the *Confederate Veteran*, Vol. XX, 1912.

Mechanicsville, Hanover County, Va., where the Seven Day's battle commenced was a little village of two or three stores and two blacksmith and two carpenter shops, and was five miles north of Richmond and one-half mile north of the Chicckahominy River. About one-third of this village was owned by my father. He lived a mile or so east of here, at which place sixteen of us were born.

In Mechanicsville I saw the raising of the first Confederate flag, and I well remember the excitement it created among the boys of the community. My brothers were largely instrumental in raising the flag and talking war, war to everybody. About this time everything was excitement over the war, and the boys used to assemble and see the Confederate soldiers drill as they were mustered in every day.

About this time our family physician, who had gone with the army, came to my father's house to dinner, and many of the neighbors assembled to hear the news. He said the Federals were rapidly approaching Richmond, and he had better send the girls to another part of the state, as he was confident there was going to be heavy fighting around home. So all were sent away except father, mother, one sister, and myself. I was then eleven years old. I well remember the parting of my sisters and our old slaves when they separated.

About this time I would assemble the many negro children at night, and as their captain I would drill them and have sham battles with stick guns, and we had a big time. All manner of rumors would come to us of the advance of McClellan's army, and at last the last Confederate soldier left us. Then my mother called me and placed around my waist a cloth belt, and in it was placed what money my father had at home. This consisted of gold, which we had ceased to use, keeping it sacredly for future needs. Confederate money only was used as exchange among the people, and those who had gold kept it hidden.

After our soldiers left, Uncle Tom came running in and said: "Marse William, dey is com for sure. My God, Marster, de woods is full of dem Yankees! Well, Marster, I wants to tell you right now: all de young niggers am going to leab you, but you is been a good marster to me, an' you can count on dis nigger stayin' with you till dis war am over." And how proud we all felt of Uncle Tom! He was one of the most aristocratic of negroes. He seldom worked in the field, just attended to the carriage team and occasionally went to market. He had a consequential air, dressed well, and bossed it over the other darkies, who looked up to him with reverence and respect. I never knew him to open a gate or shut one when a negro boy was in sight. The negroes always rated their standing from the amount of slaves and money their masters possessed. He always occupied the front seat in the gallery at the church; and when the carriage arrived at church, all the small boys stood around and watched him as he drove up. He would open the carriage door, let down the steps, and help my mother and the children out, and with a wave of the hand fold up the steps, close the door, turn his team over to the footman and go in to church.

Another of our negroes was Uncle Americus. No one knew his age, but he was supposed to be about a hundred years old. Never in my recollection had he performed any work of any kind. He would tell us children about the Revolutionary War, and they were most remarkable stories. I looked up to him in awe and admiration. When the Yankees came, he was in his glory. They would gather around him in crowds. I can see his bald head now shining in the sun, and the way he imposed on their credulity was a "caution." He was a past master in this respect. He would always ask for alms when his story was ended.

Soon after Uncle Tom told us about the coming of troops a few men rode up to the house and asked the negroes many questions, and then asked me: "Are there any Rebels around here?" I told them we were not Rebels, but Confederates. I thought at first they would kill us all, but in a few minutes their conversation with my father convinced me we were in no danger of being shot just for fun, and by the next day I had fully regained my composure and felt free to go among them and talk with them. The officers told my father they would respect his family and not willfully destroy his property, but he must stay closely upon his premises.

The next day soldiers were everywhere, putting up tents and telegraph wires, which were tacked to the trees. The wagons, each drawn by four fine mules, seemed to be in the thousands. A fine grove near the house was used as an encampment. Our large barn was also used. This barn was the headquarters for the men who did picket duty on the Chickahominy River, which at this point was occupied by McClellan on the north and Lee on the south. This was a sluggish stream about twenty-five feet wide, but there were broad, swampy bottoms on each side extending to high hills. On the south side hills was posted a battery of artillery in plain view of our home. Every evening about four o'clock a fresh regiment would relieve the one at the barn, and the other one would return to camp. I often wondered why the Confederates did not send shells into that barn, until one day an officer said they knew the Confederates knew who lived there, and they would not shell the barn or house on that account. I was allowed perfect freedom, so I mingled freely with the officers and men. Father was restricted to the immediate surroundings. No light was allowed at night.

Upon arrival of the troops all work ceased with the negroes. The cows were allowed the run of the pasture, but the boys milked as usual, and we sold the milk to the soldiers, who had plenty of everything to eat, and they would frequently give me some sugar and real coffee. Coffee in Richmond had become scarce, and we were using parched wheat instead, with sorghum molasses for sugar. Every day a lot of officers would assemble on the porch and discuss the war with father, and they always treated him with the respect his age demanded. A Major Boyd took a great fancy to us all. I have often wished that I might know whether he survived the awful days that followed.

My father was taken sick soon after they came, and Major Boyd sent a doctor to see him. When the doctor came, none of us liked him. He was so stuck up with the position he held. He said something about the "Rebels," and when he left father would not take the medicine. Boylike I mentioned this to Major Boyd, so he came the next day with another doctor. As soon as this one spoke a few words my boyish heart went right out to him, and I said: "Father, this doctor won't call us Rebels, and you will take his medicine." And he did.

There was a little pasture in front of the house with a fine stand of clover. This pasture was grazed every night by the artillery horses. One evening they put their horses in there before dark, the pasture being in plain view of the Confederate battery. I can see a big fat Dutchman now come prancing in among the trees riding one horse and having another with a halter. There were about twenty-five horses in there. Men held them to graze. When the Dutchman came riding in and before he got off his horse, I happened to look toward the Confederate line and saw four small puffs of smoke. I told father to look out, as shells were coming. They fell right among the horses and men, and such running we never saw. The Dutchman's horse, frightened, ran off with him striking a tree, and he went over the horse's head some forty feet. I never saw men laugh as those officers on the porch did when that fellow hit the ground. After that they always grazed at night.

Every day the Confederate battery on the south side of the Chickahominy would shell the woods and all around, but never any fell in our yard. A McClellan battery would reply, and when the duel would commence many officers would come into our yard for protection, as they said they knew the shells would not fall there.

The water in our yard was used by hundreds of the troops. The spring being much higher than the house, the water came up through a big pipe and then ran off to the barn. The stream was surrounded by soldiers with their canteens.

In the rear of the barn there was a small wheat field, and it was ready to cut. The negroes said that if they went to work the Confederates would throw shells at them; but Uncle Tom told them that the Confederates knew whose wheat field it was, and they went to work under his lead. A few mornings afterwards Uncle Tom and Uncle Moses came to me and said: "Don't give us away, but we can tell you where the stolen geese are. Some soldiers are behind the wheat shock picking them." The night before we lost all our geese but two or three. Now these geese were my pets; the old gander I have named Major, and I used to take them on the high hills and make them fly back home. So I went crying to the captain who had charge of the men at the barn and told him his men had stolen my geese and killed old Major. "Well," he said, "come with me, you little Rebel. We are not here to make war on geese, but to take Richmond. They shall pay you for them." So we went into the wheat field and when I saw old Major I fell down on him and cried. The captain took me up and called the men to him and made them pay me fifty cents apiece for every goose except old Major, and I took him to the house and Uncles Tom and Moses buried him for me. Now of the few geese that escaped was one given to us in 1840 by Mr. Thomas White, a relative, who moved to Missouri. He said he did not know the age of this goose, but had owned her for a number of years. She finally went through the war, escaping all the raids that Sheridan, Kilpatrick, and others made through our section. She was brought to Missouri in 1870, and was killed accidentally in 1890. She reared her young every year. She was in our own family for fifty years, and when killed was apparently young.

Before father was taken sick he had asked some privilege from the commanding officer. He told him he was originally a Union man, but Mr. Lincoln's call for troops to subdue the South had changed him, and six of his sons were in the Confederate army. The officer told him if he would take the oath he could have his request. He wanted to know what kind of oath. The next day he submitted to him the following oath for his consideration and insisted upon his subscribing to it:

"I,_____, of Hanover County, State of Virginia, do hereby solemnly swear that I will bear allegiance to the United States and support and sustain the Constitution and laws thereof; that I will maintain the national sovereignty paramount to that of all state, county, or Confederate powers; and I will discourage, discountenance, and forever oppose secession, rebellion, and disintegration of the Federal Union; that I disclaim and denounce all faith and fellowship with the so-called Confederate armies and pledge my honor, my property, and my life to the sacred performance of this, my solemn oath of allegiance to the government of the United States of America."

After reading it, my father handed it back to him and said with a voice full of fire and emotion and trembling finger pointing toward the Confederate line, his whole frame quivering: "I have six sons on yonder hill! If I sign this, it will deny me right to welcome them home; if I sign this, it will deny me right to feed them; if I sign this, it will deny me right to show to them my love and affection when whit God's will I meet them again. Never, never! How can you ask it?"

From a hill near the house the church steeples in Richmond could be plainly seen, and every Sunday morning when the church bells were ringing the sound could be plainly heard. Near this hill was our overseer's house. The overseer had gone to the army, and his family were at this house, and the officers would taunt the old lady about soon being in Richmond, saying they would capture her husband and send him home to her. One Sunday morning they came down from the hill after listening to the church bells and told her that next Sunday they would themselves ring those bells. "Well," she said, "you have been up on the his viewing the promised land, have you?" "Oh yes." "Well, don't you know the prophet Moses climbed the mount and viewed the promised land, but he never got there?" This remark amused them very much, and was the talk of the camp as long as they stayed there.

Every still afternoon they would send up balloons - "Monster things." One evening the men in the balloon reported that Lee was preparing to vacate Richmond, that they could see a big stir among the troops. They soon found out differently, as Gen. J.E.B.Stuart was starting out on his famous raid around General McClellan's army. Next morning everything was in confusion, troops galloping everywhere, and for two days they thought Lee would attack them.

On June 25, 1862, there appeared every evidence of an impending battle. Every man was in camp, orderlies were riding everywhere, and the troops were moving. The next day, June 26, we heard the first shot of the real battle. That afternoon was fought the battle of Mechanicsville and Ellerson Mill. This mill being about a mile from our house, and our house being not in line of the battle, we escaped, but shells flew all around. Father being sick, Uncle Tom and Uncle Moses carried him down into the basement and laid him on a bed where we thought it would be safer. The whole family were in this room. An old-fashioned table with drop sides stood in one corner, and every time a shell would burst close to the house a moan would come from under this table. Father called to know who it was. Under this table lay poor Uncle Tom, who cried out; "Marse William, pray for me, pray for me." The battle ceased about dark.

The porch was full of officers that night until about ten o'clock, when suddenly all left, and everything was as quiet as death the rest of the night. The next morning, June 27, we looked out and could not see a soul anywhere; so I ventured out and went up to the top story of the barn and looked over toward the Confederate lines. And as I did so I saw a man on a horse about one-half mile away. As soon as he saw me he motioned to me with his hat to come to him. I knew he was a Confederate soldier, and that was enough; so I hurried down and ran as a boy never did before toward him, and he came to meet me. It was my brother. I nearly fainted, so glad was I to see him. He took me up on his horse and carried me to General Longstreet, who asked me many questions about McClellan's army. I told him all I knew, and then in a few moments the whole of Lee's army was in motion on their way to Cold Harbor, about two miles east, where McClellan's army made another stand and where an awful and bloody battle occurred. This is the fight where the New York Zouaves of the Federal army and the New Orleans Tigers of Lee's army met, and but few lived through it.

Longstreet's Division passed right through our yard going to this battle. Lee and McClellan fought for several days.

We boys gathered bullets from the battle field and moulded them into shot to hunt with. Uncle Tom and Uncle Moses remained with us, sharing our joys and our sorrows.

The day after the battle of Cold Harbor a wounded soldier came to get a drink of water while on his way to the hospital in Richmond. He asked my father to let him rest. His wound soon began to bleed afresh, and my father dressed it over for him, and he seemed very grateful. He was an educated gentleman, so he was invited to remain with us until he got well. Being from New Orleans, he could not get home. Later, he joined my brother's command, and fought gallantly until the day before the surrender of Lee, when he gave my brother his few trinkets, asking that they be sent to his mother in new Orleans, as he would be killed that day. Before the sun set on that day this gallant Frenchman had crossed the river to meet Stonewall Jackson and his many comrades. After the war was over, his brothers came and got his body and took it to his dear old mother. She sent my mother a handsome gold watch as a slight token of her appreciation of the many favors we had conferred upon her boy.

A 1944 Alabama Photo

Source: *The Alabama Historical Quarterly*, Vol. 6, 1944

   General reunion of Confederat Veterans held in Montgomery, Ala., September 27-28, 1944. Picture taken on the portico of the Capitol near the star marking the spot where Jefferson Davis took the oath of office as President of the Confederate Government. Left to right, standing: Gen. William Banks, Houston, Tex; Gen. W. W. Alexander, Rockhill, S.C.; Gen. J. D. Ford, Marshall, Tex.; Gen. T. H. Dowling, Atlanta; Gen. J. W. Moore, Selma; col. W. H. Culpepper, Atlanta; Gen. W. M. Buck, Muskogee, Okla., and seated, the lone Negro veteran attending the Reunion, Dr. R. A. Gwynne, Birmingham, age 90 who served with his master.

Chapter VI

Newspaper Articles, 1861-1941

One of the most compelling things I have ever read regarding the Battle of Gettysburg was this one sentence found in the July 24, 1863, edition of the New York Herald. *Under the title "Incidents of the Battle" it says:*

Washington, July 10, 1863

Among the rebel prisoners who were marched through Gettysburg there were observed seven negroes in uniform and fully accoutred as soldiers.

Gregory A. Coco
On the Bloodstained Field II

Reports of Black Confederates are found in northern newspapers, including *The New York Times* and *Harper's Weekly*. On page one of the January 10, 1863, edition of *Harper's Weekly* (Vol. VII, No. 315), is an illustration of an armed black soldier in Confederate uniform. The caption reads: "Rebel Negro Pickets Seen through a Field-Glass;"

Rebel Negro Pickets

So much has been said about the wickedness of using the negro on our side in the present war that we have thought it worth while to reproduce on this page a sketch sent us from Fredericksburg by our artist, Mr. Theodore R. Davis, which is a faithful representation of what was seen by one of our officers through his field-glass, while on outpost duty at that place. As the picture shows, it represents two full-blooded negroes, fully armed, and serving as pickets in the rebel army. It has long been known to military men that the insurgents affect no scruples about the employment of their slaves in any capacity in which they may be found useful. Yet there are people here at the North who affect to be horrified at the enrollment of negroes into regiments. Let us hope that the President will not be deterred by the squeamish scruples of the kind from garrisoning the Southern forts with fighting men of any color that can be obtained.

Early in the war, southern papers contained articles about Negroes who offered to volunteer for military service and about those who conducted benefits to raise funds for local units. Later, reports were published about servants who tended the wounded, built fortifications, and performed a variety of other duties to include firing upon Union troops. As the fortunes of the Confederacy declined, editors called for the recruitment and arming of slaves—but this was not without debate that appeared in letters to editors and in featured articles.

Newspaper printing flourished throughout the war and, today, surviving editions are a gold mine for historical researchers and genealogists. And in this chapter selected articles tell the story of African American patriotism and little-known support that took place on and off the battlefield.

"TO ASSIST IN DRIVING BACK THE HORDE..."

C. Pat Cates of Woodstock, Georgia found the following article while research-ing newspapers at the Georgia State Archives in Atlanta. This article is from the *Southern Banner* published in Athens, Georgia; the issue date is May 1, 1861. The article originally appeared in the *Montgomery Advertiser.*

Tender of the Services of a Company of Negroes

We are informed that Mr. G.C. Hale, of Autnuga County, yesterday tendered to Governor Moore the services of a company of negroes, to assist in driving back the horde of abolition sycophants who are now talking so flippantly of reducing to a conquered province the Confederate States of the South. He agrees to command them himself, and guarantees that they will do effective service. What will our Black Republican enemies think of such a movement as this? We have frequently heard the slaves who accompanied their masters to the "scene of action," assert that when fighting was to be done, they wanted to shoulder their muskets and do their share of it, and we have not a shadow of a doubt but what they would be found perfectly reliable. An idea seems to have prevailed at the North, that in the event of a war between the two sections, the slaves would become rebellious. Let

them no longer lay this flattering unetion to their souls. It will avail them nothing.
--- *Montgomery Advertiser*

AN ESCAPE BY A BLACK CONFEDERATE OF THE 44TH GEORGIA VOLUNTEER INFANTRY

Source: A letter written by "Burr" of the 44th Georgia Volunteer Infantry, regarding the heroics of John, a body servant of Captain Connally; published in the October 4, 1862 issue of the *Macon Telegraph* newspaper.

I must tell you a little incident complimentary to the colored servant of Capt. Connally, Co. E, 44th Georgia. Perhaps you recollect *John*; he came into the service with his master and has been faithful to all his duties up to this time. At the battle of Boonesboro', John happened to be with our wagons, when the Yankee cavalry made a dash upon them, and among others took John prisoner. One Yankee was left to guard John while the rest sought spoils elsewhere. No sooner had they left than John asked permission of his guard to get into the wagon for his haversack of provisions, which being granted, he quickly returned with a musket, and charging the guard, compelled him to an inglorious retreat. John being thus master of the field, deemed it proper to adopt Gen. McClellan's strategic policy, and change his base, which he did by a flank movement upon our wagon trains in front. He is present as I write, and prides himself some upon his successful charge and repulsion of this Yankee guard.

"...THAT THE REBELS ORGANIZED AND EMPLOYED 'NEGRO TROOPS' "

Source: An excerpt from an article entitled "Killing Prisoners of War" from the *New York Tribune* of July 10, 1863.

KILLING PRISONERS OF WAR.

The World, in its capacity of attorney for the Slaveholders' Rebellion, premises "a full and explicit answer" to our points relating to systematic violations of the laws of war, and proceeds forthwith to evade those points entirely. It says:

"We have always doubted, and still doubt, the policy of employing negro troops. If the white men of the Free States were not able to beat the white men of the seceded States, we, for one, were not anxious to parade the inferiority."

Indeed! How does this answer our position—sustained by the most incontestable proof—that the Rebels organized and employed "negro troops" a full year before our Government could be persuaded to do any thing of the sort? You know, as well as we do, that negroes have not only grown the food whereon the Rebel armies have subsisted, but that they have dug the ditches and raised the intrenchments which sheltered those armies and enabled them to resist and repel the attacks of the Union forces. You know, too, that they began to arm and drill negro troops even before Bull Run; you have the testimony of a Rebel officer that Major Winthrop was shot by a negro slave at Great Bethel, armed and posted by his master, who had exasperated him against us by the gross falsehood that we had come down to seize the Southern slaves and sell them into a severer bondage in Cuba. Why do you not meet the facts as they are, instead of inventing others to serve your turn?

The World proceeds:

"As to the arming of slaves and the rights of those slaves, when armed, to immunity the same as inhabitants of the loyal States, is not the argument clear upon principles laid down by our own courts? Are not the inhabitants of all the

PATRIOTISM OF A COLORED MAN

Source: *The Confederate Union* (Milledgeville, Georgia) of August 26, 1863.

PATRIOTISM OF A COLORED MAN - A day or two ago a letter was received at the Treasury Department from a negro man named Henry Jones, the property of Mr. E. Cannon, of Clarkesville, in this State, which is worthy of the highest commendation and justly entitled to be imitated by those who have been hoarding their treasures during the troubles which at present affect the country. Henry places at the disposal of the Secretary of the treasury $465 in gold, which he hopes will be of some service to the Government. In his letter he speaks of "our glorious cause," and declares that the slaves of the South have a deeper interest in the establishment of Southern independence than the white population. He thinks if the Yankees are successful the negroes are destined to the most cruel treatment at their hands.

[Dispatch]

SOME ACCOUNTS FROM GEORGIA NEWSPAPERS

The following articles are contributed by Greg White of Smyrna, Georgia and are from the following period newspapers:

The *Daily Sun*, Columbus, Ga. 11 Aug. 1862
The *Macon* (Ga.) *Daily Telegraph*, 21 May 1864
The *Macon* (Ga.) *Daily Telegraph*, 10 Aug. 1864

Stonewall Jackson has an old negro man who acts in the capacity of body servant. It has become a common remark in camps, it is said, that no one except this negro body servant knows any thing of the General's plans. Some one talking to the old negro asked him how he came to be so much in the confidence of his master:

"Lord, sir," said he, "massa never tells me nothing, but the way I knows is this - Massa says his prayers twice a day, morning and night - but if he gets out of bed two or three times in the night to pray, you see I just commences packing my haversack, for I knows there will be the devil to pay next day."

\- - - - - - - - - -

A CONFEDERATE NEGRO GENERAL - A correspondent of the Houston Telegraph says I saw in a Boston paper, not long ago, a statement that we have not only negro troops but negro officers in our armies. This prodigious tale probably originated as follows:

In the army of Tennessee, a Brig. General had a negro servant who was raised with him from childhood, and who wore all his castoff clothes. Coffee was very proud of an old uniform coat of his master's; and wore it on gala days. In time of battle, mounted on a spare horse of the General, and frantic with excitement, he would charge up and down the field, beyond the reach of the shells and bullets. On one of these occasions, the enemy was in full retreat and our forces advancing, when a Sergeant, with fifteen or twenty prisoners came up with the sable General as he was careening at headlong speed over the plain.

"General," said the Sergeant, "what shall I do with these prisoners?"

"Double quick the G___ d___ rascals to the rear, was the emphatic response.

Accordingly, the humorous Sergeant trotted his Yankees down the broken road for a mile and a half and they never could be convinced afterwards that Coffee was not in the military employ of Cousin Sally Ann.

- - - - - - - - - - -

☞ A negro slave who had run away from Alabama some time ago, recognized his "young master" in the fight of Saturday at Petersburg, and, throwing down his musket, rushed to the young man and threw his arms around his neck, at the same time exclaiming, "You shan't hurt my young massa." Just at this time a cuff, not so mercifully disposed, fired at the Alabamian, but the ball instead of hitting the object aimed at, took effect in the body of the repentant slave who threw his aegis of protection around his "young massa," inflicting a severe wound upon him. Master and slave came safely off the field together, and the wound of the latter was properly attended to, and thus did his last minute repentance save him from the fate which overtook so many of his race and color on Saturday, the 30th of July, 1864.

During Saturday and Sunday nights the enemy availed himself of the darkness, to remove many of the severely wounded near his line of entrenchments, but notwithstanding this stealthy movement, many still remained Monday morning, who had laid there since Saturday beneath a broiling July sun, and famishing for water and food.

PLEASANT RUMOR.—The Washington Chronicle of the 30th, states that a rumor is current at the Federal Capital, that on Wednesday last a Confederate ram sunk a Federal gunboat on the James river. Two Yankee monitors, it adds, had been sent up the river in search of the ram.—*Rich. News.*

A negro slave who had run away from Alabama some time ago, recognized his "young master" in the fight of Saturday at Petersburg, and, throwing down his musket rushed to the young man and threw his arms around his neck, at the same time exclaiming, "You haven't hurt my young massa" Just at this time a cuff, not so mercifully disposed, fired at the Alabamian, but the ball instead of hitting the object aimed at, took effect in the body of the repentant slave who threw his arms of protection around his "young massa," inflicting a severe wound upon him.

Master and slave came safely off the field together, and the wound of the latter was properly attended to, and thus did his last minute repentance save him from the fate which overtook so many of his race and color on Saturday, the 30th of July 1864.

During Saturday and Sunday nights the enemy availed himself of the darkness to remove many of the severely wounded near big line of entrenchments, but notwithstanding this stealthy movement, many still remained Monday morning, who had laid there since Saturday beneath a broiling July sun, and famishing for water and food.

EMPLOYMENT OF SLAVES IN THE ARMY

Source: *Savannah Daily Morning News* of September 2, 1863.

A joint committee of the Alabama Legislature reported a resolution in favor of the proposition to employ slaves in the military service of the Confederate States, which proposition, we perceive, is favored by many of the people of Mississippi and Alabama. After discussion in the Alabama House, the resolution was adopted by a vote of 68 yeas to 12 nays, after striking out the words "military" before service, and "soldiers" at the end of the resolution. The resolution was amended and reads as follows:

That it is the duty of Congress to provide by law for the employment in the service of the Confederate States of America, in such situations and in such numbers as may be found absolutely necessary, the able bodied slaves of the country, whether as pioneers, sappers, and miners, cooks, nurses and teamsters.

In this form we can see no objection to the resolution.

CONFEDERATE DEAD AT ELMIRA POW CAMP ARE BURIED BY BLACK SEXTON.

Black Southerners were often called upon for burial duty and in most instances, this was done with kindness and respect. This article is about John Jones, a sexton at the infamous Elmira, New York POW camp.

Source: The November 9, 1867 edition of the *Newnan Herald* (Georgia).

A colored man, named John Jones, a former slave, is sexton and grave digger there. All these men were buried by him. He took the trouble to obtain the name of each man, the number of his regiment, and letter of his company, which he had placed upon a small head board. Each grave is so marked. Since the close of the war parties in the South have written him in regard to relatives known to have died there, and in many cases bodies have been disinterred and shipped to friends for burial in family vaults and Southern cemeteries.

To families in Georgia and Florida we will state, that if they may wish the bodies of those dear to them, who have died in prison at Elmira removed to Southern cemeteries by writing to Mr. John Jones, of Woodlawn Cemetery at Elmira, they can make arrangements to have them disinterred and shipped South. We know of many instances in which this has been done, and there would probably be more, were the fact more generally known.

A BRAVE NEGRO

From the *Daily Sun* (Columbus, Georgia) of November 26, 1861. Contributor Greg White of Smyrna, Georgia.

In the recent battle at Belmont, Lieutenant Shelton, of the 18th Arkansas regiment, had his servant Jack in the fight. Both Jack and his master were wounded, but not till they had made most heroic efforts to drive back the insolent invaders. Finally, after Jack had fired at the enemy *twenty-seven* times, he fell seriously wounded in the arm. Jack's son was upon the field, and loaded the rifle for his father, who shot at the enemy *three times* after he was upon the ground. Jack's son hid behind a tree, and when the enemy retreated they took him to Cairo and refused to let him return. Jack was taken from the field in great pain, and brought to the Overton Hospital, where he bore his sufferings with great fortitude till death relieved him of this pains yesterday. His example may throw a flood of light upon the fancied philanthropy of Abolitionism. - *Memphis Avalanche.*

A COLORED CONFEDERATE

A COLORED CONFEDERATE. — A colored man named John Phillips, who says he was a body servant of Col. Phillips, Phillips' Legion, during the war, passed through our city Friday on route from Virginia. He was wounded in the head in one of the battles in Virginia, and the ball was but recently extracted, leaving the unfortunate man totally blind. — He goes to his relatives in Atlanta now to which place a pass was given him. He ought to be kindly cared for. — *Augusta Chronicle*.

Source: *The Thomaston Herald* (Georgia) of July 25, 1874

A colored man named John Phillips, who says he was a body servant of Col. Phillips, Phillips' Legion during the war, passed through our city Friday on route from Virginia. He was wounded in the head in one of the battles in Virginia, and the ball was but recently extracted, leaving the unfortunate man totally blind. He goes to his relatives in Atlanta now to which place a pass was given him. He ought to be kindly cared for.   *Augusta Chronicle*

HOW THE "COLORED TROOPS FOUGHT NOBLY" FOR THE CONFEDERACY AT CHICKAMAUGA

Southern newspapers often reprinted articles that had previously appeared in other newspapers. This bit of forgotten history is from the February 5, 1885 edition of the *Hawkinsville* (Georgia) *Dispatch*. Historical researcher Greg White found this on microfilm in the main library of the University of Georgia, Athens. A portion of the microfilm was unreadable, but the majority of the article has been transcribed.

Mr. J. B. Briggs of Briggsville, Ky. (Muhlenberg County), says the Louisville Times, is the only person who commanded colored troops in action on the Confederate side during the war.

Mr. Briggs was Captain and assistant Quartermaster of the Fourth Regiment Tennessee Volunteer Cavalry, C.S.A. and served during the war with Wheeler and Forrest. The fourth Tennessee thus secured a full share of these recruits and was always comparatively full.

At the battle of Chickamauga the Fourth Tennessee - Cavalry was dismounted to fight as infantry, every fourth man being told off to hold horses. These horse-holders, and also all of the colored servants, were kept in the rear. The colored men numbered about 40, and having been in service a long time, had gradually armed themselves. Some of them were even better equipped than their masters, for on successful raids and battles they could follow in the rear and pick up those things the soldiers had no time to secure; so that these colored servants could each boast of one or two revolvers and a fine carbine or repeating rifle.

During all of the early part of the battle of Chickamauga, the Fourth Tennessee Cavalry had been fighting as infantry, and as it became evident that a victory was to be won, Col. McLemore, commanding, ordered Captain Briggs to return to the horse-holders, and after placing the horses, teams, etc., under charge of the servants, to bring up the quarter of the regiment in charge of the horses so that they might take part in the final triumph. Capt. Briggs, on reaching the horses, was surprised to find the colored men organized and equipped, under Daniel McLemore, colored (servant to the Colonel of the regiment), and demanding the right to go into the fight. After trying to dissuade them from this, Capt. Briggs led them up to the line of battle, which was just then preparing to assault Gen. Thomas's position. Thinking they would be of service in caring for the wounded, Capt. Briggs held them close up in line, but when the advance was ordered the negro company became enthused as well as their masters, and filled a portion of the line of advance as well as any company of the regiment.

While they had no guidon or muster roll, the burial after the battle of four of their number and the care of seven wounded at the hospital, told the tale of how well they fought that day.

UNCLE LEWIS PLAYS DIXIE

The *Southwest Times Record* of Fort Smith, Arkansas features an article on "Uncle Lewis" McConnell in the May 13, 1928 edition. This veteran was a popular fiddler at reunions and performed "Dixie" for his compatriots. Contributed by Edwin Lee Chaney of Bald Knob, Arkansas.

OLD NEGRO SLAVE ATTENDS REUNION OF CONFEDERATES

"Uncle Lewis" McConnell is Among Older Residents Of Johnson County

Clarksville, Ark., May 12, -- Lewis McConnell, negro, who makes his home at College Hill, is one of the few negro slaves of Johnson county. "Uncle Lewis," as he is better known, lived on a big farm in Missouri at the beginning of the Civil War. He and a company of other slaves, fearing they would fall into the hands of Federal soldiers, fled to Texas. At Fayetteville, "Uncle Lewis" became ill and was left there.

Later he was turned over to Captain W. H. McConnell of the Confederate army and stayed with him for the remainder of the war. A large picture of the Confederate soldiers of Johnson county is hanging in the office of Colonel E. T. McConnell, and "Uncle Lewis" is in the group.

While he was not enlisted in the Confederate army, "Uncle Lewis" says he did his part.

At the close of the war "Uncle Lewis" had become so attached to the McConnell family that he never returned to his people in Missouri and has remained in Johnson county since.

"Uncle Lewis" attended the Confederate reunion at Little Rock, and spent much time in learning to play the third part of "Dixie" on his fiddle so that he would be able to play it at the reunion.

May 13, 1923.

VALLEY

Fiddle Is Favorite

OLD NEGRO SLAVE ATTENDS REUNION OF CONFEDERATES

"Uncle Lewis" McConnell Is Among Older Residents Of Johnson County

(Special News Service)

Clarksville, Ark., May 12.—Lewis McConnell, negro, who makes his home at College hill, is one of the few negro slaves of Johnson county. "Uncle Lewis," as he is better known, lived on a big farm in Missouri at the beginning of the civil war. He and a company of other slaves, fearing they would fall into the hands of Federal soldiers, fled to Texas. At Fayetteville, "Uncle Lewis" became ill and was left there.

Later he was turned over to Captain W. H. McConnell of the Confederate army, and stayed with him for the remainder of the war. A large picture of the Confederate soldiers of Johnson county is hanging in the office of Colonel E. T. McConnell, and "Uncle Lewis" is in the group.

While he was not enlisted in the Confederate army, "Uncle Lewis" says he did his part.

At the close of the war "Uncle Lewis" had become so attached to the McConnell family that he never returned to his people in Missouri and has remained in Johnson county since.

"Uncle Lewis" attended the Confederate reunion at Little Rock, and spent much time in learning to play the third part of "Dixie" on his fiddle, so that he would be able to play it at the reunion.

STUDENTS AT HENDRIX TO SELECT OFFICERS

(Special News Service)

Conway, Ark., May 12.—At the student election to be held Tuesday morning at Hendrix college, the selections for 1928-29 officers will be made from the following nomi...

LEWIS M'CONNELL

"Uncle Lewis" McConnell, negro slave of Johnson county, is shown above with his fiddle. Uncle Lewis learned the third part of "Dixie," that he could play it at the Confederate reunion, held at Little Rock last week.

SERVED IN BOTH UNION AND
CONFEDERATE ARMIES

Source: *Vidalia Advance* (Georgia), May 26, 1941

Vidalia Negro Served Both North and South -- Charlie Hicks, 104-year-old Toombs county negro is dead. He was unique in that he served in the Confederate army for a period as body servant to his young master, was later captured and served in the Union army as cook for which he was allowed a pension. He is believed to be the only person in Georgia accredited to both the U.C.V. and the G.A.R. organizations. For many years he attended reunions of both armies and lately, being too old for the reunions, he has observed both the Memorial Day and Decoration Day dates as holidays. His death came between the two dates when he had passed his 104th birthday, and his funeral was conducted at Jordan Stream Church, of which he was a member and near which he lived for so many years of his life.

He was a substantial landowner and operated his farm until after he was a hundred years old when sons gave him such assistance as he needed. For many years he gave a barbecue on the 4th of July to which his family and white friends were invited..

A PLAN FOR RECRUITING NEGROES INTO
CONFEDERATE ARMIES OFFERED BY A GEORGIA REGI-
MENT OF INFANTRY

Source: The January 23, 1892 of *The Sunny South*, Atlanta, Georgia.

The 49th Georgia regiment was the first (and it is believed the only) regiment which suggested to General Lee a plan for recruiting the negroes for the Confederate army, after the Confederate Congress had passed the bill for that purpose.

The following document, the original of which has been deposited with the Georgia Historical Society, of Savannah, and at the request of the compilers of the Records of the Rebellion, a certified copy has been furnished to the War Department at Washington for publication in said records:

Camp Forty-ninth Georgia Regiment, Near Petersburg, March 15, 1865

Colonel W. H. Taylor. A.A.G. - Sir: The undersigned, commissioned officers of this regiment, having maturely considered the following plan for recruiting the regiment, and having freely consulted with the enlisted men who almost unanimously agree to it, respectfully submit it, through you, to the commanding general for his consideration:

First - That our companies be permitted to fill up their ranks with negroes to the maximum number, under the recent laws of Congress.

Second - That the negroes in those counties of Georgia from which our companies came be conscripted in such numbers and under such regulations as the War Department may deem proper.

Third - that after the negroes have been so conscripted, an officer or enlisted man from each company be sent home to select from the negro conscripts such who may have owners or may belong to families of whom representatives are in the company, or who, from former acquaintance with the men, may be deemed suitable to be incorporated with these companies.

For the purpose of carrying out more effectually and promptly the plan, as indicated under the third head, it is respectfully suggested that each man in the regiment be required to furnish a list of relations, friends or acquaintances in his county, of whom it is likely that negroes may be conscripted, so as to facilitate the labors of the officer or man who may be detailed to bring the negroes to the regiment.

When in former years, for pecuniary purposes, we did not consider it disgraceful to labor with negores in the same filed, or at the same work bench, we certainly will not look upon it is any other light at this time, when an end so glorious as our independence is to be achieved. We sincerely believe that the adoption throughout our army of the plan here most respectfully submitted, or some similar one to it will insure a speedy availability of the negro element in our midst for military purposes, and create, or rather cement, a reciprocal attachment between the men now in service and the negroes, highly beneficial to the service, and which would probably not be otherwise obtained.

We have the honor to be very respectfully,
J. T. Jordan, Colonel
J. B. Duggan, Major
M. Newman, Adjutant
L. E. Veal, 1st Lieut. Co. A

L. L. Williams, Capt. Cos. B and G.
J. F. Duggan, Capt. Co. C.
L. M. Andrews, Capt. Co. D.
C. R. Walden, Lieut. Co. E.
A. G. Brooks, Lieut. Co. F.
S. J. Jordan, Lieut. Co. H.
Wm. F. Mullaly, Capt. Co. I.
R. S. Anderson, Capt. Co. K.

Headquarters, Thomas's Brigade, March 18, 1865. -- Respectfully forwarded, approved.

Edward L. Thomas, Brigadier-Gen.

Headquarters Wilcox Light Division, March 21, 1865. -- Respectfully forwarded, believing that the method proposed within is the best that can be adopted.

C. M. Wilcox, Major-General.

Headquarters, Third Corps A. N. Va., March 22, 1865. -- Respectfully forwarded. The plan proposed is commended as worthy of attention and consideration.

H. Heth, Maj-Gen. Commanding.

Respectfully returned. The commanding general commends the spirit displayed by this regiment. The plan of organization which has been regarded most favorably proposes a consolidation of the regiments of ten companies as they now exist into six companies, and that the regimental organization be maintained by attaching to the six thus formed four companies of colored troops. Each regiment will then preserve its identity.

Perhaps this plan would be equally as acceptable to the 49th Georgia regiment. By command of Gen. Lee

W. H. Taylor. A. A. G.

March 27, 1865.

The above document was drawn up by Adjutant Newman on March 15th, 1865, less than a month before Gen. Lee surrendered, and at a time when every available man, black or white, was greatly needed at the "front." Although General Lee indorsed it on the 27th of the same month, it was returned to Adjutant Newman too late to be made of any service. On April 2nd a week later, he was captured at Fort Gregg, near Petersburg, having this document and other important official papers in his possession. Of the 265 gallant Confederates who manned that ill starred fort on the morning of that day, but thirty-four survivors came out of the bloody contest for its defense. Adjutant Newman saved his official papers by hiding them in the lining of his hat, where they were safe from detection during his three months captivity on Johnson's Island, in Lake Erie, to which point the prisoners were taken.

THE COLORED GENTRY ...

The *Daily Intelligencer* (Atlanta, Georgia) of December 28, 1861 reports the activities of "the colored gentry" in raising funds for Confederate causes. (Contributed by C. Pat Cates of Woodstock, Georgia.)

We notice in many of our exchanges that the colored gentry of several of the cities of the Confederacy, have displayed much loyalty and patriotism in their donations to the confederate cause. Balls have been resorted to in a great many instances from the proceeds of which liberal donations have been made. WE are not advocate of this plan to raise the wind, by which our colored gentry display their liberality and loyalty. But as it appears to be tolerated and commended every where, we do not see any good reason why the "colored folks" of Atlanta may not be heralded as having been engaged in the good work, as well as those of other cities. Hence we notice that in our own goodly city, under the management of Col. Latham's (of Campbell county) servant, in the employ of the Bank of Fulton in this place, Austin Wright, three of these balls have been given - from two of which twenty dollars have been patriotically contributed for the relleif of the families of indigent soldiers, and from a third, fifteen dollars have been contributed to the families of those darkies who are also absent in the service. The balls, of course, were conducted with all due decorum, attended with that varlegated display, which is common on all similar occassions!!

FAITHFUL TO THE END: CLASSIC
STORIES RECOUNTED

Source: These articles were drawn from an Atlanta newspaper called *The Sunny South*. The story of Old Gabe is found in the August 21, 1897 edition and the story of Westley came from the February 6, 1996 edition.

Touching Story of Old Gabe, Who Saved His Wounded Master From Drowning, and Who Sleeps Beside Him in the Family Cemetery - Both Graves Kept Green in Memory.

By Russell A. Gardner

Of all the memories associated with my childhood there are none pleasanter than my memory of the faithfulness of old uncle Gabe, my father's body servant. I was but six years of age when he performed the noble deed which endeared him to our entire family and made his memory sacred, but it impressed itself upon my childish nature with so much force I remember it more distinctly than anything connected with my early childhood.

The incidents of this narrative carry me back to the month of February, 1862, when a heavy war-cloud hung with threatening over the country. Although I was so young, I can see looking back through the years, my father's thoughtful, even sad face, as he and mother talked of the prospects for the success of the cause, the justice of which he so warmly defended, and for which he was so soon to lay down his life.

My father's regiment was a part of the Confederate army stationed at Clarksville, Tenn., prior to the fall of Fort Donnelson.

Many times have I walked over the hill where the fort at Clarksville is situated, and tried to imagine the particular spot where my father's feet have rested. There is but one spot on earth dearer to me than this, and that is the place where my father is sleeping.

As I write memories crowd upon me so, that it seems but yesterday when some one whom I did not know came to our home and told my mother that Colonel Mills and all of them had been ordered to Fort Donnelson. I did not realize what this meant, but saw my mother crying like her heart would break, and I began to cry too. When she saw this she quickly dried her own tears, and came to me and took me in her arms. "Don't cry, Robbie," she said, "God will take care of us, and we will trust in Him." And then we knelt down together and she prayed, O, so fervently, that God would protect my father and bring him back to us, that I began to cry again.

In a few minutes my father arrived to tell us good-bye, and then it was that my poor mother's heart seemed too break. But, she calmed herself, and I shall never forget the fortitude she exhibited. Never once did she say aught to turn my father from what she knew to be his duty. She clung to him and wept bitterly, while he smoothed her hair and tried in vain to console her. Even after this lapse of time I can see, as I write, the picture they made. She clinging to him with streaming eyes; he tender and sad, but firm.

After a while he put my mother gently from him, and came to where I sat sobbing, without knowing why, and kissed me, called me his dear little boy, kissed me again, and then turned once more to my mother, clasped her in his strong arms, kissed her once, twice, and was gone.

All this time old uncle Gabe had stood by, having arrived with my father, and with one hard hand brushed the tears from his old black cheeks. Now he, too, humbly bade us goodby and walked away with my father.

The following day was one of deepest anxiety for my mother. All day long we could hear the roar of the cannon, and well do I remember with what terror I listened to the rattle of the window panes.

My mother spent hours on her knees that day, but toward evening she became resigned, and sat quietly by the fire and held me in her arms.

I believe she did not close her eyes that night, for I heard her whispered prayers continually up to the time I fell asleep. I was awakened next morning by the whistle of a boat, and ere long there was a ring at the front door. Mother had already been up and dressed for some hours, and she sprang to answer the call. I shall never forgot the look that came over her face when she saw at the door a man in whose countenance she seemed to read the sad news of which he was the bearer. I heard him speak to her. He told her that Colonel Mills had been wounded, badly wounded, and that he was being brought home; that she might expect him in a few minutes.

Strange to say she did not shed one tear at this sad intelligence, but now as I remember how she had prayed, I know the hand that sustained her.

In a few minutes four men were seen approaching bearing my father on a litter, and now it was that my mother gave way to the grief I knew she felt.

As the men who had borne him placed him on his bed she knelt beside him, and the bitterness of her grief moves me now as I think of it.

Uncle Gabe had returned with my father, and when he saw my mother's deep grief he seemed to want to comfort her, but his desire found expression only in these words: "Mistriss. I saved him. I brung him back."

The physician came and after examining my father's wound looked very grave, and when asked if there was any hope sadly shook his head.

He lived only a short time, dying just at sunset that day. Shortly before the end came he asked mother and me to come near him. Mother laid her head on the pillow beside his, and I climbed up on the other side. Putting an arm around each of us he murmered a blessing, and with this his life went out. It was not till several days after my father's burial that we heard of the brave act which old uncle Gabe had performed. He never spoke of it himself, and we learned it from some who were present and witnessed it. For some reason, I never knew why, the boat which brought off the wounded had pulled off from the shore when the party that conveyed my father from the battlefileld arrived. He was placed in a canoe and paddled out into the stream where the boat waited to take him on board. As he was being lifted from the canoe the frail craft tottered, and he dropped into the water among the blocks of floating ice. He was too badly wounded to make any effort to save or help himself, and sank immediately. But his faithful old body servant had never left him, and as soon as he saw what had happened he leaped into the water and fought his way amid the floating ice to where my father was sinking. He caught him with one strong arm, and with the other swam back to the boat, where he and my father were taken on board. Thus, it is to his faithfulness and bravery that mother and I are indebted for the fact that my father is sleeping in the churchyard, rather than beneath the waters of the Cumberland.

The slaves were freed and the war ended, but old uncle Gabe never left us. Night after night have I sat in his cabin and listened to the stories of ghosts and hobgoblins which he delighted to tell, the truth of which he in his simplicity never doubted, till I was afraid to put my head outside the door.

He lived for several years after my father's death and served us faithfully to the last, and when he died he was laid by his master's side. A marble tombstone was placed at the head of his grave upon which we inscribed the simple words, "He was faithful to the end." His portrait now hangs by that of my father in our parlor, and his memory is cherished by mother and I next to that of the master he served with so much faithfulness, truth, and love.

FAITHFUL UNTO DEATH.

Story of My Colored War Servant Westly and His Splended Devotion to Me.

Your interesting paper comes to my address, and I promised to contribute once and a while something for my favorite page. Volumes could be written, and no word can express the true devotion manifested during the war by southern army servants. Westly, I beleive, was an exception to the rule. Polite and exceedingly smart, the best cook and forager in the regiment, he soon had the confidence of high officials, and had permission to go anywhere he pleased through the lines, and on many occasions reported valuable information from the Feds. Sometimes he would be gone several days, and on one occasion brought back coffee in lieu of tobacco, but always kept his own council. His devotion to me was unbounded. Often I would instruct him when a fight was on hand to remain at the rear, but often I have found him on the skirmish line or in the thickest of the fight, loaded with canteens of water for members of the mess.

He said he promised old master to look after me. A few days after the Peachtree Creek fight, near Atlanta, I obtained a furlough for thirty days to visit my home near Okolona, Miss. In my hurry I failed to obtain transportation and had to march about 100 miles to Macon. On the way I was taken sick, and Westley carried me several miles on his back, becides what little baggage we had. When we reached Macon, I put up at the best hotel, as though I had money. Hotel fare was $10 a day -- and not a cent did either of us have. Westly said if I would rely on him we would soon be all right. The first day he reported no success, and suggested that I sell him to some negro traders and give him some of the money, and he would meet me at home in a short while. I was afraid to do so, as the negroes bought were then being shipped to Louisiana and to Texas. The next day he went to the post quartermaster and reported our situation. Fortunately the quartermaster was acquainted with my grandfather and lived near my home in Mississippi. I was immediately furnished all the money necessary to buy both of us new suits of clothes, pay hotel bills and pay our way home. After the war closed Westly was still the same obedient servant, remained on the old home farm and accepted such compensation as I would give him. Twenty years ago I left him and came to Texas. I hope he still lives and will join me in the sweet bye-and-bye.

T.M. Dariel.

GEORGE BLAINE'S GRAVE

Source: Front page and inside article of *The Fairfield Reporter* (Texas) of May 20, 1904

FAIRFIELD, FREESTONE COUNTY, TEXAS, MAY 20, 1904

We publish the following touching story as our people were interested in the principals.

Old "Uncle Nick" is still with us, and his greatest pride is the portion of his life he spent with his gay young master during the bloody days of the Civil War. The article was contributed to the *Confederate Veteran* by a writer from Spring Hill, Tenn.

On one of the loveliest days of last June a sweet little girl of ten summers knelt in a field of daisies, gathering the flowers she loved. Acres of daisies whitened the hill slope all about her, and she gathered handful after handful till her arms held a great sheaf. Looking up with a sudden thought she said: "I will gather more and put them on the soldier's grave."

A little later the rays of the setting sun touched a low mound in the village cemetery decorated with flowers gathered by the hands of a little child, born long years after "the soldier" had been laid there to rest.

It was the grave of George Blaine of the Seventh Texas Regiment, who was killed at the battle of Franklin. On the eve of the battle, far from his Texas home and the sister who prayed for him there and watched for the brother who would never return; he told his negro servant that he had a cousin, the wife of Dr. Aaron C. White, living at Spring Hill, twelve miles from Franklin. He wished to be taken to their home if killed or wounded in the battle. He fell never to rise again, and the heartbroken servant took him to Spring Hill.

The writer was one of the three small children of the home who saw him for the first time in the calm majesty of death. It made an indelible impression and the pathetic burial at the village cemetery the following day is still vividlly remembered. There were no military honors, no minister to conduct a religious service, and no crowd to follow him to his last resting place. Only three little children looked on in awed silence while their father helped the faithful servant lower the body into the grave and fill in the earth, but the frame of the latter shook with sobs and the tears rained down his face as he bent to the task which hid forever from his sight the loved form of his young master.

There was mouring in every house in the village that day; the churches were turned into temporary hospitals filled with wounded and dying soldiers, and all were too busy ministering to those yet living to do honor to the dead.

"Uncle Nick" was sent on his way with his master's horse and watch, a lock of hair, etc, and later the sister wrote from Texas that he had reached her safely with these last tokens. She spoke of having her brother's body removed as soon as days of peace came, but she too died, and he was left to slumber on here.

The years slipped swiftly and silently away and almost forty had been numbered with the past when the postmaster at Spring Hill received a letter inquiring for Dr. White or some member of the family. It was from "Uncle Nick" Blaine, the faithful servant of the young soldier, asking about the grave of his master. He wrote after receiving some pressed cedar too be laid on "master's grave."

The grave has never been marked by a stone, but a wild cherry sprang up near the spot and grew into a tree. Mockingbirds build their nests there and sing requiems above his sleeping dust.

COLORED CONFEDERATE

1904. In December there is an article quoted from the *Dallas News* telling how Nic (k) Blane, colored, was given a certificate as a delegate to the Nashville U.C.V. Reunion from the W. L. Moody Camp of Fairfield, and also a certificate from the County Judge of Freestone certifing that Nick was a good citizen, good Confederate and a good Democrat. At the Reunion headquarters Nick had been refused a badge, but Gen. K. M. Van Zandt, who had commanded the Seventh Texas, personally got a badge for Nick. Later the General sent Nick a Confederate gray uniform for Christmas. Other presents included $2.50 from Col. Moody, Galveston, and an overcoat from Capt. Collett, Austin.

ARTICLES FROM *THE SAVANNAH MORNING NEWS.*

November 15, 1906

Two Colored Veterans Conspicuous in Parade - Were Body servants to W.T. Harbaum During War.

A conspicuous figure in yesterday's parade was that of Mr. W. T. Harbaum of Macon, who had with him two old negro servants that followed him through the war as body servants. These old negroes, Allen Griffin and Emanuel Pinks, are as full of the sentiment of the Confederacy as any grizzled white veteran.

Both have taken keen delight in the reunion of old friends in Savannah, and listened with close attention to the proceedings in the convention hall. Their reminiscenses, delivered in that antibellum patois so seldom heard these days, are worth the time and attention of any listener. The hair of both is almost as white as the cotton which has been the product of their toll since the days when "Dixie" put but little of the staple upon the market through the destroying touch of the iron heel of war.

Mr. Harbaum has carried these two old servants to several state reunions and they are well known to many of the veterans, who honor them almost as much as they do their white comrades.

January 21, 1912

"UNCLE RICHMOND" TELLS 'WHY THE YANKEES WON'"

"Too Many fer Us," Is Old Negro's Sage Opinion

Thomasville, Ga., Jan 20. - A familiar sight on the occasion of Gen. Lee's birthday every year is old "Uncle Richmond Mitchell, a colored veteran of the war, though not on the firiing line.

Uncle Richmond was on hand as usual this year and ready to talk to any one who would listen of the time when "Me and Marse Bob was in de war."

In 1861, when Judge Robert G. Mitchell, then Capt. Mitchell, and his brother, the late Col. W. D. Mitchell, went to fight for the Confederacy they carried Richmond along as a body servant and he stayed with them until Lee's surrender. They were members of the Twenty-ninty Georgia Regiment and Uncle Richmond counts himself as being a member of it also. When asked if he did any fighting he said, "De fightin' part wazn't my business, en while dey wuz busy whippin' de Yankees I wux looking' erroun ter see whut I could pick up fer dem ter eat, kasso dey jes couldn't keep up en fight on dat trash whut wuz give dem ter eat."

He bears the reputation among all the old soldiers who knew him in the army as being a particularly fine forager and he claims that Gen. Gordon often complimented him on his prowess in that line.

"We all could er whipped dat fight easy enough," he said, "ef we jes had de Yankees demselves ter fight, but when dey went out en picked up Irishmen en Dutchmen en dingoes en Cubians en all de other nations ter help em' dey wuz too many fer us, en das whut I tole Gineral Lee one day."

Richmond wears a number of Confederate badges which have been given him on various occasions and all the old veterans go up and shake hands with him, for they have a very kind feeling in their hearts for the old darkey and count him as one of them.

August 30, 1904

STATE PENSION SOUGHT BY NEGRO

James Clarke of Emaneul, 104 Year Old, Fought for Confederacy

Swainsboro, Ga., Aug 20 - An unusual application for a pension has been sent up from the county by Ordinary John E. Youmans. James Clarke, a full negro, said to be 104 years old, has made application for a pension as a Confederate soldier. He enlisted in Company K, Capt. Wilcox, Twenty-eighth Georgia, and was assigned as fifer. He remained in the war till its close, surrendering with his command at High Point N.C. He is now unable to work and his friends are trying to secure a pension for him upon the indigent claim, and the ground that he was a duly enlisted soldier of the Confederacy.

There is no law discriminnating between the races, and as Clarke was a free negro it is thought that Commissioner Lindsay will pass favorably upon his application. If he does it is beleived this will be the first pension given in Georgia to a negro soldier for fighting in the army of the Confederacy, although there are many negroes drawing pensions for fighting on the Union side. Commissioner Lindsay has been given all the facts in the case.

FORREST'S BODY SERVANT IS FINED

J. W. Carter, a body servant of General Nathan B. Forrest, received a degree of notoriety from this article appearing in the September 24, 1910 edition (page one) of the *Pine Bluff Daily Graphic* (Jefferson County, Arkansas). Contributed by Edwin Lee Chaney of Bald Knob, Arkansas.

FORREST'S BODY SERVANT FINED - J. W. Carter, of Little Rock, Pleaded Guilty to a Libel Charge. - Recalls a Murder - Said he Kenw Who Killed Albert McVay - Has Gold Watch Given Him By General Forrest.

J. W. Carter, of Little Rock, an old negro ex-Confederate soldier, body servannt for General N.B. Forrest and who has a gold watch presented to him by General Forrest before his death, was fined $50 in the Jefferson circuit court here yesterday by judge Grace for libel. He entered a plea of guilty to the charge and Senators H.K. Toney, of this city and J. H. Hamiter of Little Rock made an appeal to the court in behalf of their client.

Judge Grace lectured the old negro telling him that the heaviest fine in such a case was $5,000 and six months imprisonment. He intimated that the old negro's good conduct in the past promoted him to be light in punishing him and he fined the prisoner $50 and costs. Carter will pay the fine and costs and will continue to enjoy his liberty, he having been out on bond since the indictment was returned against him by the Jefferson county grand jury.

Carter's indictment resulted after the assassination of Albert McVay in this city some months ago. McVay was shot down in his home in the western suburbs of this city and to this day the officers have been unable to get a clue that might lead to the identity and arrest of the assassin. Shortly after McVay was killed Carter wrote a letter to the then Chief of Police A.J. Stewart here, telling him that he knew the name of the guilty party and mentioned a local negro, who proved an ability and fully convinced the officers that he had no connection with the murder. Carter was brought here and made an unsatisfactory statement. He was then indicted for libel. It was afterwards learned that Carter was jealous of the local negro, who admired the same woman he liked.

ONE WHO RODE WITH FORREST

The *Selma* (Alabama) *Journal* of October 16, 1912 contains this account of Boston Linam, who rode with Nathan Bedford Forrest. Menzo W. Driskell, Jr. of Selma, Alabama provides this article.

BOSTON LINAM, NEGRO VETERAN IN THE CITY

Boston Linam, of Mobile, is in the city and he is attracting quite as much attention as any of the maids, sponsors, generals, colonels or anybody else attennnnding the re-union. Boston is a eighty-year-old-negro who came through the war with General Forrest, and he has the credentials along with him to prove that he was one of the fellows who fought for the south and bled for principles which the "white folks" told him were right.

Boston has been attending the veterans reunions every year since it has been a custom to hold them. He gets to all of them, and when he goes back to Mobile he immediately begins preparing for the next re-union the following year.

This old negro formerly lived at Camden, Willcox county, and on Broad Street this morning he came face to face with Sheriff Jenkins of Wilcox. The sheriff and Boston were delighted to meet each other again, and when the old negro was told that Mr. Jenkins had been elected sheriff, he said: "Lawd, god-er-mighty man boy, you done been 'lected high shaf. I told yo you'd have good luck" and everybody had a good laugh. Boston is decorated with flags, buttons and medals from head to foot, and bears his honors quite proudly.

GENERAL LEE'S COOK TELLS HOW HE
WAS SHOT IN BATTLE

Source: The April 12, 1923 edition of *The Atlanta Journal*

Darkies Who Served in War Welcomed at Reunion - Old Fiddlers Give Concerts on Streets

NEW ORLEANS, La., April 12 - (By the Associated Press) "An when Marsa Robert wuz riding along on his big hoss in front 'uf de battle line an saw me 'side,him, he yells; 'Git away fum dis firin line, William, an git back on de animal line. Fust thing you know you'll git shot an I won't have any cook.' An' sho nuf, I gits shot a minute aftuh that; right in the wilderness, too"

So spake Rev. William Mack Lee of Norfolk, Va., body servant and cook for the Confederate chieftan as he told of his war experiences during a brief recess of the Confederate Veterans reunion. The old darkey, his coat and vest resplendent with reunion badges garnered at a score or more of such gatherings, was the center of a throng of veterans and members of the Daughters of the Confederacy. He was attired in an old gray uniform and with the half dozen other white haired negroes present held an informal reception.

The old darkies sat in the convention auditorium and were welcomed with the same cordiality that would have been shown a brigadier general. Time after time veterans, as they passed one or the other of them, would stop and shake hands. The gray uniform and the fellowship that exists between all who followed Lee and Jackson obliterated the color line.

THE SECRET OF THE BURIAL OF THE GREAT SEAL OF THE CONFEDERACY.

Source: The April 9, 1923 edition of *The Atlanta Journal News*

WASHINGTON, D.C., April 9, - Taking with him to the grave the secret of the whereabouts of the great seal of the Confederacy, which he hid away when Jefferson Davis was captured, James Jones, the colored bodyguard of the President of the Confederate states, is dead here today. The body of the faithful old servant of the sixties will be sent to Raleigh N.C., for burial on Sunday.

Throughout his long life, with its later years spent in the government service in Washington, James Jones would never reveal what became of the Confederate seal.

"Marse Jeff" had bidden that he never tell - and he never did.

Veterans of the Union and Confederate armies, newspapers, writers, curiosity seekers, and curious hunters from time to time urged Jones to reveal where he buried the great seal. They argued that the Civil War was far in the past and the seal should be produced for the inspection of the younger generation of today and generations that are to follow in a reunited country, always James Jones shook his head and to the end he maintained his silence.

The colored body guard was with Jefferson Davis when his capture was af-fected; in fact he is said to have warned his master of the approach of the enemy, but Presiden David did not escape in time. Jones accompanied President Davis to Fort Monroe where he was placed in prison.

Jones was born in Warren county North Carolina. After the war he headed a colored fire department in Raleigh and became a minor city official. He turned Republican in politics, but always voted for Representative William Ruffia Cox of North Carolina who represented the state in the house in the forty-eighth and forty-ninth congresses.

Later when Mr. Cox became secreatry of the United States senate he brought Jones to Washington with him and gave him a messenger's job in the senate. That was in 1893. Since that time he has had several jobs about the capitol and was a messenger in the senate stationery room until a short time before his death.

"...HE DID ACTUAL AND FAITHFUL SERVICE AS A SOLDIER IN MANY A BATTLE."

Source: *Palatka News* (Florida) of May 22, 1914; the ending paragraph of this copy was missing.

FOXY JOHN P. WALL CHARGES RUSSELL - With Voting to Vie a Pension to a Negro - But fails to say that it was at request of United Confederate Veterans of Florida.

At the political meeting and picnic at Silver Lake on Wednedsay, Senator John P. Wall charged his opponent W. A. Russell, with voting in favor of a special pension bill for one Jackson Junius, a negro of Monticello Jefferson county.

In his reply Mr. Russell admitted that he so voted, but took occasion too explain the vote in a way which he beleives will satisfy every fair-minded man.

Jackson Junius' special pension was asked of the legislature by the General Commandinnng the United Confederate Veterans of Florida, Gen. B. W. Patridge of Monticello. Also many other Confederate veterans of that place.

Who is Jackson Junius?

At the breaking out of hostilities he was a slave of a Mr. Henry of Jefferson county. Several of Mr. Henry's sons entered the confederate service and Jackson Junius was sent with them to serve them. Jackson served throughout the four years of the war and it is a fact that while he was never regularly enlisted, he did actual and faithful service as a soldier in many a battle.

But that isn't all. When the war closed Jackson Junius remained loyal to his old master; he was a "white man's negro;" he has always been a Democrat; he has been true to his friends.

When the carpet baggers were in contol of the State during the days of reconstruction and men like Liberty Billings and his ilk were going up and down the state stirring up hatred among the negroes and exciting them to acts of open defiance of the whites, Jackson Junius stood with his influence, like a stone wall against such depredations.

For the past 28 years the Democrats of Monticello have nominated and elected Jackson Junius a constable; his name has stood on the tail end of every democratic ticket through all these years. He was given this office, not for any special ability he posessed, but as recognition of his honest service to the white people among whom he had lived all his years as a slave and as a freedman.

This bill passed the House, but was killed in the Senate. Yes, Mr. Russell did vote to give Jackson Junius a small pension. He did it at the urgent request of the United Confederate Veterans of Florida, a body that has recognized faithfulness to a negro who fought side by side with his masters in many a bloody battle, but who because of his color is denied aid in.....

FOXY JOHN P. WALL CHARGES RUSSELL

With Voting to Give a Pension to a Negro.

BUT FAILS TO SAY THAT IT WAS AT REQUEST OF UNITED CONFEDERATE VETERANS OF FLORIDA.

At the political meeting and picnic at Silver Lake on Wednesday, Senator John P. Wall charged his opponent, W. A. Russell, with voting in favor of a special pension bill for one Jackson Junius, a negro of Monticello, Jefferson county.

In his reply Mr. Russell admitted that he so voted, but took occasion to explain the vote in a way which he believes will satisfy every fair-minded man.

Jackson Junius' special pension was asked of the legislature by the General Commanding the United Confederate Veterans of Florida, Gen. B. W. Partridge of Monticello. Also many other Confederate veterans of that place.

Who is Jackson Junius?

At the breaking out of hostilities he was a slave of a Mr. Henry of Jefferson county. Several of Mr. Henry's sons entered the confederate service and Jackson Junius was sent with them to serve them. Jackson served throughout the four years of the war, and it is a fact that while he was never regularly enlisted, he did actual and faithful service as a soldier in many a battle.

But that isn't all. When the war closed Jackson Junius remained loyal to his old master; he was a "white man's negro;" he has always been a Democrat; he has been true to his friends.

When the carpet baggers were in control of the State during the days of reconstruction, and men like Liberty Billings and his ilk were going up and down the State stirring up hatred among the negroes and exciting them to acts of open defiance of the whites, Jackson Junius stood with his influence, like a stone wall against such depredations.

For the past 24 years the Democrats of Monticello have nominated and elected Jackson Junius a constable; his name has stood on the tail end of every democratic ticket through all these years. He was given this office, not for any special ability he possessed, but as recognition of his honest service to the white people among whom he had lived all his years as a slave and as a freedman.

This bill passed the House, but was killed in the Senate. Yes, Mr. Russell did vote to give Jackson Junius a small pension. He did it at the urgent request of the United Confederate veterans of Florida, a body that has recognized faithfulness to a negro who fought side by side with his masters in many a bloody battle, but who because of his color is denied aid in

Chapter VII

Southern Memorials, Markers, and Tributes

And to you our colored friends . . . we say welcome. We can never forget your faithfulness in the darkest hours of our lives. We tender to you our hearty respect and love, for you never faltered in duty nor betrayed your trust.

Colonel William Sanford

From an address given before the Confederate Veterans of the Seventh Tennessee Regiment of Cavalry, Forrest's Corps, at the Columbia, Tennessee Reunion of September 22, 1876.

Cemetery headstones, historical markers, and stone monuments provide inscriptions that are tangible reminders of African American military service. Also, tributes to Black Confederates are found in published speeches and newspaper articles, and in the official minutes and journals of United Confederate Veteran camps.

Attempts to memorialize the Black Confederate are continuing, but there is opposition in some quarters. For instance, in the fall of 1993, the Nottoway (Virginia) Board of Supervisors voted down a proposal by a local Sons of Confederate Veterans Camp (after it was first approved) to erect a suitable monument to "the 400 African-Americans, free and slave, conscript and volunteers, from Nottoway County, who served the Confederacy." Professor Ervin L. Jordan, Jr. of the University of Virginia offers an interesting and thought-provoking analysis:

I have closely followed efforts in Virginia to honor black Confederate soldiers; to date, all have been met with uncompromising resistance by African-Americans. Somehow, this seems a pity for too many Americans, black and white, seemingly prefer to suppress this fascinating aspect of history. But as an African-American I also believe the wishes of the black community in this regard should be considered. Perhaps the day will come when the relationship between whites, African-Americans and Southern/Confederacy history will no longer be adversarial.

Rudolph Young, an African American genealogist who traces Black Confederates offers these provocative thoughts from an article appearing in the September 21, 1993 edition of the *Charlotte Observer*):

"This is a part of our shared history. It's not a matter of me being proud. I am a part of that history. The Confederate flag per se doesn't offend me. It stands for what the person holding it wants it to. If I see it at a KKK rally, I know it is a hate flag. If I see it at a Confederate veterans organization, it's a patriotic flag. If it's on the back of a pickup truck, it's being trivialized. If you want to honor your ancestors, you have to honor them regardless. You can't insult me with my own heritage."

And in an AP article of January 28, 1992 (Baton Rouge: *The New Star*), Professor Leonard Haynes of Southern University states:

"When you eliminate the Black Confederate soldier, you've eliminated the history of the south."

The following selections are drawn from southern memorials, markers, and tributes that honor Black Confederates.

A BLACK CONFEDERATE LEGISLATOR IS HONORED IN ATLANTA, 1892.

The frontispiece of an obscure hardbound book, *CONFEDERATE SCRAP-BOOK*, tells us that this work is "Copied from a scrapbook kept by a young girl during and immediately after the war, with additions from war copies of the *'Southern Literary Messenger'* and *"Illustrated News'* loaned by friends and other selections as accredited. Published for the benefit of the Memorial Bazaar, held in Richmond, April 11, 1893." The writer is Mrs. Lizzie Cary Daniel, the daughter of a Virginian and Confederate Colonel, John B. Cary.

Published by the J. L. Hill Printing Company of Richmond (1893), this book provides fascinating information as the names of the soldiers who refused to leave President Davis upon his capture, and short accounts such as this one about veteran and legislator, W. H. Styles who is honored at a meeting of Confederate veterans in Atlanta. Representative Styles, an eloquent speaker, falls into plantation dialect to add humor and levity to the proceedings.

WITH THE OLD VETS OF GEORGIA REPRESENTATIVE STYLES, THE COLORED LAW-MAKER, GETS A CANE

There were scenes at the Confederate Veterans' hall last night. The meeting of the old 'vets" was for the purpose of presenting Styles, the colored legislator from Liberty county, who voted for the acceptance of the Soldiers' Home, with a handsome gold-headed cane. They were seated around the front row near the president's chair, and President Calhoun, in a few well-turned remarks, introduced Mr. Small, who took the stand and made one of his most thrilling and eloquent speeches, presenting the cane.

SAM SMALL SPEAKS.

After entering fairly upon the purpose in view, Mr. Small said:

This man has spoken in the Georgia house sentiments in honor and defence of the men who are as much entitled to-day to the care of Georgia as they were in the days of battle when they perilled their breast at the point of the bayonet and almost courted death in the front of battle. (Applause.) With that abiding Christian faith that should govern all honest men of state, he did his duty to his name, and to his people and his God, and I honor him for it. (Much cheering.) He used to go to school with the men for whom this Soldiers' Home was built. He toted their books on his shoulder. He knew them well and loved them, and that is why he has been prompted to take the wiser course in this matter. It was a striking picture to me to see in my mind this old slave following in the footsteps of his young master to school, and then years later to see him standing in the halls of state defending the name of the Confederacy, while others of the opposite race forgot their blessed heritage. (Great cheering.) Oh, I declare to you history doesn't show a more thrilling scene than Styles, the black slave, arguing for justice to the men who rushed upon bristling bayonets while the smell of hot blood and battle came stifling over the field. (Prolonged applause.) There will always be a special page to his name on the annals of honor.

Turning to the colored man, he closed with the following:

You have honored yourself far more than we can honor you to-night with that vote you cast in the house. You stood there faithful to the duties old Georgia had placed on your black shoulders, and while those to whom jeers of the few are more than honor to the dead were wrangling against the ceptance of the home for the Confederate veterans, you stood firm to the simple faith of your old master. (Applause.)

These men here to-night are not ashamed to take you by the hand and say you are an honor to your race. (Cheers.)

With appropriate remarks, he handed the glittering cane over to the colored representative amid loud applause. The scene was one of wild enthusiasm. Men clapped their hands and shouted aloud.

THE COLORED PATRIOT'S SPEECH.

Styles, of Liberty – he is famous by that simple title – walked forward and received the handsome gift. He was deeply moved. Anybody could have seen that. He bowed his head just as one used to see the old "fo' de war" darkies bow their heads when their lords of their old South handed out the regular annual Christmas dram." The applause was deafening.

The colored law-maker finally looked up, and somebody said they saw tears trickling down his wrinkled ebony cheek, when he began to speak as follows:

"Mr. President and Gentlemen of the Confederacy: I call you men of the Confederacy, and when I do it my heart thrills with a mingled feeling of ecstasy and caressing regret at the very sound of the word. (Applause.) Confederacy! Yes, that old Southern Confederacy that fought so hard for what it felt to be right. (Cheers.) What can I say, gentlemen; what is there for a poor old servant-nigger of the past to say here and now, once more in the camps of his master's comrades? (Much applause.) Little did I dream when on the floor of the Georgia House of Representatives I contended for the rights of the Confederate soldier that I would thus be served with such pleasing reward. But I have done nothing more than my duty, nothing more than my young master who was shot down to his grave in Virginia would have been glad to see me do. (Applause.) And it's the truth I'm tellin' you that when I hear the praise you give me here to-night my heart tells me to hush and see if it ain't young marster talkin' to de old nigger." Here the applause that crowned the old colored orator's sentence shook the roof till the pictures of Lee and Jeff Davis on the wall bowed with the sway as if to nod assent, while the old Confederate war flag draped over the president's head quivered at as if it would like to be unfurled again.

"It takes me back, it does"—and the old man's face was full of smiles as he spoke—"to the time when I used to hitch his horse at the door and go along to school with his books. Bless my soul, how we boys did use to steal the horses from the lot at night and go all over the country, and the white folks, never knowin' any de better! (Laughter.) But times got war-like by and by, and my young marsters went on off to war and I went along with 'em-couldn't help it. Oh, my Lord, I would have died for 'em any minute; and I would do it again to-night, God knows. (Applause.)

STYLES GOES TO WAR.

Yes, I was in the war. But, my white friends, you know how it is with us niggers-my people-we don't love the smell of gunpowder (laughter), and I didn't stay in de war long fo' I was out of dar, 'case I didn't make no calculation ter stay dere long--see?

Styles only uses the negro dialect in his speeches when he turns to humorous sentiments, but it always brings the laugh, it is so natural with him.

"They made us able-bodied negroes put up breastworks for you white men to shoot from; you all know how it was. (Laughter.) But I soon learned a trick of the war; they had what was called a sick list (continued laughter), and I was one of the first to get sick right dar. 'Wall, you can cook,' dey said to me, and I went to cooking up at Andersonville. But all this time I had faith in old mistis; I was lookin' for her to send for me every day, till by and by she did send for me, but it cost her two good able-bodied slaves to git me out.

"Oh, well, say I don't love the grave where old mistis is buried? Tell me I don't love the mound of earth where her two sons-they were the same thing as brothers to me--are now sleeping ? I can't talk about it, white men." (Applause.)

There was earnestness in the negro's voice that told his emotion to be of the sincerest kind. It was a pathetic scene, and as the black man closed his sentence he leaned back resignedly against the stand behind him, and threw his eyes upward, remaining so for several minutes.

From this he went on to tell what praise was due to Hon. William H. Fleming for his efforts on behalf of the veterans. He said in his humble judgment, without arrogating anything to himself, and speaking simply as a negro who loved white people would speak, the gravest sorrow of State was the Senate in killing the bill for the Soldiers' Home.

He closed with an honest-hearted expression of gratitude for the gift of his handsome cane, and said be had brought along a colored friend who would, in his name, present the association with something in return. "I would to God that I had something worthier to give," he said, but I have nothing but this trifle besides my heart, which I sacrifice on this altar of the Confederate Veterans' Association."

HE GIVES HIS PICTURE.

William Betts was the friend who was called upon by Styles to give his present to the association, and, in a few well-turned phrases, he gave a cabinet-size photograph of the colored legislator, which, by motion, will be framed and enlarged and hung on the wall.

The cane Styles received was a fine ebony stick with massive gold head, upon which was engraved

W. H. STYLES,
FROM
FULTON COUNTY CONFEDERATE
VETERAN S' ASSOCIATION.
ATLANTA, GA., 1892.

He Was Dressed In Gray

From an article entitled "A Tribute to the Man in Black" in the *Confederate Veteran*, May, 1896.

Comrade C. C. Cumming, of Fort Worth, Texas, writes that Bob and Alf Taylor have just passed through the Fort in their double role of "Yankee Doodle and Dixie," and a crowded house greeted them, laughing and crying alternately at the comedy and tragedy of the "Old South" crucified under the Southern Cross "for," as Bob says, so truly, "it is the old, old South, with the print of the nails of its crucifixion in its hands." He brought to the memory of the gray heads the old "Black Mammy" and spoke of the monument in the future that would be erected to her memory for her faithfulness before and during the great struggle.

This revives the memory of a faithful man in black who followed me through from First Manassas, Leesburg, where he assisted in capturing the guns we took from Baker, to the Peninsular, the Seven Days before Richmond, Fredericksburg, the bombardment of the city December 11, and the battle, two days after, at Mayre's Heights; to Chancellorsville, the storming of Harper's Ferry, and the terrible struggle at Sharpsburg (Anteitam now), and last, Gettysburg. Here he lost his life by his fidelity to me--his 'young marster" and companion.

We were reared together on "de Ole plantation" in "Massippi." I was wounded in the Peach Orchard at Gettysburg on the second day. The fourth day found us retreating in a cold, drizzling rain. George had found an ambulance, in which I,Sergeant-Major of the Seventeenth Mississippi, and Col. Holder of that regiment, still on this side of the river, and an officer of the Twenty-first Mississippi, whose name escapes me, embarked for the happy land of Dixie. All day long we moved slower than any funeral train over the pike, only getting eight miles-to Cashtown. When night came I had to dismount from loss of blood and became a prisoner in a strange land. On the next day about sundown faithful George, who still clung to me, told me that the Yankees were coming down the road from Gettysburg and were separating the "black folks from dar marsters;" that he didn't want to be separated from me and for me to go on to prison and he'd slip over the mountains and join the regiment in retreat, and we'd meet again "ober de ribber," meaning the Potomac. We had crossed at Williamsport.

I insisted on George accepting his freedom and joining a settlement of free negroes in the vicinity of Gettvsburg, which we had passed through in going up to the battle. But he would have none of it; he wanted to stay with me always. I had him hide my sword, break it off at the hilt and stick it in a crack of the barn (that yet stands in the village) to the left of the road going away from Gettysburg, where I, with about thirty other wounded, lay. I can yet see that faithful black face and the glint of the blade as the dying rays of that day's sun flashed upon them. A canteen of water and some hard tack was the last token of his kindly care for me.

In the spring of 1865, I saw a messmate from whom I was separated on that battlefield, and he told me the fate of poor, faithful George. He had gotten through the lines safely and was marching in the rear of our retreating command, when met by a Northern lady, who had a son in our command, whom George, by chance, happened to know. He was telling her of her son, who was safe as a prisoner, when some men in blue came up. George ran and they shot and killed him. He was dressed in gray and they took him for a combatant. The lady had him buried and then joined her son in prison. She told my messmate of this and he told to the boys in camp the fate of the truest and best friend I ever had. George's prediction will come true-I feel we will meet again "over the river."

General Nathan Bedford Forrest Addresses Black Southerners

Much has been written about Nathan Bedford Forrest's ties to the founding of the "Ku Klux" but little is said of the General's relationship with the slaves who served under his command during the Civil War. In Vol. XVII, No. 4, 1953 edition of Military Affairs, published by the American Miliary Institute, Jac Weller writes:

Early in the war, Forrest's battalion had a compact well-provisioned wagon train driven by his own slaves. In large measure, the wagons and teams as well as the supplies that they carried were furnished-by Forrest himself. His teamsters were promised their freedom at the end of the war and served him faithfully long after they could easily have deserted to the enemy. His opponents had trouble understanding Forrest's personal popularity with the negroes even after the end of the war. Forty four of the original forty five teamsters remained into the last year of the war, but the attrition in mule and wagons was great.

After the war General Forrest gave keynote speeches to political and social gatherings. The following article tells of a speech before an African American audience and appeared on page one of the July 6th, 1875 edition of the *Memphis Daily Avalanche.*

"Yesterday, the 5th of July, was by general consent, observed in this city as the anniversary of American independence. The colored people turned out en masse, either individually or as members of societies, and spent the day in festivities at one of the parks, or at the Fair Grounds ....The Jubilee of the Pole Bearers [a negro political and social organization in the post-war era] at the Fair Grounds was largely attended, where, agreeable to an invitation, addresses were made by General G. J. Pillow, General N. B. Forrest and others.

Hourly trains were run on the Memphis and Charleston railroad, commencing at 8 o'clock in the morning, and at noon a large assemblage of the colored people had gathered there. The distinguished invited guests arrived about half past 12 o'clock, and, upon reaching the gate, received an evidence of their perfect equality with their hosts by being required to pay 25 cents admission. The different lodges of Independent Pole Bearers had not yet arrived, and the party spent a few minutes in walking through the spacious halls, which were arranged with tables all loaded down with meats, pies, cakes, etc., upon which a few of the earliest comers were vigorously employed.

At 1 o'clock several heavily loaded trains had arrived, and the scene inside the enclosure was a very animated one. The busy preparations for dinner and the hum of a thousand voices were now and then relieved by the sharp cries of the man peddling lemonade at a nickel a dipper full and the loud calls of the men who were raking in the quarters on the game of chuck-a-luck. Owing to the intense heat of the sun, the vast crowd was confined to the two halls and to the grand stands which overlook the race-course.

. . . At two o'clock the Pole Bearers arrived and marched from the railroad to the grounds in excellent order, with beating of drums and flying colors, the rays of a summer sun being reflected from hundreds of tin spear heads. Having reached the grand stand, Hezekiah Henley, President of the Society; John Wiseman, Grand Marshal, and Sam Farris, Assistant Grand Marshal, were introduced to the guests by Dr. Clark and after some further delay the crowd gathered on the stand and the exercises of the afternoon were commenced. During a part of the time there was considerable confusion on the stand, and at times it was difficult to hear the speakers. A disturbance occurred while General Pillow was making his address in which blows were exchanged between two colored men, but quiet was soon restored.

On the stand were General G. J. Pillow, General N. B. Forrest, Colonel M. C. Gallaway of the Appeal [newspaper], Alderman H. G. Dent, Major Minor Meriwether, Captain J. Harvey Mathes of the Ledger [newspaper], G. P. M. Turner, Dr. Clark and G. Y. Eddins.

After music by a band of colored musicians, President Henley was introduced, who said he stood before them as a representative of the Union, and as a representative of the colored race. They did not come to discuss politics, but to pull down the wall that has so long separated the two races, and to bring about peace, love and union. He hoped all would be well pleased ....

After another air performed by the band, Miss Lou Lewis, a good looking mulatto was introduced to General Forrest as the representative of the colored ladies. She carried in her hand a handsome bouquet of flowers, which she presented to the General in the following words:

"Mr. Forrest - allow me to present you this bouquet as a token of reconciliation, and an offering of peace and good will."

Much enthusiasm prevailed at this point in the exercises, President Henley proposing three cheers for the Union, which were given.

General Forrest received the flowers with a bow, and said:

"Miss Lewis, ladies and gentlemen - I accept these flowers as a token of reconciliation between the white and colored races of the South. I accept them more particularly, since they come from a lady, for if there is any one on God's great earth who loves the ladies, it is myself. This is a proud day for me. Having occupied the position I have for thirteen years, and being misunderstood by the colored race, I take this occasion to say that I am your friend. I am here as the representative of the Southern people - one that has been more maligned than any other. I assure you that every man who was in the Confederate army is your friend. We were born on the same soil, breathe the same air, live in the same land, and why should we not be brothers and sisters. When the war broke out I believed it to be my duty to fight for my country, and I did so. I came here with the jeers and sneers of a few white people, who did not think it right. I think it is right, and will do all I can to bring about harmony, peace and unity. I want to elevate every man, and to see you take your places in your shops, stores and offices. I don't propose to say anything about politics, but I want you to do as I do-go to the polls and select the best men to vote for. I feel that you are free men, I am a free man, and we can do as we please. I came here as a friend, and whenever I can serve any of you I will do so. We have one Union, one flag, one country, therefore let us stand together. Although we differ in color, we should not differ in sentiment. Many things have been said in regard to myself, and many reports circulated, which may perhaps be believed by some of you, but there are many around me who can contradict them. I have been many times in the heat of battle--oftener, perhaps, than any within the sound of my voice. Men have come to me to ask for quarter, both black and white, and I have shielded them. Do your duty as citizens, and if any are oppressed, I will be your friend. I thank you for the flowers, and assure you that I am with you in heart and hand."

The General's remarks were enthusiastically received, President Henley frequently insisting on "Rah for de Union!"

Some of the Black Confederates serving in Forrest's cavalry are found in J. P. Young's THE SEVENTH TENNESSEE CAVALRY: A HISTORY (in reprint). The following listing of men in Companies E and L are contributed by William E. Jackson Tennessee:

Colored Men with Company.

Dupree, Warner	Livingston, Essex	Mann, Frank	Allison, March
Anthony, Benjamin	Barber, Henry	Bond, Warrick	Demoss, Claiborne
Doris, Prince	Irwin, Albert (Major Mud)	Tucker, Ed	Freeman, Joseph
Robinson, Mose	Johnson, Chapman	Mann, Thomas	Walker, Dick
Jarrett, Thompson	Reed, Alexander	Taylor, Cornelius	Perkins, John
Taylor, Aaron	Wilson, John	Northcross, Henry	Haliburton, Anthony

COMPANY E.

NAME.	Rank.	Date of Enlistment.	Remarks.
J. J. Neely	Captain.		
W. J. Tate..........	Captain.	May 24, 1861	{ Wounded, June 9, 1863, at ——. Killed near Ripley, Miss., June 11, 1864.
J. P. Statler.........	Captain.	May 24, 1861	{ Wounded February 22, 1864, at Prairie Mound. Killed at Harrisburg July 14, 1864.
T. P. Harris	Lieutenant.	....	Died in service.
F. G. Patrick........	Lieutenant.		
Leon Bills..........	Lieutenant.		
W. W. McCauley....	Lieutenant.		
H. Harris...........	Lieutenant.		
W. C. Mashburn.....	Lieutenant.		
V. S. Ruffin.........	Lieutenant.	....	Killed at Athens, Ala., September, 1864.
Fisk Weaver........	Lieutenant.	....	Died in service at Abbeville, Miss.
T. W. Crawford	Lieutenant.	May 23, 1861	Absent without leave September 10, 1862.
J. W. Nelson........	1st Serg.		
A. M. Statler........	2d Serg.		

Colored Men with Company L.

Alison, Sam	Curry, Jim	O'Dell, Stephen	Taylor, George
Byers, Bill	Moore, Joe	Pugh, Jeff	Taylor, Hark
Claiborne, Henry	Nelson, Joe	Taliaferro, Dobyns	Taylor, Dick
Coltart, Ed	Pugh, Dawson		

COMPANY M.

NAME.	Rank.	Date of Enlistment.	Remarks.
James G. Haywood..	Captain.	....	Absent with leave October 30, 1862.
Benjamin T. Davis...	Captain.	....	{ Absent without leave December 31, 1863. February 29, 1864, in parole camp.
J. M. Shaw	Lieutenant.	....	Released on certificate of discharge.
W. H. Moorer.......	Lieutenant.	....	{ Absent without leave December 31, 1863. In parole camp February 29, 1864.
C. S. O. Rice........	Lieutenant.	....	Paroled December 31, 1863.
J. L. Livingston.....	Lieutenant.	....	On duty with regiment April 30, 1864.
J. H. Mann	Sergeant.	Apr. 16, 1862	{ Appointed Second Sergeant July 16, 1862 ; and First Sergeant December 1, 1862.
J. T. Green.........	Sergeant.	June 12, 1862	{ Appointed Third Sergeant October 23, 1862. Detailed as clerk at Pemberton's head-quarters December 31, 1862. Absent without leave April 30, 1864.
H. W. Keller........	Sergeant.	Apr. 16, 1862	{ On special duty at head-quarters October 30, 1862. Absent without leave December 31, 1862, and February 29, 1864.
John Haywood......	Sergeant.	May 12, 1862	{ Appointed Corporal September 20, 1862 ; First Corporal July 1, 1862. Absent without leave December 31, 1862. In prison February 29, 1864.

A NOTABLE COLORED VETERAN

BY C. M Douglas of Columbia, South Carolina

From the <u>*Confederate Veteran*</u>, Vol. II, 1894.

One of the best-known freedmen in Columbia, S. C., is old William Rose, who has been messenger for the Governor's office under every Democratic administration since 1876. His history is worthy a space in the VETERAN. He is now eighty years of age, but is still active and vigorous enough to be at his post of duty every day, and nothing delights him more than to take part in any Confederate demonstration.

William Rose was born in Charleston in 1813, and was a slave of the Barrett family of that city. He was brought to Columbia when only twelve years old, and was taught the trades of carpenter and tinner. In his younger days be went out to the Florida war as a drummer in Capt. Elmore's company, the Richland Volunteers, an organization which is still in existence, and which has made a proud record for itself in three wars. Subsequently he went through the Mexican War as a servant for Capt. (afterwards Col.) Butler, of the famous Palmetto Regiment.

But the service in which he takes the greatest pride was that in the days of the Confederacy. He was the body servant of that distinguished Carolinian, Gen. Maxey Gregg, and as soon as he heard that his beloved master had fallen on the field at Fredricksburg he rushed to his side as fast as a horse could take him, and remained with him until the end came. His description of the death of Gen. Gregg, of his reconciliation with Stonewall Jackson, and his heroic last message to the Governor of South Carolina are pathetic in the extreme and are never related by the old man without emotion.

William saw Cleveland inaugurated, and was present at the unveiling of the soldiers' monument at Richmond, and at the recent grand Confederate reunion at Birmingham. From the latter he returned laden with badges which he cherishes as souvenirs of the occasion.

For sixty years he has been identified with the Richland Volunteers, and they never parade without him. About two years ago he presented a gold medal to the company, which is now shot for as an annual prize. He never forgets Memorial Day, and no 10th of May has passed by since the close of the war without some tribute from him placed on the Gregg monument at Elmwood. Recently he has been given a small pension by the United States for services in the Florida War.

Old "Uncle" William is of a class fast passing away. They will not have successors, but all the world may witness benefactors in Southern whites until the last of them crosses the "dark river."

THE MISSISSIPPI LEGISLATURE IS MOVED BY THE STORY OF JOHN, A FAITHFUL SLAVE

Mrs. Marian Minniece of Houston, Texas writes:

I am sending you a family story of ours of a wonderful slave named John who went to war with his master Zeb. Zeb died at war but John saw that his body was returned to his family. The Mitchell family [mentioned] were the founders of Corinth, Mississippi.

The Death of Zeb

The following story concerns a letter written by L. B. Mitchell during the war. This account was written by Mrs. Don Watkins, a local researcher and historian.

The letter was dated July, 1862 and postmarked, West Point, Georgia. It is addressed to Mr. Bob Williams of Rienzi, Mississippi and reads as follows:

It pains me much to record to you the death of your beloved son Zeb. He deposed this life on Sunday nite at half after two in the morning. His illiness was short after he was taken bad. I will start him home as soon as I can get him ready. John has been a faithful servant to Zeb. I put confidence in him in getting Zeb home. I was able to wait on him in all of the last part of his illness. He had medical attention from two able physicians and was treated kindly by all the family where he boarded. His expenses will be tolorably heavy. I do not know what they will be yet. I will put them down in his black book what I pay if I have to pay any. I want John to have enough to take him home. If I do you can pay the amount to my mother that suits you.

Yours respectfully, L. B. Mitchell

This is the story behind the letter as told by Ely B. Mitchell. He said that "Bob Williams of Rienzi, sent this slave John along with his son Zeb when he enlisted. It was the custom for soldiers to take along a negro slave to wait on them when they went to war."

"John was a faithful slave and cared for his master's son in every way possible. When Zeb became sick at the Camp, located at Columbus, Georgia, about 40 miles west from the town of West Point, Georgia, John was at his side day and night. There evidently was no hospital at the Camp, or the one there was crowded, and that was the reason Zeb Williams was in a private home, where, according to the letter he was given the best of care."

"Zeb, however, died and Lt. Mitchell assumed the responsibility of seeing that Zeb's body was sent back to Rienzi, Mississippi."

"When Lt. Mitchell returned after the war he told the Williams family what he did in this emergency."

"Knowing that the journey back to Rienzi covered a distance of about 400 miles, Lt. Mitchell worked out a plan to preserve the body for the long journey."

"He burnt some charcoal and placed it, after it had cooled, in the coffin around the body of Zeb. And securing a wagon and a team of oxen and a permit he sent the negro slave John on his way to Rienzi with the body."

"It took the slave nearly eight days traveling almost constantly to make the journey. But he finally arrived at the old homeplace he had left with his master's son and there was great rejoicing as well as many tears among the Williams family and the negro slave John."

"There is an aftermath to this story. While Dr. Carroll Kendrick who lived at Kendrick, a village near Corinth, was serving in the Mississippi Legislature, a bill to grant a pension to negro slaves who served in the war with their masters came up for consideration. Dr. Kendrick told the story about this faithful negro slave to the assembly and without a dissenting vote the bill passed."

"FIDELITY IS THE WATCHWORD"

This tribute is to a free man, John Brannon, who served with the Jeff Davis Legion, Hampton's Brigade, Stuart's Cavalry Corps, Army of Northern Virginia. This article appears in the Natchez (Mississippi) Democrat, December 5, 1922, and is contributed by Lewis D. Brasell of Mobile, Alabama.

JOHN BRANNON (Contributed)

The basic action of the legislature of the State of Mississippi in distributing pensions to Confederate soldiers and servants was to honor fidelity to the cause of the Confederacy by whosoever, regardless of race or color; so as to inscribe in the history of the state a lasting memorial to the men who fought, bled and suffered for the cause, Fidelity was the keynote; fidelity was the watchword--a principle which has actuated man from the dawn of civilization. It is honored in every shape and form the world over. It is the same principle that caused the Daughters of the Confederacy to decorate each veteran with a cross of honor. It is the same principle which caused Confederate monuments to be erected all through the south; and it is the same principle that underlies the United Confederate Veterans. And it is the fidelity of the Confederate servant that induced thirty legislatures of the state of Mississippi to award pensions for 30 consecutive years for his benefit. Not only that, but the literature of the south fairly teems with the story of the fidelity of the Confederate servant. Such great writers and thinkers as Henry W. Grady, Thomas Nelson Page, Joel Chandler Harris and General Robert Toombs have immortalized the Confederate servant.

Among services performed by the Confederate servant, none was more conspicuous than that of John Brannon. He was not compelled to serve; he was born free and lived free; and he elected to serve of his own free will. And serving as he did with such grand soldiers as General Will T. Martin and Colonel Samuel Baker, he early imbibed from them that bravery, valor and devotion that won him such peculiar distinction in this class.

John Brannon was true to every other trust which was confided to him. He excelled in his profession: It is said of him that he made a thousand contracts and never broke a single one. In every storm of life he was true as steel and as brave as a lion. And his virtues and excellencies of character will cause him to be mourned by all classes of people in the community without regard to race, color or creed.

He passed away about 3:00 p.m. on Saturday, the second day of December, and was buried from the Church of the Holy Family on the following Sunday. His funeral was attended by large numbers of all classes of creeds and colors. Conspicuous among the attendants were the officers of the United Daughters of the Confederacy. The United Confederate Veterans attended in a body; and it was under a cross of Confederate flags that his remains were ushered into the church, and afterwards borne to their last resting place.

The services at the church were deeply impressive, and the sermon, delivered by Rev. Father O'Neill, was full of force and eloquence.

Beautiful floral offerings covered the grave, flanked by numerous Confederate flags.

His loss will not only be felt in Natchez and Adams county, but his legions of friends in Concordia parish. Tensas and Catahoula, in Louisiana, will long cherish his memory.

CHATTANOOGA NEGROES COMPLIMENT A CONFEDERATE

From the *Confederate Veteran*, Vol. IV, 1896

W. P. McClatchy, Commander N. B. Forrest Camp, Chattanooga, Tenn., has been honored by the negro men of that city. They presented him with a gold-headed cane. Addresses were made by J. W. White and J. G. Burge, negro lawyers there. Comrade McClatchy held the office of City Recorder (Judge of the City Court) last year, and at the expiration of his term he was greatly surprised when these men presented it as a token of their friendship and esteem, and for the just and impartial manner in which he had dealt with their race. He asked them why they had "U. C. V. 1861-65," engraved on it, and they replied that they wished to emphasize that while he was a Southern man, and a Confederate soldier, he had administered the law justly and impartially. The N. B. Forrest Camp hearing of this compliment to its commander, by a rising vote thanked the donors for their expression of confidence in and esteem for a Confederate soldier, and a Southern Democrat who had "administered the law, in wisdom, justice and moderation."

The inscription reads: "U. C. V. 1861-1865, J. W. and J. G. to W. P. McC., 1895." Which stands for United Confederate Veteran 1861 to 1865, J. B. White and J. G. Burge to W. P. McClatchy, 1895.

In a note the comrade says: I never had a present in my life that I appreciated any more than this. Every true Southerner understands and appreciates a good negro, while the negro understands that the Southern man is the best friend he has. But for the meddling of people who really care nothing for the negro, but who are prejudiced against the South, there would be no friction between the races.

Received a Cross of Honor for Bravery in Action

"UNCLE GEORGE" MATHEWSON.

George Mathewson. aged ninety years, an ex-slave. who served in the War Between the States, passed away at his home in Paris, Tenn. He was buried at Maplewood Cemetery, and Rev. P. P. Pullen, of the Fitzhgerald-Fendell Camp, U. C. V., read the Confederate ritual for the departed soldier and offered a prayer.

"Uncle George" was a faithful member of the Fitzgerald-Fendell Camp, and had been color bearer for some years. He attended many- of the reunions over the South, and his last public appearance was a reunion of his Camp. He was a servant through the war, of Dr. W. P. Smallwood, a surgeon of Company E, 12th Georgia Regiment, and received a Cross of Honor for bravery in action. He was the only representative of the camp at the Dallas reunion, and was treated with great consideration when he carried the message from his white comrades to the floor of the convention. A son of Dr. Smallwood, who resides in Fort Worth, had his father's former body guard to visit him in his home and showered him with gifts. Dressed in his uniform of a Confederate soldier with his Cross of Honor and reunion badges pinned on his breast, "Uncle George" was laid to rest till the final roll call of his comrades.

He had only one relative surviving, a son.

(Source: *Confederate Veteran,* 1927, page 469.)

THE CONFEDERATE NEGRO

By Joseph A. Mudd, Hyattsville, Maryland for the <u>*Confederate Veteran*</u>, Vol. XXIII, 1905.

The Confederate negro is the proudest being on earth. A few weeks ago I was standing at the counter of the water office, Municipal Building, in Washington, when in came a negro who, standing near by, began his business with one of the clerks. He was rather shabbily dressed, but evidently one of the "old stock," as black as ink and as ugly as Satan, eyes beaming with intelligence and a great depth of human sympathy, a countenance one loves to rest one's gaze upon, and with a bearing of modest and courteous dignity. His business over, I said to him: "How long have you been in Washington?" "Since 1870, suh." "Where did you come from?" I could see his chest swelling, and I knew the answer before it was spoken. "From Ferginny, suh." "Were your people in the war?" "Yes, suh," with a smile of enthusiasm and a bow that bespoke reverence for the memories of the olden days. "They tell me you people 'fit' some." I could almost see the lightning dart from his eyes as he straightened himself up. "'Fit?' Why, dey outfit de world, suh; never did whip us, suh. If dey hadn't starved us out, we'd been fightin' yit." As he passed me going out of the office he said: "I was wid 'em foh years, suh. I cahd my young master off de field once when I din't think he'd live till I got him to de doctor; but he's living yit." I did not tell him I was a Confederate soldier, and he didn't seem to care. He knew what he was, and that was enough.

I have never seen a Confederate negro that was not full of pride in his record. I believe this sentiment is an evidence of his patriotism as well as a testimony of his love and loyalty to his white folks. During the last year of the war I was on duty as assistant surgeon at Howard's Grove Hospital, Richmond. There were about seventy-five young negro men and about the same number of young women employed as laborers in the three divisions of the hospital. In our division there was a bright young fellow whose avowals of patriotism were so frequent and intense that we suspected his sincerity. When the proposition came to enlist the slaves, we accidentally heard that a meeting was to be held at night outside the hospital grounds to consider the matter and that this young fellow would make a speech. Taking care that no white person attended, two or three of us sneaked up in the darkness to where we could hear without being seen. He was speaking, and for a half hour we listened to a most eloquent and earnest plea for every man to enlist in our glorious cause and help to drive the ruthless invader from the sacred soil of Virginia.

A CALL FOR MEMORIALS TO BLACK CONFEDERATES

Since the end of the War Between the States, Confederate men and women have called for the construction of monuments and memorials to African-Americans who supported the Cause. Many memorials were built; others never were completed. The following articles are drawn from the *Confederate Veteran Magazine*.

HONOR FOR THE OLD-TIME NEGRO.

The time is not far distant when a monument will be erected in Montgomery, Ala., or Richmond, Va., as a tribute to the memory of the old-time Southern negro. The loyal devotion of the men and women who were slaves has had no equal in all history. They took care of the women and children whose natural protectors were with Lee and Jackson, Forrest and Joe Johnston, and were faithful to the trust.

Women during the great war did not fear to ride alone through large plantations to give directions as to the crops. These women were protected and never outraged. It was the coming of the carpetbagger, with his social equality teachings, that caused many negroes to become brutes. The old-time negro will soon be but a memory, and while a remnant survive an imposing monument should be erected as a tribute to their faithfulness. It should be a monument worth fifty thousand dollars. This money could be easily raised if the religious and secular papers in the South would take up the matter in the spirit that the cause merits.--John W. Paulett, in *the Morristown* (Tenn.) *Gazette.*
(Vol. XX, 1912)

BUILD MONUMENT TO FAITHFUL SLAVES.

Mrs. Edward Carter, of Warrenton, Va., writes: "I see in the September VETERAN the suggestion of a monument being erected in memory of the old-time Southern negroes. I hope very much that such a monument will be erected. I believe there would be a liberal response throughout the entire South to such an appeal. No people could be more faithful and more deserving of appreciation. I have the deepest veneration for their memory. Of all the monuments erected in the South, none would appeal to my heart more feelingly. Such a monument would also show to the world the devotion which existed in the South between master and servant."

(Vol XXI, 1913)

A MONUMENT TO THE FAITHFUL OLD SLAVES:

As the President of the North Carolina Division, U. D. C., I heartily indorse the following letter from Mrs. Aston, and hope the Daughters will take some decisive action in the October convention looking to the erection of this monument. The letter is addressed "to the Daughters of the Confederacy and all the women of the South." *MRS. FRED* A. OLDS.

MRS. ASTON'S *LETTER*

My Dear Sisters: Will not every one of you raise your voice with mine in making amends for a long-neglected duty in rearing a monument to our faithful old slaves?

Of all people that dwell upon the earth, I think these deserve the grandest monument. Soon all this generation will have passed away. Let us hasten with the work while some of us still survive.

Confederate veterans have for some time been speaking of raising a monument to the Southern women. We appreciate this, and thank them for their remembrance of our self-denials and hardships which tried women's souls; but what else could have been expected of us when our dear ones were at the front? While this was the case we felt we were enduring this for sacred ties of kindred and country. How different with the faithful slaves! They did it for love of masters, mistresses, and their children. How nobly did they perform their tasks! Their devotion to their owners, their faithfulness in performing their labors and caring for us during these terribly disastrous years, and their kindness at the surrender, while we were powerless and helpless, have never been surpassed or equaled.

At the time of the surrender we were entirely defenseless. Our noble, famished, ragged patriots were still away from their homes, and among us was a band of robbers who were bad counselors to our slaves. Their kindness and their devotion to us was the most beautiful this earth has ever witnessed.

From the Mason and Dixon line to the Gulf and from the Atlantic to the Gulf there was not a massacre, house-burning, or one of those unmentionable crimes which are now so common in the whole country. Think of this; 'tis wonderful. Our gratitude to God and love for the old-time servants should be boundless.

Who will say they do not deserve the greatest monument that has ever been erected? This acknowledgment from us to them of our appreciation of kindness and devotion shown by them to their former owners would be in their last days a beautiful thought. To those of their race of the present generation it would verify the character of the Southern people, their former owners, and also show the true relation that existed between master and servant.

Would it not be an act of justice for the women of the South to ask our noble men if we may not be permitted to turn this monument over to those who, if not more deserving, are equally so with our Southern sisters? I would suggest that when it is erected a tablet might be inserted bearing this inscription: "Given by the Confederate Veterans as a memorial to the women of the South, and given by them in memory of the faithfulness of our former servants."

MRS. C. GILLILAND ASTON,
49 Church Street, Asheville, N. C.

(Vol. XII, 1904)

HENRY GRADY'S TRIBUTE

Henry W. Grady, postwar editor of the *Atlanta Constitution* and one of the nation's greatest orators, paid tribute to the antebellum negro slaves. This excerpt is taken from a local history entitled *WARD'S HISTORY OF COFFEE COUNTY* (Georgia) and is probably drawn from one of Grady's speeches in the early 1900's.

It has been noted repeatedly that history records no more remarkable illustration of loyalty to trust than that manifested by the negroes of the South during the Civil War. Often left behind as the sole support and protection of the families of the Confederate soldiers, not an instance is recorded in which one violated his trust. Of this remarkable record, Georgia's matchless orator, Henry P. Grady, said in his last great speech:

"History has no parallel to the faith kept by the negro in the South during the war, often five hundred negroes to a single white man, and yet through these dusky throngs the women and children walked in safety and the unprotected homes rested in peace.

"Unmarshaled, the black batallions moved patiently to the fields in the morning to feed the armies their idleness would have starved, and at night gathered anxiously at the big house to `hear the news from Master,' though conscious that his victory made their chains enduring. Everywhere humble and kindly; body-guard of the helpless; the rough companion of the little ones; the observant friend; the silent sentry in his lowly cabin; the shrewd counselor; and when the dead came home, a mourner at the open grave.

"A thousand torches would have disbanded every Southern Army, but not one was lighted. When the master going to a war in which slavery was involved said to his slave, "I leave my home and beloved ones in your charge," the tenderness between man and master stood disclosed. And when the slave held that charge sacred through storm and temptation he gave new meaning to faith and loyalty. I rejoice that when freedom came to him after years of waiting, it was all the sweeter because the black hands from which the shackles fell were stainless of a single crime against the helpless ones confided to his care."

Virginia Tribute

Source: *Confederate Veteran, Vol. XX, 1912.*

TRIBUTE TO ALECK KEAN IN VIRGINIA.

Judge George L. Christian, of Richmond, writes of Aleck Kean, colored, as "faithful unto death:"

"Early in November, 1911, three of us, ex-members of the second company of Richmond Howitzers during the war of the sixties, honored ourselves by attending the funeral services of Aleck Kean, which took place near Green Springs, in Louisa County. The career of Aleck as an honest, upright, faithful servant and man was so conspicuous and unique that it deserves this public notice.

"When the war broke out, John Henry Vest, a son of the late James M. Vest, of Louisa, entered the Confederate army as a private in the second company of Richmond Howitzers, and took Aleck along as his body servant and cook, as was customary in those days. The 'Renfrew' mess was soon formed with Aleck as the cook, and without hesitation I affirm that he was the most faithful and efficient man in the performance of every duty pertaining to his sphere that I have ever known. His whole mind and soul seemed bent on trying to get and prepare something for his mess to eat; and if there was anything to be gotten honestly, Aleck always got the share which was coming to his mess, and he always had that share prepared in the shortest time possible and in the most delicious way in which it could have been prepared in camp. The comfort of having such a man as Aleck around us in those trying times can scarcely be described and certainly cannot be exaggerated.

"Young Mr. Vest (Aleck's young master) died in the fall of 1863, and after that Aleck, although he had offers to go to others or to return to his home, had become so attached to the members of the 'Renfrew' mess that he refused to leave them, and, with his master's consent, remained with that mess up to the very last, when he surrendered with them near Appomattox. He was always loyal, true, brave, honest, and faithful not only to the members of his mess but to every man in the 2d and 3d Howitzers, all of whom knew, respected, and admired his fidelity and efficiency.

"When the war ended, he went back to his old home. His old master, Mr. James M. Vest, gave him a little home a very short distance from his own dwelling, and it was there within hearing of his own people and always ready and willing to do their bidding that he spent the rest of his life. There was scarcely any one in all that community who was more respected by all the people, white and colored, than Aleck, and certainly no other deserved that respect and confidence more than he did. His funeral was largely attended both by white and colored, all of whom seemed anxious to attest by their presence the high regard in which he was held both as a man and a Christian.

"Such a career of fidelity, loyalty, and devotion is worthy of being published to the world and ought to stimulate others, both white and black, to strive to follow his example. Nearly every year since the formation of the Howitzer Association an invitation to its annual banquet has been sent to Aleck, and whenever he was able to do so he attended. Every member of the assocation knew and respected him, and was glad to extend to him the cordial greeting which he received at these annual gatherings."

Chapter VIII

Bivouac of the Dead:
Published Obituaries and Reminiscences

It was his commitment to the truth of history–specifically black people's con-tributions to Confederate military history–that led Eddie Brown Page III, 43, of Atlanta, to become an associate member of the Sons of Confederate Veterans.

...He was first and foremost, a historian who specialized in black history and Confederate history and how blacks contributed to Confederate military his-tory.

... "He loved putting people in shock at learning the truth," said his brother... "I'm glad that he educated me that blacks did fight on the Confederate side, and that blacks were not only slaves but slave owners...There are blacks who respect their Southern heritage, too."

From the obituary of Eddie Brown Page III, *The Atlanta Journal-Constitution*, January 15, 1998

[Note: Page, an African American musician, reenacted as a Black Confederate and often played "Dixie" for memorial services and commemorative ceremonies.]

UNCLE CHARLES RICHARDSON, VETERAN OF THE CONFEDERATE ARMY

The *Arkansas Democrate* reported in its April 24, 1929 edition that "Funeral service for Uncle Charles Richardson, 95, negro slave and veteran of the Confederate army, will be held Thursday afternoon at 3 o'clock from the colored Methodist church." The article which appeared on page six went on to say, "He drew a Confederate pension, having fought through the war with his young master who was killed, and later supplied money to take his second master, a Confederate officer and himself to St. Louis."

(Contributed by Edwin Lee Chaney of Bald Knob, Arkansas.)

"UNCLE GEORGE" MATHEWSON IS LAID TO REST IN HIS CONFEDERATE UNIFORM WITH CROSS OF HONOR PINNED TO HIS BREAST

From the *Confederate Veteran*, Vol. XXXV, 1927.

George Mathewson, aged ninety years, an ex-slave, who served in the War between the States, passed away at his home in Paris, Tenn. He was buried at Maplewood Cemetery, and Rev. P. P. Pullen, of the Fitzgerald-Kendell Camp, U. C. V., read the Confederate ritual for the departed soldier and offered a prayer.

"Uncle George" was a faithful member of the Fitzgerald-Kendell Camp, and had been color bearer for some years. He attended many of the reunions over the South, and his last public appearance was a reunion of his Camp. He was a servant through the war, of Dr. W. P. Smallwood, a surgeon of Company E, 12th Georgia Regiment, and received a Cross of Honor for bravery in action. He was the only representative of the Camp at the Dallas reunion, and was treated with great consideration when he carried the message from his white comrades to the floor of the convention. A son of Dr. Smallwood, who resides in Fort Worth, had his father's former body guard to visit him in his home and showered him with gifts. Dressed in his uniform of a Confederate soldier, with his Cross of honor and reunion badges pinned on his breast, "Uncle George" was laid to rest till the final roll call of his comrades.

He had only one relative surviving, a son.

LAST SURVIVOR OF SLAVE DAYS, SAM FISHER, DIES IN PERRY

Sam Fisher, 89-year-old antebellum negro, died here Saturday and was buried Monday. With his death, Perry lost its last slave of the sixties.

He went to the War between the States as a cook for Rev. Hammie Fleder, a Methodist preacher, and he was made a drummer boy in Mr. Fleder's company, The Southern Rights Guards, who left Perry on March 18, 1861, for Pensacola, Fla. Sam was a slave of the family of the late Judge C. C. Duncan.

White friends sent floral offerings to his funeral and the Sergt. C. C. Duncan chapter, U. D. C., sent a garland of flowers with a small Confederate flag.

(Source: *Houston Home Journal,* Perry, Georgia; October 15, 1931.)

NEGRO VETERAN GOES TO REWARD FOUGHT IN CIVIL WAR. REV. ALEXANDER HARRIS DIES AT AGE OF NINETY-ONE.

Death has claimed another citizen of the Old South, and one more veteran of the war of the Lost Cause has been laid in his last resting place, there to sleep in peace until he is awakened by the reveille on that day when the grave shall give up its dead and the long roll call is sounded.

Alexander Harris, for many years one of the leading negro citizens of the state, is dead, and there is sorrow and mourning in many a heart to-day in consequence. Though his skin was black, his heart, his soul and his life were as staunch for the right, as clean and as upright as those of any man who ever claimed the devine right of citizenship in the community. He died at his home, 525 Oglethorpe Avenue, West, yesterday afternoon at 5:15 o'clock.

Alexander Harris was never a slave. Born free and the child of free parents, he first saw the light in Savannah July 9, 1818. For the 91 years of his life he lived so that he won the respect of white and black alike.

When the Civil War commenced, Harris was chief musician for the Republican Blues, and when that organization joined the Confederate army, the faithful drummer cast his lot with them and performed valuable and gallant service for the cause he claimed as his own. While on duty at Fort Pulaski, Harris had charge of the reconstruction of the old moat, performing this task with zeal and energy. Later on he had charge of the negro laborers that constructed the other fortifications in the vicinity of Savannah, and acquitted himself with great credit. During the engagements fought by the troops with which he was associated, Harris displayed courage and fortitude.

Possessed of a good education, Harris fitted himself for the ministry, and was for many years pastor of the First Bryan Baptist Church. He did much toward the establishment of the Georgia Industrial School, and always befriended the cause of education among the negroes.

For a number of years he was custodian of the poor fund of the county, and also rendered valuable services during the yellow fever scourge which swept over the city in 1876. Many hundreds of dollars passed thorugh his hands at this time, for which he rendered a careful and accurate accounting.

The old man, although a prominent figure among the negroes of the state and an acknowledged leader of his people, always kept out of politics. He was high in the colored Masonry of the country, being a past grand master in that organization. It was largely due to his efforts that the colored Masonic Widows and Orphans Home of Georgia was established.

The news that the old man is dead will be received with sorrow. The surviving war members of the Republican Blues will attend his funeral in a body and pay their last tribute to the memory of the dead. Harris was almost the last of the old time negroes who were so interwoven with the sacred history of the Old South. He will be laid to rest to-morrow afternoon, the funeral exercises taking place at the church of which he was formerly pastor.

(Source: *Savannah Morning News*; Oct. 10, 1909)

WHITE VETERANS PAY TRIBUTE OF RESPECT
Attend Funeral of Colored Minister Veteran.

Several of the surviving war members of the Reuplican Blues paid a last tribute of respect to their old drummer, Rev. Alexander Harris, former pastor of the First Bryan Baptist Church, colored, yesterday afternoon, when they attended his funeral from the church, on West Broad Street near Waldburg.

Together with the veterans of the Blues several other veterans and their relatives attended the funeral. These occupied a prominent position in the church, where seats had been reserved for them. A beautiful floral offering, designed in the form of a cross, was sent by the Blues.

Among those who were present were Maj. E. S. Elliott, Capt. William Spencer, Capt. W. D. Dixon, Capt. J. J. Gaudry, Joseph M. Solomons, I. A. Solomons, C. A. Marmetstein, A. B. Collins, J. Gardner, Lemuel Downs, William Metzgar, Henry Smith, L. C. Cornell, J. S. Silva, and A. B. Laroche.

The funeral service was conducted by Rev. George Dwelle of Augusta, a friend of the deceased since boyhood, and with whom he had a mutual agreement that whichever died first, the other was to conduct the funeral service.

Rev. Dwelle spoke very feelingly of his friend and of the good he had done through an upright and faithful life, admonishing his bearers to take his example and follow in his footsteps. He told in detail of his acquaintance with the dead pastor of the church, and of the good work he had done for the members of his race in his religious work, in the cause of education, and in the colored masonic order.

The funeral was attended by the colored masons and a large number of the members of the church and other colored people of the city. Besides the floral design sent by the Blues there were a number of others sent by the white friends of the deceased.

(Source: *Savannah Morning News*; October 12, 1909)

"...ALL SEND LOVE TO THE 'OLD REBEL NEGRO.'"

This article appeared in the *Mobile* (Alabama) *Register*, 1906, and is contributed by Lewis D. Brasell.

Colored Confederate
Who Has Applied To Legislature For Pension And Whom Sons And Veterans Are Aiding, Pending The Issue.

(New Orleans Picayune.)

Robert Shropshire, the old negro Confederate Veteran, was born at Nashville, Tennessee., and is now about 73 years old. He was a member of Company A, Fifth Texas Cavalry or Second Regiment, Sibley's Brigade. He served as teamster and was sworn in and paid monthly in the Confederate army. Robert belonged to Major John Shropshire, who was killed in a battle at Glorietta, out near the Texas line. After the death of his master, Robert belonged to Mrs. Robert Shropshire, who is living and gives Robert the best of recommendations. Robert continued to serve in the army as teamster with the brother of his former master, Captain Ben Shropshire, until the end of the war. He then went with Captain Shropshire to Holly Springs,

Miss., and was there wounded by a piece of a shell, which cut him in the head, and he was disabled for a long time. At the close of the war he worked on steamboats. Previous to this he went to Columbus, Texas, to his mistress, Mrs. Robert Shropshire, where he remained a few months.

Although 73 years old Robert is as loyal to the Confederate cause as ever. He is very feeble, and has made application for a pension from the state, and is perhaps the only colored man in the state entitled to a pension. He is a familiar figure at all the reunions, the last one he attended being held at Baton Rouge, Aug. 9...

The following extract from a letter written by a well known gentleman of this city to a prominent member of the last Legislature shows the felling existing among the old soldiers for Bob. He said: "As a Confederate soldier and one who appreciates the services rendered during the four years of untold hardships, or rather undescribable hardships, I would request of you that you introduce a bill in the House granting a pension to the old and faithful colored man, Robert Shropshire. From personal observations I know that Robert was true and faithful and bears the marks of a wound which nearly resulted fatally, obtained at Holly Springs, Miss. It will be a very small matter for the great State of Louisiana to recognize the services of this poor old negro in his old age."

What could be more sincere than the sentiments expressed in a letter received by Bob a few days since from a white comrade in Texas. He addresses Bob as "Dear Bob and comrade," and says:

"You did not say if you took part in the reunion at New Orleans. I wanted to come just to see you, but could not leave home. I wrote you about Charley Shropshire's death, also Mr. Dick died some time back. Only a few of our old boys are living. Bob, I will enclose you a one dollor bill and want you to acknowledge receipt of it and tell me if you had a good time at the reunion. Bob, I will never forget you and our trip home in 1862 through the mountains of New Mexico, when you had the smallpox and no one would go near you in the wagon but myself. And, afterwards, when you had gotten well and I had the measles, you stayed by me as I had you. On our trip alone from San Antonio you stuck to me when I was so sick. And this trip, Bob, in heart, bound one white man and one negro together. You had lost your master in the battle of Glorietta. I had lost my health, but to each other we stood true, and are today enjoying the blessings that were bestowed on but a few of those old boys. Long life Bob. Nora and the boys all send love to the 'Old Rebel Negro.' Write soon to your old comrade and friend."

It is the hope of many that Bob's services will be recognized. He can not live much longer, and when he passes to the Great Beyond it should be with the feeling that his white comrades appreciated the bravery and devotion and suffering of old Bob, and that it was also recognized by the state.

During the past week the Army of Tennessee and Camp Beauregard, Sons of Veterans, each appropriated $2.50 a month for Bob's relief.

"HE WAS DRESSED IN GRAY"

From an article entitled "A Tribute to the Man in Black" in the _Confederate Veteran_, May 1896.

Comrade C. C. Cumming, of Fort Worth, Texas, writes that Bob and Alf Taylor have just passed through the Fort in their double role of "Yankee Doodle and Dixie," and a crowded house greeted them, laughing and crying alternately at the comedy and tragedy of the "Old South" crucified under the Southern Cross, "for," as Bob says, so truly, "it is the old, old South, with the print of the nails of its crucifixion in its hands." He brought to the memory of the gray heads the old "Black Mammy," and spoke of the monument in the future that would be erected to her memory for her faithfulness before and during the great struggle.

This revives the memory of a faithful man in black who followed me through from First Manassas, Leesburg, where he assisted in capturing the guns we took from Baker, to the Peninsular, the Seven Days before Richmond, Fredericksburg, the bombardment of the city December 11, and the battle, two days after, at Marye's Heights; to Chancellorsville, the storming of Harper's Ferry, and the terrible struggle at Sharpsburg (Antietam now), and last, Gettysburg. Here he lost his life by his fidelity to me–his "young marster" and companion. We were reared together on "de ole plantation" in "Massippi."

I was wounded in the Peach Orchard at Gettysburg on the second day. The fourth day found us retreating in a cold, drizzling rain. George had found an ambulance, in which I, Sergeant Major of the Seventeenth Mississippi, and Col. Holder of that regiment, (still on this side of the river), and an officer of the Twenty-first Mississippi, whose name escapes me, embarked for the happy land of Dixie. All day long we moved slower than any funeral train over the pike, only getting eight miles–to Cashtown. When night came I had to dismount from loss of blood and became a prisoner in a strange land. On the next day about sundown faithful George, who still clung to me, told me that the Yankees were coming down the road from Gettysburg and were separating the "black folks from dar marsters;" that he didn't want to be separated from me and for me to go on to prison and he'd slip over the mountains and join the regiment in retreat, and we'd meet again "ober de ribber," meaning the Potomac. We had crossed at Williamsport.

I insisted on George accepting his freedom and joining a settlement of free negroes in the vicinity of Gettysburg, which we had passed through in going up to the battle. But he would have none of it; he wanted to stay with me always. I had him hide my sword, break it off at the hilt and stick it in a crack of the barn (that yet stands in the village) to the left of the road going away from Gettysburg, where I, with about thirty other wounded, lay. I can yet see that faithful black face and the glint of the blade as the dying rays of that day's sun flashed upon them. A canteen of water and some hard tack was the last token of his kindly care for me.

In the spring of 1865, I saw a messmate from whom I was separated on that battlefield, and he told me the fate of poor, faithful George. He had gotten through the lines safely and was marching in the rear of our retreating command, when met by a Northern lady, who had a son in our command, whom George, by chance, happened to know. He was telling her of her son, who was safe as a prisoner, when some men in blue came up. George ran and they shot and killed him. He was dressed in gray and they took him for a combatant. The lady had him buried and then joined her son in prison. She told my messmate of this and he told to the boys in camp the fate of the truest and best friend I ever had. George's prediction will come true–I feel we will meet again "over the river."

A BLACK CONFEDERATE IS REMEMBERED

From the *Huntsville* (Alabama) *Times* of August 31, 1929.

Calvin Scruggs, aged negro and life long resident of this city, died yesterday morning at his home on Madison Street after an illness of several months.

His passing marks the almost complete obliteration of the old war time negroes and faithful servitors of the families, some of whom have long been mere names in this community.

Born about 1845, he was reaching manhood at the time of the War Between the States and took part in the local turmoil.

His reminiscences of those battle-torn days were exact and colorful. Birth and circumstances made him a slave without the bonds of slavery, and during the period of reconstruction, where all slaves were freed, he chose to cast his lot in with that of the family to which he had previously belonged, and to which he remained faithful until his death.

His loss will be regretted by members of Huntsville's older families who admired and respected him.

Note from Contributor Elliott R. Matthews of Athens, Alabama: Calvin Scruggs was born on the plantation of my great-great grandfather, in Madison County, Alabama. I remember him quite well, as a child. From his birth to his death, he was a member of my family for five generations. He was one of those individuals, who place their sense of loyalty above all.

A Georgian Drummer

Ned Bailor, a colored man of Brunswick, died last week. During the war he served as drummer for the fourth Georgia regiment, and had the same position in the Brunswick Riflemen until his death. In respect to his memory the Riflemen escorted his remains to the cemetery.

(Source: *Middle Georgia Times*, Thomaston, Georgia; December 26, 1885.)

A "Striker" for General Price, CSA
George Williams, Slave During Civil War, Dies At Central; 92 Years Old

After a two months illness, George Williams, 92, pioneer colored resident of Silver City, where he had lived since the early 70's, died last Thursday morning at the home of his daughter, Mrs. Emma Gilbert, at Central.

Williams was born at Nashivlle, Tenn., June 15, 1843, of slave parents, and as a child, with a brother and sister, was sold as a slave.

During the Civil War, he served as a "striker" for General Price of the Confederate army and participated in many battles, forced marches and exciting skirmishes with Union troops, narrowly escaping death or capture a number of times. He could recount his war experiences vividly.

In 1864, he accompanied General Price and a detachment of Confederate soldiers to Texas, the party being headed for Mexico, but they were not permitted at first to cross the river at Eagle Pass, Mexico at the time being engaged in war.

A few years later Williams came to Silver City, which has since been his home. He lived here in the boom mining days when Chloride Flat, Pinos Altoe and Georgetown were big camps. He took part in many brushes with marauding bands of Indians throughtout this district, fighting with the citizen soldiers and regular Army troops.

At the time of his death, Williams owned a residence on Market street, corner of Arizona, which had been his home for more than 50 years. He reared a family of several children. He was the adviser and counsellor of the colored people here most of his life, and as a citizen enjoyed the confidence and respect of the community.

Surviving is a son, Alec Williams, who was born here, and now is a resident of Kansas City, Mo., being a letter carrier, under the Civil Service, there. The son arrived Sunday for the funeral. A daughter, Mrs. Emma Gilbert, Central, also survives, and an aged sister, Mrs. Hattie Hester, Des Moines, Iowa.

The funeral was held yesterday afternoon at the Catholic church, with burial in the Catholic cemetery. Many friends attended the services. Cox's Mortuary directed the funeral.

(Source: *Silver City Independent* (New Mexico) of August 22, 1934.

Slave Freed by Civil War Dies at Central; Funeral Held Monday

Funeral services for George Williams, 92, a colored slave during the Civil War, were held Monday afternoon at the Catholic church, with the burial in the Catholic cemetery. Arrangements were in charge of W. B. Cox Inc.

The aged Southerner died Thursday morning at Central, where he had been ill from the infirmities of old age for over two months. He was at the home of his daughter, Mrs. Emma Gilbert, at the time of his death.

Born at Nashville on June 15, 1843, as a slave, Williams had an interesting background of the Civil war days that he recalled with a marked vividness.

His family was purchased from a slave trader by Col. Joe Davis and he lived with him on his plantation until 18??.

With his brother Henry he was taken into Col. Sidney Jackman's company which moved down the Missouri river between Booneville and Roachport. After several skirmishes with the federals, Col. Jackman's detachment reached Shreveport, La., where he was left to guard Colonel Jackman's family.

In 1864, Jackman, General Price and Shelby, forced to retreat by the federals, headed for Mexico with a wagon train, planning to join the French in their fight with the Mexicans.

A Mexican general refused to let them cross, but did offer to buy the wagon train to keep it from being captured by the Yankees. Williams was still with Colonel Jackman on this excursion.

The colonel drove a deal with the Mexicans whereby the rebels were allowed to remain in Mexico until after the war ended in 1865.

Following the war Williams came to Silver City and remained here throughout his life until just a few months ago when he went to Central to reside with his sister. He reared a family of several children. His life here was spent as a law abiding citizen and he enjoyed the respect of many friends. For several years he lived at the corner of Market and Arizona streets and this house belonged to him at the time of his death.

His only surviving son, Alex Williams, arrived here Sunday for the funeral Monday. He is a ... in Kansass City. Others left to morn his death are his daughter, Mrs. Gilbert of Central, and an aged sister Mrs. Hattie Hester, Des Moines, Iw.

(Source: *Silver City Enterprise* (New Mexico) of August 31, 1934.

The contributor, Laurence Fletcher Talbott, Ph.D., writes: It would seem that Georgia Williams is unequivocally a Confederate Veteran of some note. I was especially interested in his post war life as a citizen of Silver City and his seeing action against "marauding bands of Indians." He was a fine example of the veteran contributing to his community. His descendants married into Hispanic families, and they soon 'passed' into that community.

A CAUSE FOR TEARS AND SORROW TO THE WRITER

This article entitled "A Black Skin, But White Soul" is from the _Confederate Veteran,_ Vol. XII, 1904.

The loyal old Southern plantation negroes, like their friends and former masters, the Confederate veterans, are fast passing away. One of these, "Uncle" Jim Gass, recently died in Bonham, Tex., and Comrade W. T. Gass, editor of the Hopkins County *Democrat*, whose slave he was, pays this tribute:

"The announcement of the sudden death of this faithful and honest old man was a cause for tears and sorrow to the writer. The faithful negro carried us around in his arms and on his sturdy back and shoulders in infancy, and we grew older taught us to swim, to fish, to hunt, and to ride. He was black, but he had a whiter soul and purer life than hundreds of boys and men we have known with white skins. When the war clouds of 1861 came, although but a boy of fifteen, I enlisted in the Confederate service. Jim came to me and said: 'Marse Will, I want to go wid you to de war. I'll stay wid you and never leave you.' My mother was a widow, father having died a short time before, and I explained to Jim that we both couldn't leave home at once; that one of us would have to stay to care for her and four brothers and sisters younger than myself. The argument was unanswerable. 'Dat's a fact, Marse Will; I specks I'm de one to stay.'

"Looking back through the mist and tears of forty-one years, it is a melancholy pleasure to testify to the faithfulness of our trusty old slave and companion of boyhood, for he was as true to his trust as was any Confederate soldier true to his flag during all those four years of war, blood, fire, and blockade. And when, in May, 1865, I returned home, I found Jim still at his post of duty. With two horses and a wagon he had been making numerous trips to Shreveport, taking down flour and trading it for sugar and molasses, helping my widowed mother to keep the wolf from the door, Jim being her mainstay and chief purveyor of the commissary department. Peace to his ashes!"

Levi Miller "...one of the few colored men regularly enlisted in the Confederate army."

Richard C. Radi of Granite Springs, New York writes:

Our research has revealed a Black member by the name of Levi Miller. I have enclosed photo copies of two different obituaries of Comrade Miller from the Winchester Evening Star.

In addition, I refer you to "A History of the Laurel Brigade" by Captain William N. McDonald (1907), page #476 where he lists in the Roster of Company H, 12th Virginia Cavalry, 3 members that he brackets as "Colored". I have no further information on these men.

LEVI MILLER HAS A GOOD WAR RECORD

The body of Levi Miller, one of the few colored men regularly enlisted in the Confederate Army during the Civil War, who died at Opequon, this county, yesterday morning, will be taken on Monday to Lexington, Va., for burial.

There are still many ex-Confederate soldiers in this section who recall Levi Miller's service in the Confederate Army and much regret was expressed at his death. There has come to light a letter written on June 6, 1907, at Jewett, Texas, from J. E. Anderson, the last Captain of Company C, Fifth Texas Regiment, in which Levi Miller was enlisted. It was directed to the late B. C. Shull, of this county, who was chairman of the Confederate Pension Board of Frederick County. The letter gives Levi Miller's civil war record, written by his commanding officer, and throws an interesting light on the war career of the colored man who has just died here. Capt. Anderson said:

Colored "Rebels" War Record.

"Levi Miller served as a servant for Capt. McBride and Capt. J. E. Anderson, of Company C, Fifth Texas Regiment, during the entire war from 1861 to 1865. When our company arrived in Richmond in September, 1861, Capt. J. J. McBride wrote his brother who lived in Rockbridge county, Va., to bring us one of his servants (slaves), and he brought us Levi Miller who was with us during all the fighting around Richmond in the year 1862, and in the Maryland campaign. Capt. McBride was wounded in battle in the battle of Manassas August 31, 1862. Levi Miller stayed at the hospital and nursed the Captain until he recoverd and both rejoined the company in time for the Fredericksburg fight December 1862. He was on the Suffolk campaign in the spring of 1863.

"He was in the Pennsylvania campaign and at New Castle and Chambersburg he met several negroes whom he knew (I think some of them were related to him) and who had run away from Virginia. They tried to get Levi to desert but he would not. He went with us to Georgia and was in the battle of Chickamauga, Georgia, and in the campaign around Chattanooga, Tenn. He was with us during the severe cold winter of 1863-64 in the campaign of Knoxville and East Tennessee.

"Fighting With The South."

In the spring of 1864 we returned to Virginia and rejoined General Lee's army. In the battle of the Wilderness, Va., where General Lee started to lead the Texas brigade in a charge and the men turned his horse and made him go to rear before we would charge–for we would not see him killed–Capt. McBride, during the desperate fighting had both legs broken and was considered to be fatally wounded. This occurred in the early morning of May 6, 1864. Levi Miller was at that time with the wagon trains and did not know of the Captain being wounded until he got to Spottsylvania Courthouse where we arrived on the morning of May 8. On the morning of May 10th Levi Miller brought to me a haversack of rations and in order to get to me in our little temporary ditch and breastworks, had to cross an open field of about 200 yards and as he came across the field in full run the enemy's sharpshooters clipped the dirt all around him. I told him he could not go back until night as those sharpshooters would get him. I gave him directions where he could find Capt. McBride and as soon as it got dark for him to go and nurse the captain until he died and then return to me.

About two o'clock on that day I saw from the maneuvres of the enemy in our front that they were fixing to charge us and I told Levi Miller that he would get a chance to get in a battle. He asked for a gun and ammunition. We had several extra guns in our ditch and the men gave him a gun and ammunition. About 4 p.m. the enemy made a rushing charge. Levi Miller stood by my side and man never fought harder and better than he did and when the enemy tried to cross our little breastworks and we clubbed and bayonetted them off, no one used his bayonet with more skill and effect than Levi Miller. During the fight the shout of my men was "Give 'em hell, Lee!"

Levi Enrolled As Confederate Soldier.

After the fight was over, one of the men made a motion that Levi Miller be enrolled as a full member of the company. I put the motion and of course it passed unanimously and I immediately enrolled his name as a full member of the company, which roll I have yet in my possession.

"As soon as dark came Levi Miller went to Capt. McBride who was taken to a hospital at Charlottesville, Va., and Levi Miller stayed and nursed him until October, 1865 which was some time after the war closed. Capt. McBride returned to Texas and died there in 1880. He owed his life to Levi Miller's good nursing.

"Levi Miller was never absent a day from the army except when nursing Capt. McBride. No better servant was in General Lee's army. If anyone was sick in camp he was always ready to wait on them. He was a pet with every man in the company. Thousands of faithful and generous acts I could write to you if space and time would permit.

"My company was Company C, Fifth Texas Regiment, Texas Brigade, Hood's Division, Longstreet's Corps, Army of Northern Virginia. Out of a company of 142 men I had but nine left to surrender with me at Appomattox, Va."

(Source: *Winchester Evening Star* (Virginia) of Nov. 11, 1921.)

He Wore The Gray In Morton's Battery

Source: *Confederate Veteran* (Nashville), Volume 9, No. 5, May, 1901.

With the batteries of Capt. John W. Morton, Gen. Forrest's chief of artillery, there were two negroes, Bob Morton, a cook, and Ed Patterson, the hostler for the captain, both of whom served with the artillery throughout the war. Ed Patterson, whose fidelity and loyalty stoutly withstood the test of battle and even of capture, still survives. He is a respected householder and property owner, near Nashville, and delights to recall the time when he wore the gray in Morton's Battery. Everybody in the artillery service of Forrest knew and liked Ed. He took good care of the horses, and performed his duties with unflagging good humor.

On one occasion it was feared that Ed was lost to the battery. In the terrific fight at Parker's Cross Roads, when Morton's men, behind the guns, were almost overwhelmed by superior numbers of the enemy in a sudden charge, about twenty members of the battery were run over and captured. Ed was among them. He was missed, notwithstanding the confusion of the disaster, and the temporary reverse of the almost invariably successful artillerists was regarded by them as aggravated by the loss of their diligent hostler. Capt. Morton particularly mourned his absence. One morning, a few days after the battle, he rode into the camp of the battery, mounted upon a superb horse, whose caparison denoted it the property of an officer of no mean rank.

"Hallo, Ed! Where did you come from?" was the artillery chief's greeting.

"I des come f'om de Yankees," responded Ed complacently, as he dismounted and stood proudly eying the steed.

"How did you get away, and where did you get that horse?"

"Wall, sah; dey taken us all along. When we got out o' sight o' y' all, I notice dat dey didn't 'pear to notice me, an' when dey got to whar dey was gwine into camp, I sort o' got away. De Yankees des seed me ridin' 'roun', an' I 'spec' maybe dey thought I was waitin' on some o' de officers. I des went on th'ough de woods. I seed a heap o' dead men wid blue coats on, an' a heap of 'em what was 'live, too. D'rectly I come to a big road. I seed one o' our boys walkin' what 'ad done los' his horse. I axed him which erway Marse John went. He knowed me, an' said de artillery done gone down dis road. I kep' on, an' passed a heap o' our men walkin'. I asked 'em which er way de artillery done gone, an' dey said, 'Down dis road.' I kep' on an' kep' on 'til I got here, an' dat's why I'm here, Marse John. Dey took yo' horse away f'om me, but I done got you a better one, sho. No, sah; dey didn't 'par to notice me at all. When I was comin' on I seed some mighty nice-lookin' hosses tied in de bushes, an' ez dey wan' nobody noticin' I tuck 'n' pick me out one, an' des got on dis 'n' and rid him to hunt y' all. I seed a blue overcoat layin' on de groun', an' I took 'n' put it on. An' it's a good one, too, Marse John."

Mr. Charles K. Barrow writes:

I came across the enclosed in the Wednesday, October 16, 1912 copy of *The Selma Journal*.

Boston Linam, Negro Veteran In The City

Boston Linam, of Mobile, is in the city and he is attracting quite as much attention as any of the maids, sponsors, generals, colonels or anybody else attending the re-uion. Boston is an eighty-year-old negro who came through the war with General Forrest, and he has the credentials along with him to prove that he was one of the fellows who fought for the south and bled for principles which his "white folks" told him were right.

Boston has been attending the veterans re-unions every year since it has been a custom to hold them. He gets to all of them, and when he goes back to Mobile he immediately begins preparing for the next re-union the following year.

This old negro formerly lived at Camden, Wilcox county, and on Broad street this morning he came face to face with Sheriff Jenkins of Wilcox. The sheriff and Boston were delighted to meet each other again, and when the old negro was told that Mr. Jenkins had been elected sheriff, he said: "Lawd, God-er-mighty man boy, you done been 'lected high shaf. I told you' you'd have good luck," and everybody had a good laugh. Boston is decorated with flags, buttons and medals from head to foot, and bears his honors quite proudly.

Notable Tribute To Amos Rucker
Ex-Slave and Confederate Soldier Given Remarkable Funeral.

**Dressed in Confederate Gray With
a Battleflag Above Him, Rucker
Went to His Last Sleep.
General Evans Officiates.**

In the presence of a remarkable congregation of people, white and black, that filled the chapel and crowded out into the street for almost half a block, and while he lay in his coffin dressed in a Confederate uniform and wrapped in the mantle of praise of two races, funeral services over the body of Amos Rucker, colored, ex-slave and Confederate soldier, were held yesterday afternoon at 3 o'clock, in the chapel of Hilburn & Pools, on Hunter street.

It was one of the most remarkable funerals ever held in Atlanta.

The services were conducted by General Clement A. Evans. General Evans offered a beautiful prayer, as did Rev. Dr. T. P. Cleveland. A few of the faithful old negro's favorite hymns were sung, and with the recitation of a poem by Captain "Tip" Harrison, "When Rucker Called the Roll," the services were concluded.

On top of the casket was a Confederate battleflag, with the emblems–crossed guns, a cannon and a Confederate battleship. The flag was encircled by a silver wreath. Many other exquisite floral offerings covered the casket, flowers being sent by some of the most prominent families in the city.

Among the floral designs on the casket were those sent by the Daughters of the Confederacy and Camp Walker, United Confederate Veterans.

Desiring to show their respect for the old negro, D. C. J. Cleburne, first cousin of General Cleburne, who owned the old negro during the slavery days, and his son, Dr. Ronaryne Cleburne, both attended the funeral services yesterday afternoon.

The following prominent citizens were the pallbearers to Southview cemetery, where the body was interred; Ex-Governor Allen D. Candler, General A. J. West, Dr. Amos Fox, Judge W. Lowndes Calhoun, J. Bid Holland, Frank A. Hilburn and R. G. Ozburne.

(Source: *The Atlanta Constitution*, October 13, 1905.)

CONFEDERATE DEAD AT ELMIRA POW CAMP ARE BURIED BY BLACK SEXTON

The Confederate dead were often laid to rest by Black Southerners. In many instances, kindness and consideration is shown towards the deceased and their families. This article about John Jones, sexton at Elmira, New York, is taken from the November 9, 1867 edition of the *Newnan* (Georgia) *Herald*; contributed by Greg White of Smyrna, Georgia.

Confederate Dead at Elmira

The *Savannah Republican* says:

We have long been intending to make public a fact known to us, but it has heretofore slipped our memory; and we think it will prove a matter of interest to our readers in Georgia and Florida, and especially to many whose husbands, brothers and sons may have died while in prison. It is well known that a large prison camp was located at Elmira, New York, where, as many as from ten to fifteen thousand Confederates were confined at one time. The many diseases incidental to prison life decimated their numbers; that dreadful scourge–the smallpox prevailed to a great extent. Many unused to the rigor of severe Northern winters became victims of consumption; and on a plateau in Woodlawn Cemetery, at that place, the graves of over three thousand men give mournful evidence of the visitations of death in the camp.

A colored man, named John Jones, a former slave, is sexton and grave digger there. All these men were buried by him. He took the trouble to obtain the name of each man, the number of his regiment, and letter of his company, which he had placed upon a small head board. Each grave is so marked. Since the close of the war parties in the South have written him in regard to relatives known to have died there, and in many cases bodies have been disinterred and shipped to friends for burial in family vaults and Southern cemeteries.

To families in Georgia and Florida we will state, that if they may wish the bodies of those dear to them, who have died in prison at Elmira removed to Southern cemeteries, by writing to Mr. John Jones, of Woodlawn Cemetary at Elmira, they can make arrangements to have them disinterred and shipped South. We know of many instances in which this has been done, and there would probably be more, were the fact more generally known.

A BLACK CONFEDERATE APPEARS ON THE LIST OF DEAD AT CAMP DOUGLAS, ILLINOIS

Appearing in the *Memphis* (Tennessee) *Appeal* of October 8, 1863 is a list of those who died as Confederate P. O. W.'s at Camp Douglas, Illinois. Among the dead are a young Black Confederate, Hardin Blackwell of Ward's Company, 3rd Kentucky, who died of gunshot wounds. Although this article mentions the "excellent sanitary arrangements" at Camp Douglas, it is now documented that prisoners in this camp died in great numbers.

CAMP DOUGLAS.

List of Deaths Among the Prisoners—Sanitary Condition—New Arrivals—Change.

From the Chicago Times, 2 th ult.]

Thanks to the excellent sanitary arrangements lately made at Camp Douglas. the mortality among the prisoners bears a very small proportion to those of last year. The prisoners now in camp have occupied their present quarters nearly seven weeks, and, out of more than three thousand. the number of deaths is but fifteen. This is at the rate of three and a half per cent. per annum, which, considering the condition in which many of them arrived, and the fact that the climate is not the one to which they have been accustomed, is lower than the average of camp mortality. The following are the names of those deceased since the arrival of the prisoners in Chicago, with the date and proximate cause of death:

Jas F Estes 48th Tennessee, company I, Sept 4th.

Henry Nevitt, 4th Kentucky company K, September 3d gaft itis.

James E Cook, 3d Kentucky, company D, August 20th. d. sentery.

James D Hanna, 8th Kentucky, company C, August 28th, typhomal fever.

A Marshall, 6th Kentucky, company C, September 9th. dysentery.

James Mathers, 3d Tennessee, typhoid fever, September 5th.

James Floyd, 8th Kentucky, company H, dysentery.

William Ansay, 51st Alabama, company E, September 10th, dysentery.

Martin Rodgers, 3d Kentucky, company G, September 18th, remittent fever.

Hardin Blackwell. 3d Kentucky, Ward's company, a black boy, died of gunshot wounds, September 22d.

H Haydn, 6th Kentucky, company A, August 30th, pneumonia.

W Shot, Jack May's battalion, company A, September 9th, pneumonia.

F O Coeurly, 27th Tennessee, company H, September 5th, dysentery.

John Sullivan, 3d Kentucky, company G, September 20th, pneumonia.

M Patton, 8th Kentucky, company B, September 22d, intermittent fever.

Rev. Alexander Harris, a prominent pastor in Savannah, served as a Confederate musician. Note: the UDC Cross of Honor is placed in front of his monument

Chapter IX

Contemporary Perspectives

BATON ROUGE (AP) – The role of blacks in the Civil War is misunderstood, and blacks in the south hold a common heritage with whites, a philosophy professor says.

"When you eliminate the black Confederate soldier, you've eliminated the history of the South," said Leonard Haynes, professor of philosophy at Southern University, a student of the Civil War and a former Methodist minister.

. . . Haynes, 69, says he will talk about blacks who served on the side of the Confederacy–a topic that is barely known much less understood.

As many as 50,000 blacks fought for the South...They included "free men of color," blacks who owned slaves themselves and slaves who went to war with their masters.

. . . "It's a part of our history," Haynes said.

From *The News Star* (Louisiana), January 28, 1992
Headline: [African American] Professor says blacks share Civil War
legacy with whites

The Unlikely Story of Blacks Who Were Loyal to Dixie

by J. K. Obatala

Even slaves, especially the house servants, sometimes played a part in The Cause, serving bravely under the Stars and Bars

Despite reams of writings on the "New South," few artists, intellectuals or scholars have come to grips with Southern history. We still tend to characterize the current state of affairs in the South as a "Second Reconstruction." The truth, it seems to me, is that Southern race relations are more on the order of a New Confederacy than a Second Reconstruction. Reconstruction was characterized by the estrangement of black and white. The Confederate era, on the other hand, was a period which produced a considerable amount of cooperation between whites and those blacks who remained loyal to the South during the war. While it is true that the vision of the devoted slave, working loyally for his master's cause, is largely myth, there were outstanding and memorable instances of black patriotism among slaves and "free men of color." The blacks in these instances were not merely passive participants in the Southern cause; they were serving to protect their homes.

An early indication of Afro-American involvement in the Confederate cause was the enthusiasm with which many blacks endorsed secession. As the various state legislatures announced their decisions, ardent patriotism was displayed among some of the slaves. In April 1861 a group of Afro-Americans in Petersburg, Virginia, who had volunteerecd to work on fortifications in Norfolk, held a mass rally at the courthouse square. They were presented with a Confederate flag by the former mayor, John Dodson, who promised the volunteers "a rich reward of praise, and merit, from a thankful people."

The black spokesman, Charles Tinsley, a bricklayer, accepted the flag and responded, "We are willing to aid Virginia's cause to the utmost of our ability...and we promise unhesitating obedience to all orders that may be given us."

New Orleans' blacks not only staged what historian Benjamin Quarles, in The Negro in the Civil War, termed a "monster mass meeting," but they also organized two regiments of "Native Guards"–this to make good their expressed commitment "to take arms at a moment's notice and fight shoulder to shoulder with other citizens." The guards were eventually joined with the state militia, and paraded with white troops in November 1861. The black companies even supplied most of their own arms. (They did not, however, stay with the Confederacy.)

Incredible though it seems, many slaves made financial and material contributions to the Confederacy. In Alabama, William Yancey's slaves brought $60 worth of watermelons to Montgomery for the soldiers. A South Carolina slave was moved to contribute his life savings–$5. Some slaves turned their formidable talents for showmanship into sources of funds for the Confederacy. Even the most fervent fire-eaters in Charleston must have been somewhat subdued by the "Confederate Ethiopian Serenaders," a group of slave singers who turned over the returns from one of their concerts to help finance the production of gunboats and munitions. "It became a custom," noted E. Merton Coulter in *The Confederate States of America,* 1861-1865, "for slaves to hold balls and concerts and give the money...to aid soldiers' families and to other patriotic causes."

Some skepticism about ultimate loyalty

Within certain Confederate circles, however, the black patriot was seen with jaundiced and perennially suspecting eyes. Many white leaders were conscious of their would-be allies' reputation for being more or less geniuses, as Bell Irvin Wiley put it in Southern Negroes, 1861-1865, at "anticipating what a white person would like to hear, and saying it in a way pleasing to the whites." That concern was evident in a notation by Mary Boykin Chesnut, wife of a former U.S. Senator and military aide to Jefferson Davis, in her unusually candid A Diary From Dixie. "Mr. Chesnut's Negroes offered to fight for him if he would arm them," she recorded, in a March 18, 1862, entry. "He pretended to believe them."

Such skepticism was not altogether unfounded; thousands of blacks had already sought refuge behind the Federal front. Not long after Mrs. Chesnut's notation, a Confederate regiment of free Negroes offered their services to the Union's General Butler when he entered New Orleans. He declined that offer but later recruited freed slaves, and in September 1862 the First Regiment Louisiana Native Guards was mustered into the Union Army.

White "purists" formed still another obstacle to black involvement. Writing in Atlanta's Southern Confederacy, the editor said, "The idea of a lot of buck negroes and saucy house gals meeting in a public hall, and dancing, fiddling, sweating and fuming to raise funds for our sick soldiers, is supremely ridiculous."

A scene from GWTW

Yet the use of blacks in some jobs was not only widely approved but provided for by the Confederate Congress. Unsurprisingly, most of these occupations fall under the rubric of military labor. Slaves and free blacks formed an abundant, economic, efficient and well-seasoned work force. They also helped conserve white manpower. "Every 'Sambo' wielding a shovel," Wiley observed, "released a 'Johnny' for the ranks."

One well-known testament to the worth of the black military worker is his appearance in Margaret Mitchell's Gone With the Wind. The scene is a surprise encounter between Scarlett and Big Sam, the black foreman of Tara. Scarlett, riding in a carriage with Rhett Butler, meets Sam in a crowd of "sweating black men with picks and shovels over their shoulders, shepherded along by an officer and a squad of men wearing the insignia of the engineering corps..."

"What are you boys doing so far away from Tara? You've run away, I'll be bound..."

"Runned away?" answered Big Sam. "No'm, us ain' runned away. Dey done sont an' tuck us, kase us wuz de fo' bigges' an' stronges' han's at Tara." His white teeth showed proudly. "Dey specially sont fer me, kase Ah could sing so good. Yas'm, Mist' Frank Kennedy, he come by an' tuck us."

"But why, Big Sam?"

"Lawd, Miss Scarlett! Ain' you heard? Us is ter dig de ditches for de w'ite gempmums ter hide in w'en de Yankees comes."

But the black Confederate laborer did a lot more than dig ditches. He carried the wounded, tended the sick, drove the teams, moved the guns, raised redoubts, grew the crops and cooked the food–to name but a few random chores. Thus, since planters grew increasingly reluctant to release their slaves to the military, the government thought it urgent enough to pass an Impressment Act in 1863. As amended a year later, it provided for the impressment of up to 20,000 slaves. Not all workers were impressed. Many of the cooks were either body servants or free blacks and made up an important contingent in the Confederate Army. Before the government began allocating four cooks to a company, some soldiers chipped in and hired their own. Such extraordinary measures were more than justified, according to a Southern journalist who reported biscuits cooked by white Confederate soldiers, "which if hurled against the side of a house or tree, would stick there through a heavy rain storm."

Many black cooks were also adept and resourceful foragers. Among the more famous was "General Boeyguard" who earned his reputation during Lee's invasion of Pennsylvania in 1863. He would leave the march at reveille and not be seen again until evening–at which time the six officers in his mess were liberally indulged with assorted delights from the tables, orchards and barnyards of the local Pennsylvania Dutch farmers.

Cook Bill Doins acquired his nickname from his habit of referring to his cooking utensils as "my doins." A free black, he was working on a Chesapeake Bay oyster boat when Virginia seceded. On hearing the news, the entire crew quit, and Bill joined the Confederate Army. After the Battle of Antietam when Lee retired his forces across the Potomac, Doins received an order for an issue of cooked rations. There was plenty of flour nearby, but the pots and pans were miles ahead in another wagon. Doins had the flour brought down to the river, mixed the dough in barrels, adding river water as he needed it. He ordered a picket fence cut down for firewood. As the barrels were broken, the heads were used first to cook the bread on, then for additional fuel.

The blacks loyal to Dixie

Cooks were not the most renowned of black military personnel. That status belonged to the ubiquitous "body servant." He was usually a slave, charged with attending to the personal needs of his master, probably an officer. In effect, he was a true Johnny Reb. He fought, foraged, captured prisoners, was himself captured and often died. And when white Johnny marched, it was often to black Johnny's music. His loyalty was legendary.

In The Confederates States of America, 1861-1865, Coulter published a drawing from Harper's Weekly (October 1861) showing a black musician beating a bass drum in an army recruiting parade at Woodstock, Virginia. And Wiley found that Josephus Black and two other servants of General John B. Gordon provided the music to which his regiment marched. Interestingly enough, Confederate law required that black and white musicians receive equal pay.

No less interesting were certain remarkable acts of personal and political loyalty. Mary Boykin Chesnut made note of a Columbia, South Carolina, black who braved the battlefield, shells bursting all around, to bring his master a bucket of ham and rice! The Linden Jeffersonian on August 8, 1862, carried a report from the Richmond front, which told of a servant named Nathan who was captured by a Federal officer. "The Negro was sent to a spring to procure some water for his new master. But instead of performing that task he kept on his way to the Confederate lines where on his arrival he presented himself to [the commanding general] together with two horses which he captured from the Yankees on his 'masterly retreat!'" Nathan was returned to his old master's service.

Captain George Baylor of the 12th Virginia Cavalry recalled how one of his servants "rendered himself obnoxious to the Yankees" by directing some Federal troops across the Potomac at Harper's Ferry, where a detachment of Baylor's men awaited them.

During the Battle of Brandy Station, two of Baylor's servants named Tom and Overton supplied themselves with arms left by retreating Federal troops and "joined in the company charges." They "succeeded in capturing a Yankee Negro...and brought him safely into camp." The servants were "highly delighted" with their trophy, Baylor said, and they held on to him for several months. They made the prisoner rub down their master's horses, fetch firewood and water, and "do other chores about the camp."

Slave recalled serving guns

Body servants, although the most likely to be in the midst of the fighting, probably were not the only ones to see combat with Rebel forces. It is difficult to separate the apocryphal anecdotes from the historical. James Munro McPherson, in *The Negro's Civil War*, published a statement (purged of its plantation dialect) by John Parker, a slave who served in the Battle of Bull Run: "I arrived at the Junction two days before the action commenced. They immediately placed me in one of the batteries. There were four colored men in our battery. I don't know how many there were in the others. We opened fire about ten o'clock...couldn't see the Yankees at all and only fired at random. Sometimes they were concealed in the woods and then we guessed our aim...My work was to hand the balls and swab out the cannon. In this, we took turns. The officers aimed the guns; we fired grape shots. The balls from the Yankee guns felled thick all around. In one battery, a shell burst and killed twenty, the rest ran..." The fact that grape was not used in field pieces during the Civil War points up the problems for the serious student of the war. It may have been a case of mislabeling, or it may have been fantasy.

A *New York Times* correspondent with Grant in 1863 wrote, "The guns of the rebel battery were manned almost wholly by Negroes, a single white man, or perhaps two, directing operations." Unfortunately, Confederate sources to reinforce this story are lacking.

By that year, the ranks of the Confederate army were dismally depleted and slaves and free blacks formed a veritable fountain of military youth. But when the press, and later General Patrick Ronayne Cleburne, suggested arming slaves, Jefferson Davis suppressed the question. Georgia's Governor Joseph E. Brown felt that "when we establish the fact that they are a military people we destory our theory that they are unfit to be free..."

Although Cleburne's proposal aroused consternation, his idea was later approved by Robert E. Lee and in March 1865–after much political haggling–the Confedreate Congress finally passed a bill authorizing the use of slaves as troops. The act contained no antislavery clause, but it was generally assumed that those who served would be freed.

By the time the first black companies were raised the fate of the Confederacy was sealed. There were fascinated onlookers when freshly outfitted black troops paraded in Richmond, but it appears to have been more of an opera-bouffe affair than a solemn occasion. "A little more than a week later," noted historian E. Merton Coulter, "Richmond had fallen and with it the Confederacy."

But why would blacks fight in the first place? Why would they support in any shape or form a regime committed to their own subjugation? James H. Brewer, writing in *The Confederate Negro: Virginia's Craftsmen and Military Laborers*, suggests that they were "denigrated, corroded by degradation, and psychologically disabled by oppression." Indeed, it is too often forgotten that the world of the slaves was limited to the plantation; and that the plantation system simply wasn't designed to turn out Eldridge Cleavers or Andrew Youngs.

Yet thousands of ignorant and denigrated blacks went over to the Federal side, so there were other operative factors. One was money. Free blacks earned up to $30 a month in the army, plus upkeep for themselves and their families. Slaves made money trading in whiskey, food, horses and other bounty from their foraging missions. Nathan, the servant who escaped from the Yankees with two horses, made a net profit of $50 on one and kept the other for his personal use. Slaves even lent money to white soldiers and charged them interest.

The quest for freedom also played a key role in black Confederate thoughts. Army life offered slaves an opportunity to escape plantation routine and to travel. There was also the likelihood of being manumitted on good service. Then, too, it was widely believed among blacks that freedom was inevitable no matter who won the war. In this opinion they were supported by many insightful whites, including Jefferson Davis, Robert E. Lee, Patrick Cleburne and, of course, the infinitely perceptive Mary Boykin Chestnut of Charleston.

Local attachment also prompted many blacks to come to the aid of the Confederacy. Many house servants felt secure in their environment and preferred not to change. Wise slave owners strove to inculcate that attitude in all their bondsmen. Jefferson Davis even established a system of self-government on his plantation. Slaves had their own court before which offenders appeared prior to being punished. Consequently, when Vicksburg fell in 1863, the Davis slaves refused to follow the Federal army. Soldiers had to physically remove some of them. And by 1865, almost all of them had drifted back.

The corollary, of course, is that the Rebel black seems to have had at least a primitive, instinctive feeling that his fortunes were tied inextricably to those of the South. That he was a Southerner. In this regard, the black Confederate–far more than the Reconstruction politicians who were appendages of the Republican North– was the prototype of the modern, middle-class black of the "New South." In fact, it was a strong sense of regional pride that helped generate the Civil Rights movement of the 1950s and '60s. This is clearly evident in the imagery invoked by Dr. Martin Luther King in his famous March on Washington address, in which he envisioned the day when black and white Southerners would come together and create a new social order.

The new order is symbolized for me, to some extent, by Jimmy Carter and Andrew Young, and by the President's friendly feud with National Urban League director Vernon Jordan. But these highly publicized relationships were also fore-shadowed in the Confederate era.

When Jefferson Davis was captured at Irwinsville, Georgia, after fleeing Rich-mond, he had with him James Jones, his coachman and valet. Jones sounded an alarm as Union troops closed in on the forest where Davis was in hiding. He threw a raincoat around the fallen president's shoulders (Union soldiers later reported that Davis had been captured in a dress). And, finally, Jones claimed that Davis gave him the Confederate Seal to hide.

The irony is arresting, for the legacy of James Jones and other Confederates has been inherited by the very groups from which a number of today's prominent national figures have come–the black middle and upper classes. Leaders like Jor-dan and Young, who come from educated families, with deep roots in the South, may conjure up to us the ghosts of martyred Union soldiers and runaway slaves. But in fact their historical ancestors might just have worn the butternut of the Old South rather than the blue of the Union Army.

(J.K. Obatala, a free lance writer, is an expert on the roles of African Americans in history. This article was originally published in *Smithsonian*, March, 1979.)

BLACK FIGHTERS FOR THE SOUTH

by Sheldon Vanauken

The fierce loyalty and dedication of white Southerners–most of whom had never owned a slave–in repelling the northern invaders in the War of Southern Independence cannot be questioned. When asked by a northern soldier why he fought, the captured Southerner succinctly replied: "Because you're here!"

The whole story for many a Confederate soldier: invaders. "Northern flags in South winds flutter," say the war-time words of "Dixie": To arms! To arms! And conquer peace for Dixie." It was the Athenians at Marathon against the Persian host. Or Churchill's England against the Nazis. "To live or die for Dixie!" And tens of thousands of Southerners fought and died for Virginia or Carolina or Georgia– for Dixie.

But, while the loyalty and dedication of the Confederates under arms–white men, since blacks could not be enrolled–cannot be doubted, what did black South-erners feel? It is widely accepted–because the victors write the history books–that Southern blacks, groaning under slavery, were hoping and praying for Northern victory and their own liberation. But there were no pollsters in those days; this image of the blacks is no more than an assumption–a guess. We know, of course, that there were some blacks who ran away to the North via the "Underground

Railway": but we also know that the murderous John Brown, capturing the arsenal at Harpers Ferry, Virginia, in order to hand out muskets to the slaves who would rise, found that the slaves were uninterested in rising against their masters. Thus there is reason to doubt the popular assumption of black hostility to the Confederate cause. It is fair to assume that the attitudes of Virginian blacks would not be greatly different from that of blacks in South Carolina or in Louisiana? And a further assumption appears reasonable; that the attitudes of certain black Southerners would not be decidedly different from those of their families and friends.

The failed invasion of South Carolina to relieve Fort Sumter was, as intended by Mr. Lincoln, the beginning of the War, but real combat began with the invasion of Virginia in 1861. Shortly thereafter the Lynchburg, Virginia, newspaper reported that seventy black freemen had formed a company pledged to defend Virginia–and the paper adds: "Three cheers for the patriotic Negroes of Lynchburg." At about the same time another company of sixty black freemen marched into Richmond under a big Confederatte flag, asking to be allowed to fight the invaders. There were nearly 200,000 free blacks in the South, many of whom wanted to fight for the Confederacy. And in Petersburg blacks volunteered to help in raising fortifications and held a mass rally. The Mayor presented them with a Confederate flag, amidst cheers. The black leader accepted it proudly, saying "We are willing to help Virginia's case to the utmost." Somewhat later when Union forces were besieging Yorktown, the bluecoats were plagued by a deadly accurate sharpshooter. When he was finally located and killed, he turned out to be a black Virginian. Do the descendants of those men, one wonders, still cherish the Stars and Bars? Do they even remember? And what of the descendants of the three and a half thousand blacks who themselves owned black slaves? As early as 1830 there were some 13,000 slaves with black masters. Who remembers this? Or have the memories been blanked out by the waves of propaganda against the Confederacy?

Although, by law, blacks were not allowed a combat role, many of the military bands were black. And many officers had black body-servants with them. In late 1862 one of these servants was captured and told he was now free. Hired by a Union officer as a servant, he was sent to a spring for water. He trudged off towards the spring, and then simply kept going, along with two Yankee horses, back to his own Confederate regiment. "A masterly retreat," said the general.

In 1863 Captain Arthur Freemantle of the English Coldstream Guards, who was with Lee, told of an even more masterly retreat. A black servant who had been captured returned to his Confederate lines wearing a blue uniform and bringing a Yankee prisoner dressed in his old rags. Captain Freemantle in his book also speaks of "the detestation and contempt" with which the Southern blacks with the Army spoke of the Yankees. Not much "groaning under slavery" here. Another Englishman with the Confederate army told of a black who deserted to the Union, revealing the location of the Confederate batteries. Later that black man was recaptured. Was he then whipped by his white officer? On the contrary, a delegation of black servants asked to be allowed to punish the deserter, and this was granted. Thereupon the Englishman reported, the black deserter turned over to the loyal blacks "met a death at their hands more violent than any white person's anger could have suggested." How would those Confederate blacks have regarded today's blacks who want to tear downt he Southern flag? And do the great-grandchildren of those loyal Confederate blacks still pass on this story?

At Brandy Station in 1863 an officer's black servant lured a detachment of bluecoats into a Southern ambush. And, during the great cavalry battle two black servants grabbed Yankee muskets and–no doubt–with Rebel yells–joined the 12th Virginia charge and captured a Union soldier.

Another black servant, a cook, was himself captured, and he refused the oath that would have freed him. "I'm a Jeff Davis man," he said; and he steadfastly remained a prisoner despite all offers of freedom for the rest of the war. Was this story of loyal fortitude remembered in his family?

These are, to be sure, isolated incidents, yet there were no doubt many similar stories that were never written down. At all events, they do strongly suggest a massive black loyalty–the very opposite of the "groaning under slavery" myth. No doubt there were those who groaned under slavery, but the idea that all blacks felt oppressed under cruel masters and regarded the Southern Cross Battle Flag with loathing simply cannot be true. They simply did not see the Confederacy as wicked; that is left to those who never knew it. All over the South, the only plantations were being run by the women and old men; the slaves could have risen against Ol' Massa or Ol' Miss–the young white men were off with the Army–but they did not rise. And the loyalty of the black servants with the armies was surely not diametrically opposite to the feelings of their families and friends at home.

There were many calls for the blacks to be enlisted in the fighting units, calls, as we have seen, from blacks as well as whites. General Lee himself urged it strongly. Until November 1864 President Davis resisted this idea, but finally he yielded, and in the following year, 1865, the C. S. Congress authorized it. Virginia alone was to enroll 300,000 black men. A massive black army from the whole of the Confederacy. And the blacks enrolled in the army were to be emancipated. Obviously, it would mean the end of slavery. But it was too late, although a few units were formed; the Confederacy was collapsing. Whether it would have made a difference in the outcome if the black regiments had been formed can never be known.

Regardless of the outcome, it is a pity that the enrollment of the blacks did not occur. The emancipated blacks would then owe their freedom to the Confederacy, so that today it would not be a propaganda enemy. Moreover, if blacks and whites had fought together against the Yankees, that comradeship would have been a bond in later years. Even today, according to *The Enduring South*, the Southern whites and Southern blacks are closer in their values than Southern whites and Northern whites.

But there's one thing more to be said of the decision by President Davis and the Congress of the Confederate States: the decision itself proves beyond question that the representatives of the white South cared more for independence than for slavery. The decision is proof of that. If one or the other had to be sacrificed – independence or slavery – slavery must go. Therefore it cannot be said that the South fought primarily for slavery. But the South's fight for independence was almost over, and with its fall the old idea of the voluntary Union perished.

The late Sheldon Vanauken, a writer, poet, and personal friend of C. S. Lewis, is the author of *A Severe Mercy*, a national best-seller, and *Glittering Illusion: English Sympathy for the Southern Confederacy.* This article appeared in *Southern Partisan,* 4th Quarter, 1992.

AFFIDAVIT OF SGT. EDDIE BROWN PAGE, III, IN U.S. DISTRICT COURT, 1994

U. S. Judge Orinda Evans heard arguments in a U.S. District Court hearing in Atlanta, Georgia on Monday, November 21, 1994 to determine if the Confederate battle emblem should be removed from the Georgia state flag. Plaintiff James Coleman had brought suit against Governor Zell Miller and the State of Georgia. Ironically, it was Miller who was unsuccessfully attempted to change the state flag in his first term as governor.

Eddie Brown Page, a sergeant in the Georgia Army National Guard and a Black Confederate reenactor, was called to testify for the defendants. After hearing Sgt. Page's testimony, the case was later dismissed.

(Contributed by Charles Park and the CSA Historical Preservation Society, Rock Hill, South Carolina.)

IN THE UNITED STATES DISTRICT COURT
FOR THE NORTHERN DISTRICT OF GEORGIA
ATLANTA DIVISION

JAMES ANDREW COLEMAN
    Plaintiff,

v.

ZELL MILLER, GOVERNOR OF
THE STATE OF GEORGIA

CIVIL ACTION FILE
NO. 1 : 94 - CV - 1673 - ODE

and

THE STATE OF GEORGIA,
Defendants.

AFFIDAVIT OF STAFF SGT. EDDIE BROWN PAGE, III

Personally appeared before the undersigned officer, duly authorized by law to administer oaths, STAFF SGT. EDDIE BROWN PAGE, III, and states the following:

1.

My name is Eddie Brown Page, III. I have personal knowledge of the matters addressed in this Affidavit. I am over the age of majority and am suffering for no legal disabilities.

2.

I make this affidavit for use in the above-styled case and for any other lawful and proper use of this Court.

3.

I am a native Atlantan and Georgian. I am an African-American and a patriotic Southerner. I am a graduate of from Georgia State University. I also attended Clark-Atlanta University, graduated from Atlanta Metropolitan Collge, Atlanta Area Technical School and Joseph E. Brown High School in Atlanta. I am currently a full-time student again at Atlanta Area Technical School and serve on the student government as Representative of Automotive Technology Program and President of the Vocational Industrial Club of America (VICA) chapter; I am also the post-secondary State of Georgia Historian of VICA for all Georgia post-secondary schools and technical colleges, for the 1994-95 term. I am a free-lance professional musician of Local 148-462 of the American Federation of Musicians, Atlanta Federation of Musicians Chapter. I am also a music teacher at the Gate City Heritage Preparatory School, teaching grades 1-4. I work as a cashier-clerk at the West End Newsstand. I am a soldier with the 116th Army Band of the Georgia National Guard. My rank is Staff Sergeant. My duties are double-reed section leader and unit career counselor. I am an honor graduate of basic combat training at Fort Jackson, South Carolina – squad leader of the cycle. I am also a graduate of Georgia Military Institute, honor graduate, basic Non-Commissioned Officer course; graduate of the basic retention NCO course, Camp Robinson, Arkansas; graduate of the NCO battle skills course at Camp Robinson, Arkansas; graduate of the senior ROTC advanced camp, Fort Bragg, North Carolina.

4.

The lineage of my current service unit (the 116th Army Band of the Georgia National Guard) dates back to 1862, under Jefferson Davis, President of the Confederacy and Joseph E. Brown, Governor of Georgia. Based on my own study of my unit's history, a significant number of African-Americans served in the Confederate militias as musicians, as I do presently in the Guard, and they were decreed by the Confederate Congress to receive the same pay as Whites; musicians in the Union Army received unequal pay.

5.

As a native Georgian, I was born under the "1879" Georgia memorial flag, based on the Confederate Stars and Bars, but enlisted under and have continuously served under the 1956 Georgia flag with the cross of St. Andrew, also known as the Confederate battle flag. I am a distinguished graduate and alumnus of Joseph Emerson Brown High School of Atlanta, Georgia, named after a Governor of Georgia during the War Between the States who later became Chief Justice of the Georgia Supreme Court and U. S. Senator from GEorgia (Governor Brown was also the first president of the Atlanta Board of Education and champion of public education as an alumni of the University of Georgia). The "nickname" and "mascot" of Brown High School was the "Rebels." Its colors were Confederate gray and infantry royal blue, dedicated as a living memorial to the Confederacy, like our current Georgia flag. As a member of the Brown High Rebel Band, I wore an authentic reproduction of the uniform worn by my African-American forefathers who served in that capacity during the War Between the States. "Dixie" was the school song (this song was made famous by Ohioan Dan Emmett and composed by two Black minstrels, the Snowden brothers, who taught the song to Emmett). The school flag was the Confederate battle flag. As an eighth grader at Brown High School, I was taunted by one White schoolmate who told me to "put that flag down" because it was a "white man's symbol," and that it didn't belong to me and for me to "get my own" symbol. As a result, I embarked upon the study of my African-American Southern heritage and my forefathers' contributions to the Confederate States of America.

6.

My many years of study on this subject show that Blacks made significant contributions to the Confederate war effort as free people of color and as slaves. I found out that while President Abraham Lincoln was resolute in refusing to use Blacks as soldiers, the Confederate States from the beginning used African-Americans for all army chores and even as fighting men. Black men furnished most of the cooks, mess attendants, teamsters, stablemen, builders of fortifications, brakemen, baggagemen, track layers and porters, and were also musicians and combatants or bodyguards. Black women served as nurses in the Confederate military services.

7.

For me, as a native of the South and as a soldier, the St. Andrew's cross on the Georgia flag symbolizes <u>my</u> heritage – respect for the courage and sacrifice of my patriotic forefathers, free people of color and slaves, for the constitutional principle of sovereignty of the states of the founding fathers – and not racism, current events or the institution of "slavery." For me, the Confederate symbolism of the current state flag should be understood as representing and acknowledging the contributions of African Americans, Native Americans and Jewish persons, as well as European Americans, that is, a multicultural heritage. To do so would strip the Confederate symbolism of its racial potency and would underscore our common heritage. I directly rebut those who see in the St. Andrews Cross a symbol of white supremacy, segregation and "state's rights".

FURTHER, AFFIANT SAYETH NOT.

656 Eddie Brown Page, III GAARNG
EDDIE BROWN PAGE, III

Sworn to and subscribed before
me this / _3rd_ day of _December_ 1994.

Sandra C. Kennell
Notary Public

My Commission Expires: Notary Public, Douglas County, Georgia
My Commission Expires March 24, 1934

Note: Eddie Brown Page III died on January 13, 1998 as a result of a gunshot wound that was inflicted during an attempted robbery near his home in Southwest Atlanta. For more information, please see the obituary posted in the *Atlanta Constitution*.

Eddie Brown Page III, Black Confederate Reenactor (Musician), leading a February 4, 1995, tribute to General John B. Gordon, Atlanta, Georgia.

Courtesy of Calvin E. Johnson, Jr.

UNDERSTANDING THE STILLNESS

By Bill Maxwell

On a recent morning, standing on a windswept hill in the Virginia village of Appomattox Court House, I traveled back in time, into the soul of America.

As a U.S. citizen whose great grandparents had been slaves, I wanted to stand on the ground where the Civil War ended. I wanted to see where Confederate Gen. Robert E. Lee and Union Gen. Ulysses S. Grant had faced each other in Wilmer McLean's living room.

Why, I thought, did historian Bruce Catton title one of his Civil War books "A Stillness at Appomattox"? I didn't know. But on this balmy morning, gazing at miles of brown grasss and undulating hills stretching toward the Appomattox River, I got a clue as I was enveloped in silence.

Unlike many black Americans who discount everything related to the Civil War, I'm awed by it.

How can any sane black person ignore the event that marks the most important turning point in the history of black peoples worldwide? That remains America's greatest national tragedy? I believe that if we want to understand Southerners – white and black – we must understand the Civil War.

Walking where the defeated Lee had saluted Grant on April 9, 1865, I regretted that Lee, the most beloved general of all time, had been humiliated. I didn't regret that the South lost the War. But because I'm a proud Southerner who has a strong sense of history, I feel a deep kinship with Lee and the thousands of soldiers who died.

I abhor the idea of the Confederacy, the system that debased all human life. As for the individual men who followed Lee, however, I have the utmost respect. They, creatures of their historical time and place, acted on their shared moral imperative.

To Southerners, the Yankees were foreign invaders. Dixie, though made up of temporal farms and towns, was a transcendental mosaic worth dying for, a condition of the spirit.

I had these thoughts as voices softly echoed in the courthouse museum and as I read the captions beneath wartime memorabilia. Slowly, I realized that I had stopped judging the rightness or wrongness of what had occurred more than a century earlier.

Seeing the illustration of Hannah – a slave who was the only casualty of Lee's surrender – I remembered the evil of slavery, that "peculiar institution."

Why did a random bullet find this woman just as Lee and Grant were preparing to silence their guns? Why such a cruel, paradoxical fate? Surely, her death held meaning beyond Appomattox, beyond the room where she was cooking her master's meal.

I was unaccountably inspired as I turned away from the illustration and climbed the stairs to the second floor. Here, displays of authentic relics of the war, including uniforms, weapons and original papers lined the walls.

But nothing inspired me more than the spectacle of the surrendered battle flag of the 61st Virginia Infantry. In reality, the banner is a tattered, torn, stitched and smudged piece of cloth. To the brave men who held it aloft in bloody campaigns, however, it was a living symbol of their esprit de corps.

Staring at this battle emblem, I thought of today's Southerners who sport the "Stars and Bars" on pickup trucks. Do they understand the meaning of the flag? Can they visualize the bloodshed? The courage? The cause?

Do they understand the words of Lee – "I would rather die a thousand deaths" – after his decision to surrender? Do they understand his utter humiliation after returning to his troops? "Boys, I have done the best I could for you," he said with typical dignity. "Go home now, and if you make as good citizens as you have soldiers, you will do well, and I shall always be proud of you."

Leaving Appomattox, I marveled at the simple beauty of the place and imagined the two great generals riding toward the McLean House. I thought, too, of Hannah. Again, the silence, the stillness returned.

Bill Maxwell, a journalist for the *St. Petersburg Times* (Florida), offers insight from the perspective of a contemporary black southerner. In the spring of 1994, this article appeared on national wire services and was carried by newspapers around the country.

"A Score of Faithful Confederates," reunion photo. *Confederate Veteran* (Vol. XVIII, 1910).

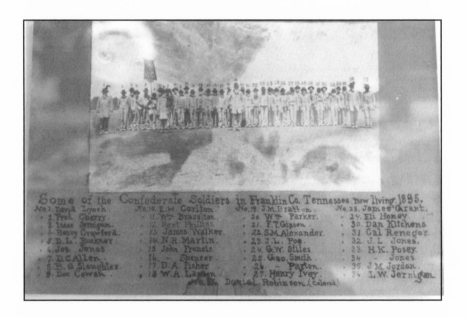

This archival photo includes a listing of "Some of the Confederate Soldiers in Franklin Co. Tennessee now living, 1895," A numeral is written by each name so that each soldier can be identified in the photograph. Included is "No. 37, Daniel Robinson (colored)."

Contributed by James and Carolyn Bell

The Editors

J. H. Segars, a native of Eatonton, Georgia, is author and editor of a number of Civil War books to include *The Bell Irvin Wiley Reader* and *Life in Dixie During the War.*

Charles Kelly Barrow, a social studies teacher at Flint River Academy and Historian-in-Chief, SCV, is a member of the Georgia Civil War Commission and co-editor of *Forgotten Confederates: An Anthology About Black Southerners.*

Southern Lion Book Sale!

BLACK SOUTHERNERS IN CONFEDERATE ARMIES provides historical documentation to suggest that large numbers of African Americans served as Southern allies. In this intriguing volume, readers will encounter selections drawn from a wise variety of reliable sources to include official records, veterans' accounts, newspaper articles, and published reports. This book is enlightening - and mind-boggling! Over 225 pages with photographs; soft-cover; $16

TRUTHS OF HISTORY: A HISTORICAL PERSPECTIVE OF THE CIVIL WAR FROM THE SOUTHERN VIEWPOINT by Mildred Lewis Rutherford. Now available in reprint for the first time since 1920! This provocative book provides an interpretation of Civil War history that is rarely found in modern texts. Few scholars were more keenly aware of the heart, mind, and soul of the South than this national orator and Grand Historian of the UDC. 192 pages; soft cover; $14.

FORGOTTEN CONFEDERATES: AN ANTHOLOGY ABOUT BLACK SOUTHERNERS who served in Confederate armies. This extraordinary book, edited by Charles K. Barrow, J. H. Segars and R. R. Rosenburg, examines the role of African Americans who served within Southern armies. Includes information drawn from official records and original source material, and narratives written by veterans. 34 photographs and illustrations; 194 pages; $15.

ANDERSONVILLE: THE SOUTHERN PERSPECTIVE Finally, the true story of Confederate Camp Sumpter as seen through the eyes of Southerners, past and present. Articles by William R. Scaife, Mauriel Joslyn, Edwin C. Bearss, Heinrich Wirz, Edward A. Pollard, and others. 46 photos and maps, 192 pages, $12.

IN SEARCH OF CONFEDERATE ANCESTORS by J. H. Segars. The acclaimed "how-to" guide for both beginning genealogists and more experienced family researchers. Contains step-by-step instructions for finding your Civil War ancestors. Now in the fifth printing; 112 pages, 45 photos and charts; $10.

To order: Please send check or money order
(plus $1.50 per book shipping) to
Southern Lion Books, P.O. Box 347163, Atlanta, GA 30334

For notable books about the South, please see our web site:
southernlion.com

Publish your next book

with assistance from
the Southern Heritage Press
and Southern Lion Books, Inc. Publishing Group.

Ideal for
- Family History and Genealogy books.
- Church Histories.
- Historical Society Publications

We provide full consultations, manuscript review, typesetting, and printing. We oversee the entire production process and produce books that meet your approval. All of this for a reasonable price.

For information, contact us at
Southern Lion Books
P.O. Box 347163
Atlanta, GA 30034

e-mail: slbooks@hotmail.com

Independent Typestyles

Professional Typesetting
for the Discriminating Author

Custom typesetting delivered print-ready

For information:
Brenda Brothers
1612 Golden Valley Drive
Christiana, TN 37037-6152

(615) 896-6344

E-Mail: brendabrothers@att.net